The Faithful Prepper
A Christian Perspective on Prepping

by

Aden Tate

Post-Apocalyptic Fiction & Survival Nonfiction

www.PrepperPress.com

The Faithful Prepper
A Christian Perspective on Prepping

ISBN 978-1-939473-88-2
Printed in the United States of America.
Prepper Press Trade Paperback Edition: July 2019
Prepper Press is a division of Kennebec Publishing, LLC

To Yellowhead
I killed a snake in the kitchen last week.
This seemed like the right place to tell you.

Table of Contents

Introduction

Prepping: the act of preparing one's self and one's family for potential future disaster by stockpiling necessary food, water, supplies, and knowledge.

Disaster is a subject laced with questions. I believe this is why the apocalypse, natural disasters, and terrorism are hot subjects in today's books and movies. We enjoy the moral dilemmas that these situations create. What would we do if neighbors began coming to our door begging for food when we barely have enough to feed our own family to begin with? How would we secure our homes from marauders in such a world? What would we do if our kids desperately needed medicine during a disaster?

And I don't think that these questions are necessarily far out in left field. If you're reading this, odds are you don't either. Natural disasters are increasing on a global scale. Terrorism seems to have taken the forefront in the news. Experts warn that another worldwide pandemic is only a matter of time. And it's an understanding of these facts that has caused people to begin looking at things differently.

We live in an incredibly fragile society, and in some ways, one that is more fragile than it has ever been before. With the decline of the family farm, most communities can no longer produce the food that they need to feed their own residents. With our increased reliance on electricity, we have lost many of the skillsets that are needed to survive in a world without it.

Preppers understand these things, and seek to rectify the situation with their own families. However, as Christians there are going to be different ways that we not only engage with these threats, but how we respond to them as well.

How do charity, witnessing, taking care of our families, and other aspects of the Christian walk tie in with prepping? This book was written as a response to questions such as those. I trust that you will find it helpful.

Chapter 1
What's Going on in the World?
"It takes one unexpected event to change the course of one's life."[1]

Disasters are increasing worldwide.[2] That's a fact. Disaster fatalities are increasing worldwide as well.[3] This points to our disasters becoming more and more deadly. Whether that be due to increased population density (an earthquake hits more people), increased vulnerable populations (we're living longer, and old people are more vulnerable), increased reliance on technology, or just increased devastation as a direct result of the disaster, isn't the point. The point is that disasters are becoming more prevalent and more dangerous than ever before.

Thomas Malthus actually wrote a rather interesting paper on the earth's population and food supply a few hundred years ago. In it, he predicted that at some point the earth would not be able to produce the resources needed to feed an exponentially growing human population. At some point, he theorized, a crises of some sort would occur.[4]

Now, I'm not a huge believer in Thomas Malthus. I just don't see it. Some people do, I don't. So there. We're not producing nearly as much food as we could. And I think faced with the crises of a worldwide famine, that not only would more people begin growing their own food (rather than growing grass in their back yard), but that we'd find innovative new farming and gardening methods as well to produce even *more* food. Mankind is endlessly creative. Plus, I think the Malthusian idea of mandatory birth limits is entirely wicked/ ridiculous.

There's an interesting science known as chaos theory, and though it doesn't exactly deal with disasters such as tornadoes, earthquakes, and the like directly, it does have ramifications for them. Basically, chaos theory offers that there are times when there is no pattern. The pattern that existed beforehand breaks, and havoc plays out through the system. It's a fascinating, relatively new science, and I highly recommend image searching "fractals" if you'd like to see some of the mathematical representations of it.

Mathematicians have a formula regarding population growth that perfectly demonstrates chaos, though. The formula is known as the logistic difference equation, and for years it was a cool way to demonstrate how human population would grow. A mathematician named Robert May was tinkering around with the equation and found that at a particular point within the equation, chaos entered. The equation no longer performed as it did initially, and large checks and balances were found within the equation.[5]

This is where those who disagree with me on the whole Thomas Malthus stuff would scream and shout. If we know that the human population is increasing exponentially, and we know that at a particular point in the logistic difference equation we're screwed, then shouldn't we expect chaos to happen soon?

Let's take a moment to look at simple logistics. Currently, 2% in the First World feed the other 98%.[6] What that means is that people no longer have the time, resources, knowledge, or desire needed to produce their own food. As a result, they're dependent not only on the 2% that actually produces the food, but on the people who ship the food to them as well. Sure, some people out there may have a small summer garden that they plant every year, but the odds that that garden is producing enough food for that family to live off are very slim. The odds that same family knows how to properly and safely preserve the food that they are producing in that garden for leaner times is even slimmer. Just ask around. How many people do you honestly know (who aren't retired) that know how to can food? The only people I know who still do this where I live are seniors!

This is where I believe the difference lies: with any disaster, yeah, this small amount of food producers could be an issue. But does that automatically mean that once the human population reaches X that we're screwed? I don't think so. Logistic difference equations work fine for wolves, rabbits, deer, and butterfly populations, who pretty much follow the same patterns they have for all of history. But as I mentioned, *humans* have technology. Humans can change things. A wolf, bunny, deer, or butterfly can't.

> The Spanish flu of 1918 was bad, there's no doubt about it. But one of the reasons that it wasn't *worse* was because a large portion of Americans during this time not only had stored canned foods available in their larder but farmed as well.[7] I would argue that people were "closer to the earth" back then. They knew what it took to grow food, to raise cattle, and how butchering a hog or chicken was sometimes the best course of action for both the animals and the farmer. I talk to people now about butchering a chicken

and they act as if I'm the most heartless person they've ever met! I can remember watching a survival show called *Fat Guys in the Woods* a few years back. I loved it. On one of the episodes, some of the contestants (who have been starving in the woods, mind you) captured a wild boar and now had to butcher it. The grown men were crying and dry heaving afterwards! What kind of man cries after he kills a wild pig? Like it or not, that's the current state of society that we live in. People aren't "close to the earth," and as a result, don't know what it takes to get the food that's on their plates.

If a similar pandemic influenza swept throughout the globe, would the States be in as resilient of a position as they were then?

Now consider the fact that the average food item travels roughly 1,500 miles from its original farm to your plate.[8] That is an incredibly long chain of supply. And though there is certainly a growing local food movement gaining ground (no pun intended), does your current locale produce enough food to feed all of the people in it? I'd venture a guess the answer is no. Now what happens should something happen to that chain of supply? What happens when the trucks quit rolling into the city? When the food trucks quit coming, the food supply evaporates.

It wouldn't take much to accomplish this. An Electromagnetic Pulse (EMP), widespread flooding, pandemic, a trucker strike, an attack on our electrical grid, or OPEC refusing to sell the States oil could all potentially lead to this result.

What about grocery stores, though? Surely they would have plenty of food stored in the warehouses, right?

Unfortunately, this isn't so. Most Western businesses, particularly grocery stores, now follow a concept known as kanban.[9] Kanban was a Japanese concept. It's the idea that if we order the goods that we need right as we need them, we save money and make the business more profitable. By not keeping a stockpile of goods on-hand, space is saved from having to be utilized as storage, energy is saved from having to keep the good from extreme temperatures, and less waste is produced from the good potentially going bad on the business owner's hands. The model does make businesses more profitable.

The disadvantage to this is that it makes the business more dependent on distributors and less resilient to hiccups. In our grocery store example, if the distributor doesn't bring more sugary cereal, there's not going to be anything other than what was on the shelf before. Kanban makes the chain of supply more vulnerable to disaster and emergencies.

Any time you increase the chain of supply's length you simultaneously increase your vulnerability. Why? Because there are more cogs to the system, and the more cogs there are, the more you have to worry about everything running smoothly. Just ask Napoleon on this one. What happens when you try to invade the heart of Russia in the middle of the winter thousands of miles away from France when everything has to be delivered by foot, horse, or sail? You end up with a recipe for disaster.

Disasters have incredibly long reaches as well. Very often, you don't have to fight just one. One disaster leads to another, which leads to another, creating a domino effect that compounds the problem as time goes on. For example, a devastating earthquake can lead to a tsunami that wipes out coastal regions, causing widespread flooding in the process. The ground can't handle the saturation and mudslides result, killing dozens in the process. The tsunami also caused a chemical spill at a nearby factory which has been seeping into the floodwaters which people are wading through to find safety. This chemical is caustic, and has caused a lot of burns on people who've touched the water. The government attempts to help with the situation, but as usual, botches it, leading to political unrest and instability in the area. This in turn can lead to further issues.

Do you see how this works? It's a larger version of the Butterfly Effect at play here! One action leads to another bigger action, which leads to bigger options, and so on and so on.

Disasters Through Recent History
Are disasters of that magnitude even really something that happen? Could they happen to you? Well, let's take a quick look through some of the disasters to strike the U.S. within the past century or so.

The Galveston Hurricane – 1900
Around 6,000-8,000 people were killed, and there was an estimated $30-40 million in property damage.[10]

The Dust Bowl – 1930s
Massive unemployment, starvation, and kids dying from dust pneumonia.[10]

The Heat Wave Incident – 1980 summer
>1,200 deaths, and $20 billion in property damage.[10]

Hurricane Katrina – August 29, 2005
Nearly 2,000 dead, >1,000,000 left homeless, and >$100 billion dollars in damage. The most destructive storm in US history.[11]

Batman movie theater shooting
Twelve killed and 58 injured when James Holmes opened fire on a midnight screening of *The Dark Knight Rises* on July 20, 2012 in Aurora, TX.[12]

Superstorm Sandy – 2012
Destroyed around 650,000 homes, left 9 million without power, killed 125 in the U.S., and had an estimated damage of $62 billion.[13]

Birmingham, Alabama snowstorm – January 28, 2014
Two inches of snow (you Yankees are laughing) left the city in a state of gridlock for *days*.[14]

Dallas, Texas shooting – July 7, 2016.
Micah Xavier, a Black Lives Matter advocate, opened fire on police officers from a skyscraper during a protest, murdering 5 of them.[15]

Las Vegas Jason Aldean concert shooting – 2017
59 were killed and 590 injured when gunfire erupted during a country music concert in Las Vegas. Highly suspicious circumstances.[16]

Puerto Rico hurricane – 2018
100% of the island lost power; 30" high floodwaters that were often sewer-ridden; potentially 4,600 fatalities; and $94 billion dollars in damage.[17]

All the Muslim terrorist attacks
There's really too many to list here. But remember 9/11, the 2017 Lower Manhattan van attack, the 2016 Ohio State attack, 2016 NY and NJ bombings, the Pulse nightclub incident, the 2015 San Bernardino attack, and numerous other acid, van, knife, and IED attacks.

It's interesting how despite all of the evidence that things are pretty fragile, people fail to prepare themselves still.
Chew the cud over these facts for a while, and tell me how any of

this makes sense.

The American Red Cross (ARC) did a study that found only 46% of Americans had enough supplies to shelter at home in the case of a pandemic flu.[18] I'd argue those numbers are incredibly liberal as well. How many average Joes do you know that could actually shelter at home for any length of time? The average Joe has something like 3 days of food available in their home? Just how long did the ARC think that people would shelter at home? Two days? So, really I think that number's a joke. Pandemic influenza probably isn't as large of a risk though compared to simple power outages. And knowing that, this next statistic doesn't make much sense to me:

Families with children of special healthcare needs were no more prepared than the general population when studied.[18]

Shoot. Wouldn't you think that if you knew your own child had to have gluten-free food, special medication, or electronic medical equipment to *live* that you would do what you could to ensure they would be taken care of perchance the power goes out? This same study by the ARC found that most families in fact aren't prepared to be self-sufficient for any period longer than 3 days following a disaster.[18] That proves my not-able-to-shelter with pandemic theory, doesn't it? If you really want to be able to shelter in for a pandemic, 3 months' worth of goods is a much better place to start.[19]

Looking further, even the Federal Emergency Management Agency (FEMA) says that we need to be more prepared as a nation for potential disasters. They push really hard for that. This can be seen in the FEMA Ready campaign, which had a three-pronged message: 1) be informed; 2) make a plan; 3) build a kit. And though I think you can take this line of thinking too far ("I didn't go to the doctor because worse off people may show up, and I'd just be diverting resources from people who need them more."), prepared households *do* actually lessen the burden on response resources.[20] That means that since you prepped, things as a whole in your community may go a whole lot better than they would if there wasn't a sizeable prepper movement already in existence there.

> Did you know that the Japanese actually store a couple of days' worth of emergency rations in their homes?[21] It seems that earthquakes, nuclear reactors, and tsunamis have taught them a thing or two most refuse to learn.

This was evidenced during Hurricane Katrina. The Superdome was set up as a refugee camp (and it was nasty), and tens of thousands of people were evacuated out of New Orleans. FEMA wasn't even capable of dealing with all the various aspects of the disaster. Katrina was simply too big. The damage caused by Katrina was so catastrophic and so widespread that it was virtually impossible for FEMA to resupply even the *basic* necessities such as food and water.[22]

Why place yourself in a position where you are solely living in the now, where perchance something bad happens, you're left to rely on unreliable government aid? The answer to that is beyond me, but people do it.

Even the Centers for Disease Control and Prevention (CDC) thinks that people should prep more. In what I think was a brilliant piece of marketing, the CDC published a zombie novella a few years back during the hay day of *The Walking Dead* that not only got people interested in prepping, but taught them some of the steps they would need to take if they wanted to be able to survive for any length of time after a disaster, whether that be a zombie apocalypse or not.[23] I actually think that the zombie craze of the past decade has helped to boost prepping as well. It's gotten people thinking about what they would do should some type of post-apocalyptic disaster take place, and they've become more interested in survival information as a result.

What Are Some of the Threats?
My intention here isn't to be a fearmonger. I'm solely highlighting some of the potential threats that even government officials have pointed out.

Biological Weapons Attack
"A large scale biological weapons attack by a terrorist organization is probably not a matter of 'if' but a matter of 'when'".[24]

We know that al-Qaeda has expressed interest in biological weapons. There are various resources online for terrorists to use to create their own biological weapons. *Silent Death* by Uncle Fester is an online book that details the production and dissemination of bioweapons. A North Korean defector was recently found with anthrax antibodies in his system.[25] Biopreparat was the Soviet clandestine offensive biological weapons program that researched heavily. After the collapse of the Soviet Union, a lot of their infectious agents simply disappeared.[26] T2 mycotoxins were found in Iraqi warheads during Desert Storm.[27,28] The Vietnamese utilized "yellow rain" mycotoxin attacks during the Vietnam War.[29] The Rajneesh cult utilized salmonella in laced water and at local

7

buffets to influence elections in Oregon. To date, it's the largest bioterrorist attack on US soil (that we know of).[30] Aum Shinrikyo, another Japanese cult, utilized sarin on their infamous subway attack, and also collected anthrax, Q-fever, Ebola, and botulinum toxin as well.[31] Prior to 9/11, the small bioterrorism group within the CDC who said we needed to prepare for biological terrorism were viewed as doomsayers. Then anthrax letters started being mailed out and that opinion changed rather quickly.[32]

The point is that this stuff is out there, it's relatively easy to create and distribute compared to nukes, and it's hard to trace.

EMP

The threat of an electromagnetic pulse (EMP) is something that some are concerned about as well. Awareness for this threat has been increasing in recent years as a result of several books, such as: Ted Koppel's *Lights Out*, William Forstchen's *One Second After*, and David Crawford's *Lights Out*.[33] An EMP, many claim, would wipe out all non-protected electronics in an incredibly wide range. Vehicles, gas stations, hospitals, medical supplies, refrigerators, and anything else that utilizes electricity would either have their electrical components fried, or no longer have power. As you can imagine, this would quickly lead to widespread death due to the people who need electricity to live, such as people needing daily doses of refrigerated medicine (e.g. diabetics), people in areas with extremes of temperature, people who were currently aboard planes, and people who need dialysis or other regular medical procedures which rely on electricity.

If vehicles are no longer working, many modern farms would be unable to grow, harvest, or deliver their food. People would slowly starve to death. Up to 90% of the US population would die as a result.[34]

The most probable method for an EMP blast would be via either a nuclear missile or an EMP bomb detonated high above the U.S. Such a blast could have the capacity to wipe out all electricity through many states.

Hyperinflation

James Wesley Rawles, founder of SurvivalBlog.com, believes this is one of the more credible scenarios, and writes about it in his excellent book *Patriots*. When $500 this month is only worth $200 next month, things get ugly fast. In the past, hyperinflation occurred when 40% of government expenditures were financed by printing more money. When this happens, it can lead to civil unrest, regime change, and dictatorships.[35] It destroys peoples' savings, making a year's worth of work disappear overnight.

Within the U.S., the Federal Reserve System (the Fed) controls the money supply, and therefore has great influence over inflation. The more they print, the more inflation goes up. As Brad Lyles says, "Inflation is the inevitable result of government intervention...into the economy."[36]

Check this out though:

"There is no subtler, no surer means of overturning the existing...society than to debauch the currency (by a continuing process of inflation). (This) process engages all the hidden forces of economic law on the side of destruction, and does it in a manner which not one man in a million is able to diagnose." - John Keynes quoting Lenin[37]

That's pretty creepy noting the rise of socialists and anti-Americans within the US lately, isn't it? Just take a look at some of the modern examples of inflation that we can see from recent history:

In May 1949, China saw an inflation rate of 4,210%.

In January 1994, Yugoslavia saw an inflation rate of 313,000,000%.

In November 2008, Zimbabwe saw an inflation rate of 79,600,000,000%.[38]

By January 2019, Venezuela is expected to see an inflation rate of 1,000,000%.[39]

Riots

Riots can happen for many reasons, but let's just assume they're from another highly-publicized shooting by a cop. They happen. Ferguson, Los Angeles, Baltimore and several other cities have all been hit by rather severe riots in the past that can make it unsafe. Avoid windows, understand that riot control chemicals affect *all*, and never drive toward the police if you don't want to end up looking like a sponge (full of holes) afterwards in these situations.[40]

Power Outages

The average American loses power 1x every 9 months.[41] Knowing that, shouldn't you at least have some method available to ensure that the food and medication you keep in your fridge and freezers doesn't go bad? What if that power outage occurs in the dead of winter? Do you have ways to keep your family warm? Ways to cook? Actual cash in case the local stores can't accept credit card?

Terrorism

The world has always faced terrorism, but after 9/11, it was brought to the forefront of everyone's minds. And for good reason. There's been a

500% increase in terrorist websites over the past 10 years.[42] You can barely turn on the news nowadays without hearing of another terrorist attack somewhere. We know that it's increasing worldwide, and we know that these people aren't stupid. I don't even think they're insane, as the media will commonly lead you to believe. I think they're *wicked*, and there's an important distinction to be made there.

Terrorists purposefully look for soft targets that are both easier and cheaper to cause massive damage at.[43] Hospitals, malls, movie theaters, and schools just don't have the security that prominent military targets do (*and* often have zero weapon policies in place). As a result, they get targeted by groups such as ISIS when it comes to choosing the next target.

I like what Matthew Stein has to say on the issue. "Emergency preparedness is cheap disaster and terrorism insurance."[44] Should terrorism hit close to home, being prepared helps to ensure that things will run more smoothly for you compared to the next guy.

Pandemic

There have been a number of pandemics throughout human history, and according to experts, we're past due for another one. One of the most prominent pandemic threats comes from influenza, commonly referred to as "the flu." On average, pandemic influenza occurs every 3-4 decades when a new, incredibly virulent strain of the virus mutates.[45] According to the US National Strategy for Pandemic Influenza Implementation Plan, if there was a modern U.S. pandemic, anywhere from 200,000 – 2,000,000 people would die in the U.S. alone.[46]

Is it even a real threat though? According to the CDC it is. Here's some of the recent flu scares that we've seen:

- 1997 H5N1 – bird flu made the jump to people in Hong Kong. Six out of the eighteen people who were infected died (a 33% fatality rate).
- 2003 H5N1 – two people identified with infection of this very rare strain. Two people died, but one never had samples taken to identify the virus. Though we're not talking about a lot of people here, this is an incredibly dangerous strain.[47]
- Late 2014 – 2015 – H5N8 influenza – a highly pathogenic bird flu spread to birds in the U.S. from Asia. Fifteen different states were hit and 50.4 million chickens and turkeys had to be slaughtered as a result.[48]

Since 1997 there have been greater than 1,826 human infections and

784 deaths worldwide caused by H5N1.[49]

So, you can see that pandemic flu isn't just a theoretical threat. It's a *recurring* threat that the world faces on a regular basis. What could the world expect if pandemic flu once again became a reality of greater proportions?

Martial law would be a very real possibility should things get bad. Anytime an epidemic hits an area hard enough, the emergency response system struggles to respond. The emergency phone lines become overloaded, and it becomes very difficult for police to respond in a timely manner. When you add the fact that police may be placed on security details at hospitals or quarantine sites, it makes sense that the police will be unable to stop crime any distance away from these zones.

Should quarantines be ordered, the local area could be blocked off from the outside world. This is one of the action plans listed within the National Strategy for Pandemic Influenza Implementation Plan.[50] This blocking of roads would most likely not be done by the police, but by members of the National Guard.

So, perchance a pandemic influenza strain swept across the globe, there are pretty good odds that you would not have quick access to the police, crime would increase in your area, sick people would attempt to break their quarantines, and your local community would be blocked off from the rest of the world.

Knowing that is the case, do you have what it takes to protect, feed, and take care of your family for a reasonable period of time? The average infection in a localized area can last 6-8 weeks, so wouldn't that make storing at least 6-8 weeks of supplies a reasonable precaution should you be concerned about pandemic influenza?[51] I say at least, because you may in fact want to store more. Once a pandemic flu has been identified, it'll likely take somewhere in the ballpark of 4-6 months before a vaccine has been developed, tested, and *begin* to be produced.[52] And who's to say that you'll be anywhere near the top of the list when it comes to getting those vaccines? To add even further concern, as of 2008, there were only two companies – Sanofi Pasteur and Chiron Corporation – that produced over 95% of the US supply of flu vaccines.[53] What happens if one of those companies goes down?

"Oh, that could never happen. You're being dramatic."

Well, in 2004-2005, the vaccination supply was essentially cut in half when one of those two suppliers faced manufacturing issues.[53] Who's to say that couldn't happen again?

Here's some other pandemic facts to think about:

- Should things get really bad, 20-30% of the global population could develop influenza.[54]
- On average, most symptoms show at 2 days post-infection, though this range is from 1-4 days.[55] It's important to note that some will be asymptomatic carriers of influenza who will infect others without feeling any of the symptoms themselves.[56]
- The human flu is primarily spread person-to-person via aerosolized droplets when a person speaks, sneezes, or coughs.[57] However, it can be spread via fomites (inanimate objects such as doorknobs), and can remain viable on such surfaces for up to 48 hours.[57]
- The average flu-infected person transmits the infection to 2 other people.[58]

If you really want to keep track of the flu within your area, utilize the CDC's flu tracker website, particularly FluView.[59] There are resources within the site that will allow you to know just how bad flu is in your area. And this isn't just for *pandemic* influenzas either. I keep regular tabs on FluView every flu season to know how alert I need to be to the issue. The flu map by the CDC is comprised of the reports that come into it from doctor offices across the nation. When doctor offices and hospitals intake patients with flu, that data then gets sent to the CDC, who compiles maps and statistics based on the incoming data.

Flunearyou.org is another neat way to track the incidence of flu within your area. It's a crowdsourced website where users click on how they are currently feeling and if they have symptoms. The data is then compiled in real time, and users can see how many cases of flu there are within their specific locale. Though it may not be as accurate as the CDC numbers (people could lie, not everybody knows about the site, sick people may not be able to access the site, etc.), it can still help to give you a basic idea of where things are at in your region.

Another monitoring system that you can use for pandemic flu is just to watch the news. For some reason, I've noticed a lot of these new flu strains start in China. The way the system is geared within the States though, things really begin to kick into overdrive once the first North American human case is confirmed. Strict measures begin to be laid down very quickly by that point, so you may want to be ready before then.

Conclusion

These are just some of the many concerns that preppers attempt to mitigate their risk towards. There are others, but I feel that the above are more likely ones, and therefore the only ones worthy of being discussed. Regardless of what you believe to be a threat, the truth remains that storing just basic materials can help you be better prepared for the entire spectrum of threats.

Chapter 2
Is Prepping Biblical?

Some of the first questions that Christians may have when it comes to prepping are these: is it biblical? Is prepping something that a Christian *can* do? Is it something that Christians can engage in without guilt? The answer to these questions is a resounding yes. In fact, there are numerous examples within Scripture where we can find of people "prepping."

The very first instance occurs with Noah.

And God said to Noah, "The end of all flesh has come before Me, for the earth is filled with violence through them; and behold, I will destroy them with the earth. Make yourself an ark of gopherwood; make rooms in the ark, and cover it inside and outside with pitch. – Genesis 6:13-14

Thus Noah did; according to all that God commanded him, so he did. – Genesis 6:22

Noah prepped. How else can you explain it? God told Noah that the end of the world was coming. Not a famine. Not a drought. Quite literally the end of the world, and it was going to be via a worldwide flood. Armed with this new knowledge, Noah wasn't expected to just sit back and do nothing, to sit back and wait on miraculous deus ex machina (though I'm not arguing what God did *wasn't* miraculous here). No. Noah was given specific instructions by God that he needed to prepare for this catastrophe. He needed to build an ark to specific dimensions, out of specific wood, with specific rooms.

Noah knew that absolute catastrophe was coming - in this case, the destruction of mankind - and he did something to get his family out of it alive. Now was he specifically instructed by God to do something about it? Yeah, absolutely. Nobody's denying that. But the point is that Noah didn't just sit on his butt and wait for the flood to come. He spent the interim preparing for it.

The next example of prepping within the Bible takes place just a few pages away during Joseph's lifetime. Pharaoh had had two separate dreams that were revealed to be warnings about the state of food that would be available for the next 14 years. There were going to be 7 years of plenty; 7 years where the earth would just straight up *produce*. Crops were going to grow great, and thus, livestock was going to fare great as well.

But when those 7 years were over, things were going to change. There were going to be 7 years of famine so bad that the previous 7 years of plenty would essentially be forgotten. It would be like they never even happened.

But check out Joseph's advice to Pharaoh:

Now therefore, let Pharaoh select a discerning and wise man, and set him over the land of Egypt. Let Pharaoh do this, and let him appoint officers over the land, to collect one-fifth of the produce of the land of Egypt in the seven plentiful years. And let them gather all the food of those good years that are coming, and store up grain under the authority of Pharaoh, and let them keep food in the cities. Then that food shall be as a reserve for the land for the seven years of famine which shall be in the land of Egypt, that the land may not perish during the famine. – Genesis 41:33-36

Joseph told Pharaoh that the wise thing to do was to store food! To prepare for the lean times ahead! He doesn't say that they just need to sit back and to "trust God" and do nothing. No, Joseph is saying that they need to prepare, or they are going to die. He understands God's providence. The guy had been thrown in a pit, sold into slavery, accused of attempted rape, languished in prison for years, and just interpreted Pharaoh's *dreams*. Yet he had lived through it all, and I would argue that he trusted God throughout it judging by his attitude as described in Genesis 39:21-23. People don't typically go to prison with such a great attitude towards things that the jailkeeper puts them in charge of things. That's exactly what happened with Joseph though.

Though holding on to this belief in God's providence, Joseph knows that they need to do something or they are going to starve. Pharaoh puts him in charge of storing food, and for the next 7 years that's exactly what Joseph does. He makes sure they produce, he stores what they produce, and he keeps records of what they produce for as long as he can (until they have so much that it's impossible to keep counting – Gen. 41:49).

Sure enough, the famine comes, and it's just as bad as Pharaoh's dream (an act of Providence) had warned.

The famine was in all lands, but in all the land of Egypt there was bread. – Genesis 41:54b

People were starving. But not Egypt. In Egypt things weren't that bad. Why? Because *they had prepared.* They knew what was coming, and they were willing to do something about it to prevent needless suffering in their own lives and the lives of their families.

"But suffering is part of a Christian's calling. It is what we're supposed to do."

Wait, what? Where the heck did you find that? I've heard this before, and it comes across as spiritual masochism to me. Yeah, suffering is a part of life. Yeah, Jesus said that we were going to face a lot of trials and tribulations and that the world would hate us. I get that. But if you really believe that we are to intentionally seek out suffering, then you need to quit going to doctors, and quit eating while you're at it. We should still avoid suffering if we can. It's not supposed to be something that we actively seek out.

> *But the Lord was with Joseph and showed him mercy, and He gave him favor in the sight of the keeper of the prison. And the keeper of the prison committed to Joseph's hand all the prisoners who were in the prison; whatever they did there, it was his doing. The keeper of the prison did not look into anything that was under Joseph's authority, because the Lord was with him; and whatever he did, the Lord made it prosper. - Genesis 39:21-23*

Does that mean that every decision we make is going to be rosy? No way! I've had plenty of uncomfortable conversations with people that I most certainly did *not* want to have, but I knew that *having* them was what I was supposed to do. In some cases, those conversations led to strained friendships. But if you stopped somebody from engaging in a substance abuse addiction that they were killing themselves with, you've probably done the right thing.

> *So all countries came to Joseph in Egypt to buy grain, because the famine was severe in all lands. - Genesis 41:57*

What I am saying is this – a lot of times people think that the most miserable option available is the correct one. In some cases, that might be the case. Moving to somewhere else may be the miserable decision on the surface, but it may be the correct one if that is where you're being called. However, don't let misery be your North Star on what decisions you are to make. Your guiding lights should instead be prayer, the Holy Spirit, the Bible, a multitude of counselors, and logic.

I raise crops and sell them, so I like to consider myself something of a farmer. Part of the farm is chickens, bees, a dog, and a cat. What happens if I don't take care of these animals? They cannot get food and water for themselves (they're kept in fenced in areas). Those animals' well-being is entirely dependent upon me. Would it be morally ok for me to just go on a week-long vacation somewhere and leave those animals without food, water, or anyone to take care of them? I don't think so.

Proverbs 12:10a says, "A righteous man regards the life of his animal."

If I want to be a righteous man, then part of my job is to take care of my animals. I believe that it's this basic understanding that is the root cause of why farmers will often ensure that their animals are fed before they eat their own breakfast every morning. The farmer can get breakfast whenever, but the farmer's animals rely upon him.

I realized after a power outage a few years ago, that no power means no water from the well. I wanted to ensure that my animals could drink and eat perchance I'm not able to get to the store to buy feed, or perchance the power goes out, and as a result, I keep extra bags of feed on hand and had rain barrels installed.

Do I think that you must have those things handy to not sin? By no means, but that verse is the reason that I do everything that I can, within reason, to ensure that my animals are cared for.

It's interesting to note that the Egyptians storing of food also saved the lives of thousands from other countries. *Because* of Joseph's preparing, people didn't die. He was able to sell grain to those that needed it who otherwise would have no recourse to turn to when hunger set it (Genesis 41:57). Genesis even delves into a more personal aspect of this with the story of Joseph's brothers coming to him to buy food. What if Joseph hadn't prepared? Would his brothers - his family – have been able to eat? Where would they have gone? What would they have resorted to? These are all questions that, thankfully, didn't have to be answered because Joseph *prepared*.

On a further interesting note, look at what happened to the people as the famine progressed. First, they lost all their money (47:14-15), then they lost their livestock – their means of producing food and making money (47:16-17), then they lost their land and their freedom (47:18-23). So, we can see from both the life of Noah and of Joseph that the act of preparing for catastrophe saved lives.

As J.P. from survivalblog.com has noted, "There are events that have the potential to destroy lives in the future, and it is only wise to prepare for events such as these."[1]

Some people may try to detract from this, and oftentimes they'll use Scripture to back up their own opinions on the subject. I learned quite some time ago though that just because somebody slaps a Bible verse onto the end of what they say, it doesn't necessarily make it Scriptural. People do all kinds of stupid things because of twisting Scripture, and I think we need to remember that. It is possible to be a spiritual sounding fool. The Bible's pretty clear on that as well.

I mean, even Satan used Scripture against Jesus while Jesus was being tempted in the desert. In Matthew 4:5-6, Satan straight up tells Jesus that He should prove who He is by jumping off the tippy-top of the temple because after all, Psalm 91:11-12 say that His angels would protect Him. Jesus uses Scripture right on back against Satan, and they move on. Look at the lives of the Pharisees. These were spiritual-sounding guys to whom Jesus had much to say. Look at Eliphaz, Bildad, and Zophar in the book of Job. These were all people who *sounded* spiritual, but couldn't have been more wrong. So just because somebody says something with a Bible verse behind it, it doesn't automatically mean they are right. You must examine the *whole* of Scripture to make sure you're not doing or saying something *really* stupid.

I like the example of the Bereans in the book of Acts. They closely inspected everything that Paul had to say by examining it against Scripture. It says that "*they received the word with all readiness, and searched the Scriptures daily to find out whether these things were so*" that Paul and Silas were preaching (Acts 17:11). They had inquisitive minds, and weren't going to accept things willy-nilly without examining for themselves what the Bible had to say about the subject at hand.

> *And whoever gives one of these little ones only a cup of cold water in the name of a disciple, assuredly, I say to you, he shall by no means lose his reward.* **- Matthew 10:42**

For example, a lot of detractors from prepping will often quote Matthew 6:19-21:

Do not lay up for yourselves treasures on earth, where moth and rust destroy and where thieves break in and steal; but lay up for yourselves treasures in heaven, where neither moth nor rust destroys and where thieves do not break in and steal. For where your treasure is, there your heart will be also.

People will use this passage to claim that to store up treasure is evil. That if you are prepping, if you are getting ready for catastrophe by laying up stores of supplies, that you are sinning; because after all, the Bible makes it very clear that we are not to do that. Doesn't it prove right here in Matthew that if you *do* store supplies that your heart is not seeking after God but after *material possessions*?

Take a closer look. That's not what this passage is talking about at all.

What this passage is referring to is the need to be more concerned over our spiritual treasure than our earthly treasure. Our spiritual treasure cannot fade. It's in heaven and it lasts for eternity! That's pretty cool! That doesn't mean that it's wrong to prepare and store things that we need in case of future crisis though. It doesn't even mean that it's wrong to have nice things. It means that we are to guard our hearts – the wellspring of life (Proverbs 4:23) – and that we are to treasure heavenly things more than earthly things (Col. 3:2).

I think charity is one of the things that can help with this, and the Bible makes it clear that charity is one of the ways that we actually *build* heavenly treasure as well. Just look at Matthew 10:42. If we give a cup of cold water in Jesus' name, we receive a reward. Focusing on a pressing problem that desperately needs immediate attention is not wrong. You *need* to build an emergency fund. Not having a few grand tucked away can quickly spell disaster when the car dies, the contracts end, or you contract mononucleosis. Working hard on pressing problems is what prepping is, and to do so is not wrong.

Shoot, if it was, then should we really study the book of Nehemiah?

After all, that's the underlying objective of the whole book! Jerusalem's walls were destroyed, and they needed to build them up fast. It's hard to defend a city against invaders with spears, swords, and arrows if you don't have proper walls. Nehemiah 4:6 says that the reason the wall was built halfway so quickly was because "*the people had a mind to work.*" They were working for an important purpose really fast!

And with good reason, because the Arabs, the Ammonites, and the Ashdodites were planning to attack Jerusalem at any moment (4:7)! If the Israelites were unable to get the walls up quick enough, their chances of survival were slim. And so, they worked on a collective purpose with all haste to protect their lives, their families, and their property. There was nothing wrong with this.

"Yes, but you're worrying. And that makes all the difference. That's why I have a problem with prepping. You're worrying about the future. Haven't you read Luke 12:22-29?"

Detractors from prepping will often resort to Luke 12:22-29. Unfortunately, they're twisting the truth of these verses.

Then He said to His disciples, 'Therefore I say to you, do not worry about your life, what you will eat; nor about the body, what you will put on. Life is more than food, and the body is more than clothing. Consider the ravens, for they neither sow nor reap, which have neither storehouse nor barn; and God feeds them. Of how much more value are you than the birds? And which of you by worrying can add one cubit to his stature? If you then are not able to do the least, why are you anxious for the rest? Consider the lilies, how they grow: they neither toil nor spin; and yet I say to you, even Solomon in all his glory was not arrayed like one of these. If then God so clothes the grass, which today is in the field and tomorrow is thrown into the oven, how much more will He clothe you, O you of little faith? And do not seek what you should eat or what you should drink, nor have an anxious mind.

These are great verses. They've helped me a lot. But prepping is not what Jesus is condemning here. No, these verses are about *worrying*. Prepping does not equate to worrying. These verses are telling us that we need to trust in God and His provision, but that by no means absolves us from doing work on our part. Did Joseph sit back and expect God to do the work because he "didn't want to worry?" No, he got off his butt and did what needed to be done, and saved hundreds of thousands (if not millions) of lives in the process.

{ **I often wonder if part of the problem that many Christians have with prepping is that it** } involves a plan. I mean after all, how many times have we heard that "man proposes, and God disposes," or that "if you want to make God laugh, tell Him your plans." And while I do agree that God's plans are often not our own, I think that gleaning from these witticisms that planning is wrong is to glean the wrong lesson.

As Benjamin Franklin said, "If you fail to plan, you plan to fail."

Planning is *not* evil. There is nothing wrong with having an action plan for how things should work, with how you're going to tackle your debt, how you're going to save to start up that business, or how to prepare for disaster. And I think a lot of people have gotten it into their head that it *is* wrong. Instead, what I think that we should glean from this is that we do need to plan – we can't flippantly float through life on the breeze. We need to be flexible enough to understand that plans sometimes change, that sometimes getting to our goal takes us on a different route than we had mapped out, and that sometimes there are going to be unforeseen obstacles in our path that we must work out.

Did Joseph sit back and expect God to do the work? Did he just pray that the silos would be magically filled overnight? What about Noah? Did he pray that a boat would just pop up out of nowhere? No way! In both cases, these men trusted in God, they knew that He ultimately controlled the outcome, but they were willing to do something about it in the meantime.

Let's look further at some specific verses in Proverbs (one of my favorite books).

A prudent man foresees evil and hides himself, but the simple pass on and are punished. – Proverbs 22:3

A prudent man foresees evil and hides himself; the simple pass on and are punished. – Proverbs 27:12

That's interesting. Solomon gives us this same advice *twice*. He must want us to pay attention here. So, it's the *wise* man that knows bad stuff is coming and does what it takes to ensure that he's going to be okay. Alright, and how do we know if there's trouble coming down the pipeline? Well, by understanding human nature. By staying informed as to what is going on not just in your own community, but in the world as well. By seeking wise counsel. By increasing knowledge.

Ask any older person in your community, and they'll most likely tell you that it seems as if we're getting storms that are much worse than what they've experienced in the past. Heck, I can even vouch for this in my community. Where I live, we used to *never* get tornadoes. For 20 something years there wasn't a single one where I live. I used to tell friends from out of state that that was one of the great things about living here, that there are no twisters.

Over the past few years we've had *dozens* in nearby cities in my state. What the heck happened?! Just last night one touched down right near my friend's house *in the middle of the city* and tore through massive trees and wrecked some buildings. It was the first one in my city in almost *70 years*. I can't go into my day job today because 19,000+ people are out of power, my company being one of them. Where on earth did all this come from?

Statistics show this as well. Weather-related disasters are increasing.[2]

So, if we know from statistics that weather-related disasters are increasing, and if we know from anecdotal experience as well, wouldn't it be wise to ensure that our family is well-fed, warm, and cared for should one of those storms/disasters strike anywhere near where we are? What's wrong with that?

Let's look further in Proverbs:

He who gathers in summer is a wise son; he who sleeps in harvest is a son who causes shame. – Proverbs 10:5

The lazy man will not plow because of winter; he will beg during the harvest and have nothing. – Proverbs 20:4

Go to the ant, you sluggard! Consider her ways and be wise, which, having no captain, overseer or ruler, provides her supplies in the summer, and gathers her food in the harvest. – Proverbs 6:6-8

So, we know that working before winter is wise. Typically, winter is pretty cold. There's snow and ice. Plants die off or go into a dormant mode. Not much food is being produced. The Proverbs verses above show that it is the wise man who ensures he is working during the summer - the time of abundance - to ensure that he and his family are provided for during the winter - the lean times.

Dependence on God doesn't mean that we should not do what it takes to prepare ourselves for difficult times and situations. As P.H. from survivalblog.com states, "God is in charge, but that doesn't make doing *nothing* a wise call."[3] Nobody denies that disaster and hard times are an inescapable aspect of life. If you've been around long enough, you *know* this. Knowing this, it is foolish to act as if there is nothing wrong with the world.

Look at Proverbs 24:30-34:

I went by the field of the lazy man, and by the vineyard of the man devoid of understanding; and there it was, all overgrown with thorns; its surface was covered with nettles; its stone wall was broken down. When I saw it, I considered it well; I looked on it and received instruction: a little sleep, a little slumber, a little folding of the hands to rest; so shall your poverty come like a prowler, and your need like an armed man.

You *need* materials to live. Clothes. Shelter. Food. Medical supplies. Money. Storing supplies during the times of plenty to survive the times of famine and drought is not unbiblical, but a wise course of action. Doing nothing – laziness – leads to need. And though need isn't necessarily directly tied to laziness every time (sometimes circumstances are out of our control) it most certainly can be a factor.

This can be further demonstrated by the following verses:

Do not love sleep, lest you come to poverty; open your eyes, and you will be satisfied with bread. – Proverbs 20:13

He who has a slack hand becomes poor, but the hand of the diligent makes rich. He who gathers in summer is a wise son; he who sleeps in harvest is a son who causes shame. – Proverbs 10:4-5

The desire of the lazy man kills him, for his hands refuse to labor. – Proverbs 21:25

It's interesting to note how people don't seem to have a problem with prepping after the garbage has already rained down. *After* the lights go out, *after* the hurricane hits, *after* the blizzard rolls through, *that's* when people decide they suddenly need to take care of their families through physical provisions. Why is that? "Well, because now it's okay. To do it beforehand would have just been being paranoid." But is it really being paranoid if you were preparing for something that actually happened? Wouldn't it have been better to just have the stuff in place in the first place? That way you don't have to frantically run to the grocery store aisles looking for the scraps of what's left while your family stays at home (or in the car) surrounded by a bunch of desperate people who are willing to resort to desperate actions. And if you don't even get the supplies that your family needs while you are putting them in danger without your presence, or with the environment that you have placed them in, was the risk really worth in the end? To have it in the first place is the wisest course of action here.

As we can see, there are numerous examples within Scripture that show preparing for disaster is not an unbiblical concept. And in many cases, refusing to do so when risk of danger is *clearly* coming down the pipeline is not an expression of a super-faith, but one of a super-stupidity.

Chapter 3
Is Prepping a Lack of Faith in God?

We've been talking about whether prepping is biblical or not, and we've seen several passages in Scripture that show it is something we can engage in without guilt. However, some critics will press deeper, and I'd argue be a little hyper-spiritual, and say that prepping is actually a lack of faith.

Let's discuss that a bit.

"Your prepping is a sign that you lack faith in God's provision."

Gag.

What a bunch of garbage. But it's one of the most commonly used arguments you'll hear from people arguing against preparing for future catastrophe. These people often cite Matthew 6:25-34:

Therefore I say to you, do not worry about your life, what you will eat or what you will drink; nor about your body, what you will put on. Is not life more than food and the body more than clothing? Look at the birds of the air, for they neither sow nor reap nor gather into barns; yet your heavenly Father feeds them. Are you not of more value than they? Which of you by worrying can add one cubit to his stature? So why do you worry about clothing? Consider the lilies of the field, how they grow: they neither toil nor spin; and yet I say to you that even Solomon in all his glory was not arrayed like one of these. Now if God so clothes the grass of the field, which today is, and tomorrow is thrown into the oven, will He not much more clothe you, O you of little faith? Therefore do not worry, saying, 'What shall we eat?' or 'What shall we drink?' or 'What shall we wear?' For your heavenly Father knows that you need all these things. But seek first the kingdom of God and His righteousness, and all these things shall be added to you. Therefore do not worry about tomorrow, for tomorrow will worry about its own things. Sufficient for the day is its own trouble.

They'll then use this passage to state that God will take care of them and that to prepare for potential crises in the future is to show a distinct lack of faith. However, this is not only an unbiblical idea, but it's also inconsistent logic, *and* a twisting of Scripture. I'd *also* argue that it is a sign of laziness and pride.

These same Christians citing that God's provision means that they don't have to do anything to prepare for future lean times *most likely* still have health insurance. They *most likely* wear seat belts. They *most likely* avoid cigarettes, save for retirement, get their kids vaccinations, change their car's tires before they go bald, and so on. Why? Not because they don't believe in God's provision. No, they do it because they understand (in those situations) that there are consequences for refusing to take preventive action.

That's the whole concept behind insurance. People buy it just in case something bad happens. Just in case their little kid breaks a bone playing T-ball they'll not get socked by a gigantic medical bill that will leave their family in a financially precarious situation. People buy health insurance to protect their family. It's something we buy in times of plenty to shore ourselves up against trouble during times of storms. Nobody hopes they'll end up in a car accident, but if we do end up in one, we're grateful for auto insurance.

If you resist acting to prevent something bad from happening, are you really demonstrating faith or are you just being lazy, fatalistic, and potentially apathetic? People regularly go to work and clock in. Why? To earn a paycheck. If they don't, they can't afford food and shelter. If you refused work as a way to demonstrate superior faith in God's provision, you're not demonstrating anything other than your own laziness and stupidity.

I've met people like this before.

People who felt guilty because they asked their wife to wear a seat belt. They thought their doing so was proof that they didn't trust in God's provision for their wife's safe journey. Wouldn't reminding your wife to engage in doing something to keep herself from flying through a windshield and cracking open her skull be *more* Christ-like? You show you *care and love* by engaging in such actions, not that you lack faith.

Wouldn't that same logic make police officers an unchristian idea?

Why do we need cops to serve and protect if we are to solely trust in God's provision? And if it's unchristian to utilize cops when you see the neighbor beating his wife in the backyard, doesn't that by extension make even *being* a cop unchristian? Wouldn't this apply to EMS workers as well? Don't call 911, don't do something proactive to save the life of your father suffering from a heart attack on the floor. Heck, don't even do CPR. Do nothing proactive at all, because to do so is to prove that you do not trust in God's provision.

I've heard this logic used from a self-defense standpoint as well. A pastor said that if his wife was being raped on the living room floor *in front of him* that he would stand back and do nothing (I'm not making this up), because to do so would be to intervene with God's plan. God is sovereign after all. He obviously planned for his wife to be raped in front of his own eyes. For that man to do anything to save his wife would be sin, according to him.

Holy smokes, if I came across somebody trying to do that with *my* wife, I'd paint the walls with their brains. The forensics team would need shovels and buckets to get that guy out of there.

Shoot, you could carry this logic down to where it's even wrong to be a doctor. Just let the disease run its course. Broke your leg? Too bad. Deal with it. Fixing it's a sin. You're an epidemiologist? How could you ever call yourself a disciple of Christ? You halt the spread of divinely-ordained disease and illness!

That's all ridiculous, isn't it? Nobody would believe that junk!

Now let's apply that same logic to prepping: is it really a sign of unfaithfulness to make sure that you and your family have what you need to survive a disaster (financial, health, natural disaster, etc.) by storing food and supplies?

> I find it interesting how people often think it's okay for the government to plan for contingencies, and to prep for the future, but it's wrong for the individual to do so. Why is it ok for FEMA to stockpile food, but it's a lack of faith on my part to have enough food stored to keep my family fed should a disaster happen? Both FEMA and I believe the same thing on this point, but for me it's wrong, and for them it's okay?
>
> Let's take this a step further.
>
> New Orleans *knew* about the threat from Hurricane Katrina yet lacked the mitigation and preparation to truly do anything about it.[1] Would you consider this responsible? Heck, no you wouldn't!
>
> Now if this was irresponsible on the government level, what about the individual level? If you knew a devastating storm was coming your way and you did absolutely nothing to prepare yourself and your family for it, would that be considered responsible?

It's funny how that works, isn't it? And yet despite the strange looks and hurtful comments you may receive now, when that person's power goes out, who are they most likely to turn to? The person they know is prepared. Nobody calls the man with no power, no food, no water, and no skills for help keeping their newly born infant warm and fed when the power goes out. They call the guy (because *now* it's okay to do something – they're suffering) who's done what it takes to ensure his family is going to be warm, clothed, fed, and taken care of.

As Patrice Lewis of rural-revolution.com says, "If you fold your hands and refuse to help yourself because of your sincere belief that God will give you full pantries when times get tough, then that's slothful. It smacks of arrogance. You're expecting Him to do the work He commands *you* to do."[2]

The Thessalonians seemed to be having a problem with a similar outlook. By the time that 2 Thessalonians had been written, the church there had been led astray by a few false teachers who were causing the people to believe Christ's return was so imminent that there was no need to work. As a result, they decided to sell their houses and lands, quit their jobs, and sit on hilltops awaiting the return of Christ.[3] It sounds like a spiritual response, but it was far from it. Paul had some harsh words for them. As 2 Thessalonians 3:10 states,

For even when we were with you, we commanded you this: If anyone will not work, neither shall he eat.

If you don't do the work, don't expect the outcome you want!

I knew somebody once who said they really needed a car. They prayed and prayed for one, but absolutely refused to get a job to work and save for one. That never made sense to me. And they never got their car either.

"God gives every bird its food, but does not throw it into the nest." – J.G. Holland[4]

I believe that working can be an expression of faith itself. Let's look back at the example of Noah. Isn't it interesting to find that he's inserted into the "Hall of Faith" in the book of Hebrews? Take a look:

By faith Noah, being divinely warned of things not yet seen, moved with godly fear, prepared an ark for the saving of his household, by which he condemned the world and became heir of the righteousness which is according to faith. – Hebrews 11:7

> One of the coolest examples I've gotten to see of a man doing what it takes to prepare his family happened via a contact I made through Craigslist. All while growing up I had several gumball machines that were placed in local businesses. It was a fun source of a little passive income as a teen, and with 3-4 locations, I made about $150 dollars a month just sitting back and doing nothing.
>
> I eventually moved, and decided to sell the

gumball machines. The man I sold them to had recently broken both of his legs and couldn't work as a result. He bought the gumball machines from me because he still needed some sort of income despite being hurt.

I just thought there was something really cool about that. Here was a guy that'd just broke both his legs. He didn't just sit back and say, "Well, everything will be alright. We'll be provided for." He got off his butt and did something. He was proactive about things rather than passive. He was willing to take the necessary steps to ensure that his family was just a little better prepared to weather a current storm.

I hope those machines served him well, and that God has blessed his efforts.

No, prepping isn't a lack of faith in God's provision at all. I'd argue that an additional reason that people get all high and mighty and self-righteous against those who prep is a result of Normalcy Bias. Normalcy Bias is a mindset that says "it can't happen to me" or "It's never happened before, so therefore it can't." It's the idea that tomorrow, and the next day, will be like the days before. You can see the problem with this kind of thinking.

Normalcy Bias is an all-or-nothing mindset. Either there'll be a zombie apocalypse, or nothing will happen, and the zombie apocalypse is a ridiculous idea, so it's probably just going to be nothing. There's no in-between here. There's no concept of month-long power outages, hurricanes that devastate an area, or anything else. It's one extreme or the other.

God doesn't throw free groceries in your cart, or magically fill your pantry with oatmeal, cereal, and bread. He expects you to work to do so.

And that brings me to the next subject…

Chapter 4
Biblical Perspectives on Charity Post-Disaster

The Bible is very clear on charity. As Christians, it's part of our job. God commands it, and we're to do it. Knowing this, how can we apply it to prepping? Obviously, if you've spent time, money, and sweat preparing in order to protect yourself and your family for when disaster strikes, you've at least earned the right to use those resources, right? If you just gave away everything you've been working for, you've done nothing but prepare to be a big humanitarian aid center to those who might not have been as wise as you were, while you sit back and starve in the cold.

There's a whole lot to unpack here, and I'd like to expand on a couple key questions that must be faced when it comes to prepping and charity post-disaster:

1) Is it necessary?
2) Who do we give to?
3) To what extent do we give?
4) What do we give?
5) How do we give safely?

Is It Necessary?
Whoever shuts his ears to the cry of the poor will also cry himself and not be heard. – Proverbs 21:13

He who gives to the poor will not lack, but he who hides his eyes will have many curses. – Proverbs 28:27

Post-disaster is one of the times people need help most. Sure, there's always going to be people out there who need help, but when a twister slams through your city, there's most likely going to be a *whole* lot more of those people, and they are going to have concrete, tangible needs.

I think the Bible is pretty clear that we are to be charitable just as a part of who we are. It's not something that we only do some of the time, but something we need as a fiber of our being. As these verses above from Proverbs state, I don't want to be somebody who's cursed by the Lord. I don't want to be the guy who cries out to God for help, but isn't answered because I plugged my ears to everybody else's cries.

"Nope. I ain't givin'. I worked for it. It's mine."

I don't want that to be my constant attitude. I first discovered this verse a couple of years ago, and it's stuck with me.

And you shall remember the Lord your God, for it is He who gives you power to get wealth..." – *Deuteronomy 8:18*

I try to remember that. It's God who even gives me the ability to get up every morning so that I *can* work to earn a paycheck. If you've ever worked in the medical field, you quickly realize just how fortunate you are. I've met people who would give anything to walk, speak, swallow, or breathe - but they can't.

What I have is only because God has given me the ability to work for it. I got it through His grace. So, as a result, I'm thankful for my ability to earn wealth, but I simultaneously strive not to forget that He is the source of my blessings and that He often uses people to be blessings to others.

Psalm 112 goes on to describe characteristics of the man that fears the Lord and delights in His commandments. There's an entire list of awesome attributes that are ascribed to men who fear the Lord, but check out what it says in verse 9:

He has dispersed abroad, he has given to the poor...

A righteous man knows that biblical charity is a part of who he is.

Keep looking at what these other verses in Proverbs say:

There is one who scatters, yet increases more; and there is one who withholds more than is right, but it leads to poverty. The generous soul will be made rich, and he who waters will also be watered himself. – Proverbs 11:24-25

He who has a generous eye will be blessed, for he gives of his bread to the poor. – Proverbs 22:9

He who has pity on the poor lends to the Lord, and He will pay back what he has given. – Proverbs 19:17

Blessed is he who considers the poor; the Lord will deliver him in time of trouble. The Lord will preserve him and keep him alive, and he will be blessed on the earth; you will not deliver him to the will of his enemies. The Lord will strengthen him on his bed of illness: You will sustain him on his sickbed. – Psalm 41:1-3

Check this out. These verses say that if we are charitable, generous, and if we give to the poor, that we will be blessed for it! This isn't prosperity gospel. I'm not saying that if you give $100 God will give you $200 back. What I am saying is that the Bible is *very* clear that those who are generous will be blessed by God. Take Proverbs 19:17, for example. If God says that He will pay back what you've given (which I don't think necessarily means an exact dollar amount), He's going to bless you back for what you've done! Who doesn't want to be blessed by God? Who can you trust more than God to fulfill what they say? What happens when God makes a promise? He answers it, and often with style!

That's pretty exciting.

Plus, look at all those other blessings that are mentioned in Psalm 41. There's 6 separate things that God says He'll do if we consider the poor! Take a closer look at those, because I think they're worth your study.

And speaking about God's blessing, check out this:

But this I say: He who sows sparingly will also reap sparingly, and he who sows bountifully will also reap bountifully. So let each one give as he purposes in his heart, not grudgingly or of necessity; for God loves a cheerful giver. And God is able to make all grace abound toward you, that you, always having all sufficiency in all things, may have an abundance for every good work. – 2 Corinthians 9:6-8

We're not blessed solely for our own benefit. Sure, I do think that God blesses us with some things solely for our own benefit. Ecclesiastes and 1 Timothy 6:17 confirm that it's not bad to have something that you enjoy. But God also blesses us so that we can in turn bless others.

Doesn't 2 Corinthians 9:11 show this?

While you are enriched in everything for all liberality, which causes thanksgiving through us to God.

Lastly, check out what Luke 3:11 says (this is John the Baptist speaking):

He answered and said to them, "He who has two tunics, let him give to him who has none; and he who has food, let him do likewise."

It's kind of hard to do this if you don't have food or clothes to begin with! All the more reason to ensure you are prepping a little extra to ensure that you *can* help others when bad things happen.

Moving on, we know that works *aren't* necessary to our salvation. We can't earn salvation. It's a gift. That being said though, we do know that good works should be a natural outflowing of the love that we have for Christ and for others.

"Faith without works is dead" (James 2:26). So, if we love Christ as we say we do, then we have the responsibility of doing good works when it is within our power to do so.

Check out 1 John 3:17:

But whoever has this world's goods, and sees his brother in need, and shuts up his heart from him, how does the love of God abide in him?

That's pretty straightforward, isn't it? I want the love of God to be in me! I want God to know it, and I want the people around me to know it as well. This is one of the reasons that I think if you're going to prep, it is wise to prep with charity in mind.

Who Do We Give To?

Things get tricky with charity post-disaster. Some of the situations are just so strange. I wouldn't be able to turn away close friends or family. I suppose this may be easier for me because I get along great with my family. If you hate your brother, it may be a more difficult decision.

I think there are some further issues here that we should go over.

1. Utilize the Holy Spirit – Isn't it great? How we can hear direction from the Creator of the universe? If you're struggling with wisdom in a situation, *ask* for it. What does James 1:5 say? That if we *ask* for wisdom, God will give it to us! In some situations, human logic is only going to be able to take you so far. The Holy Spirit can give one the discretion to know what action it is that we are to take.

2. Utilize a woman's discretion – My Dad has harped on this my entire life. He's pointed out that there have been many instances where he just wasn't sure what the appropriate choice was. In these cases, he consults Mom. For some reason, women have the innate ability to "feel out" a situation. If something just doesn't "feel" right to her, then there's a good chance you need to reassess the situation. Obviously, I think this depends on the woman you ask; is she a believer, someone you trust, somebody you see wisdom in?

3. Don't forget about the Good Samaritan – What happened in the Good Samaritan story of Luke 10:25-37? A Jewish man was ambushed, robbed, beaten to a pulp, and left for dead along the side of the road. Who helped him? A Samaritan, despite the Jews and Samaritans detesting each other for generations. This is something to keep in mind.

To What Extent Do We Give?

As J.M. of survivalblog.com has pointed out, this is most likely going to depend on a number of factors.[1]

For starters, what are the circumstances? Are we talking about a short-term power outage of a week, or are we talking about a Hurricane Katrina or larger event where society has disintegrated and you're on your own for months?

If it's a short-term event, and you have good reason to believe that it's all going to be resolved within a couple of days, then I think you could *potentially* give a little more than a long-term event. With a short-term event, you obviously want to ensure that your family has enough so that they're provided for, but you would *most likely* be able to spare a bit more to others around you.

As Patrice Lewis has pointed out, this is probably a good idea just for the fact that people have long memories post-disaster.[2] Your neighbors will remember if you were the stingy Scrooge who had warm food and blankets yet turned them down when they asked for help, leaving their little kids cold and hungry. Good luck having a positive relationship with them after that, or relying on their help if *you* needed it.

If we're talking about a large-scale disaster (pandemic, terrorist attack, EMP, devastating hurricane, etc.), then you're going to have to be more careful. If you have very good reason to believe that it's going to be months before things go back to normal, you need to be very selective. You don't want your family to suffer, and you don't want to attract unwanted attention. You can, and should, give in these situations, just be more careful.

The next factor that might determine charity post-disaster would be the attitude of the recipient. If the person is banging on your door *demanding* that you give them shelter and threatening you if you don't, then I wouldn't be too inclined to help. If they're arguing that you're not giving them enough, then I'm not going to be much inclined to help further. If they're saying they'll return with backup, that they're staying with you whether you like it or not, or similar statements, then I'd start to get angry.

However, if the person is genuinely grateful for what they've received, they're humble about it, and you can tell they appreciate your help from the bottom of their heart, then I'd probably be willing to help them out even more.

Lastly, I think your current resources will help you to reach a conclusion as to what you should give. If you have years of food stored up, then you can give a more than the person who only has a month's worth. You start to end up in sticky situations here. If you know your family only has limited food left, at some point you have to start saying no.

Matthew 25:1-9 illustrates this.

Then the kingdom of heaven shall be likened to ten virgins who took their lamps and went out to meet the bridegroom. Now five of them were wise, and five were foolish. Those who were foolish took their lamps and took no oil with them, but the wise took oil in their vessels with their lamps. But while the bridegroom was delayed, they all slumbered and slept.

And at midnight a cry was heard: 'Behold, the bridegroom is coming; go out to meet him!' Then all those virgins arose and trimmed their lamps. And the foolish said to the wise, 'Give us some of your oil, for our lamps are going out.' But the wise answered, saying, 'No, lest there should not be enough for us and you; but go rather to those who sell, and buy for yourselves.'

What would have happened had the virgins given of the oil that was needed for them? They would have been screwed. You have to know your boundaries.

What Do We Give?

This one's pretty easy and fun to work with. The answer? Anything you would find useful in their predicament and that you are okay sparing. Preppers are good at putting themselves in these types of what-if scenarios. It's what allows us to make better preparations! To get you started though, here are a few ideas of things that would be useful:

- Canned food
- Dried food (mashed potatoes/dehydrated milk/cereals/ oatmeal/etc.)
- Infant formula
- Diapers
- Feminine hygiene products
- Batteries
- Flashlights
- Blankets
- Water
- Soap
- Warm clothes
- Fire starter kits
- Rope
- Ponchos
- Tarps/black plastic sheeting
- Candles

I have seen some lists out there that include bullets. I'm pretty hesitant on that one. If I'm already hesitant to help somebody out for safety reasons, do I really want to be giving them something that can help them to take me or someone else out?

If it was a trusted friend that needed extra ammo to defend his family, then yeah, sure. But giving a random stranger ammunition just doesn't sit well with me.

How Do We Give Safely?

This part gets tricky. We've established that as Christians, charity is part of our duty. It's part of what makes us Christians. Yet post-disaster, charity can often be an easy avenue for evil to enter the lives of those who solely had good intentions. Our faith tells us that we are to give, but the logic of the situation tells us that we also need to ensure that our friends and family are taken care of first.

What happens if the person to whom you give food demands more? What if they come back with a big, angry, well-armed group that decides they're going to *take* what you have by force because they *need* it more? What happens if they demand to be let into your group/retreat/house/etc.? What if opening the door for a woman with two kids gets you shot in the head by a man hidden in the trees?

I'm not here to pound you with imaginative "what-ifs." These are things that have actually happened to people! Mankind is imaginatively evil, and often seeks out creative ways to steal what they want. You must be prepared for this not only mentally, but from a security standpoint as well.

What good does it do to let a group of four men into your house to give them food if they kill you, rape your wife, and take everything you've got?

Zero. It does zero good.

I've heard the arguments on how we're supposed to give to all and not attempt to distinguish between the tare and the wheat, but I really think that's foolish. If I know somebody sitting on the street begging for food is quite literally a fraud, that he has a nice house, a nice car, and that he makes $5,000 a week begging, giving to him is not being charitable. It's being stupid.

These things happen. I was walking downtown and saw a homeless man on a blanket begging for money with his dog. I walk into a store, come out, and it's a *different* man sitting on that same blanket with the same dog. What happened to the prior guy (I actually asked him)? His response? "Uhhhh, I'm filling in for my buddy."

We need to be wise with our charity. Don't separate your heart from your brain.

With post-disaster situations, you need to find the balance between doing nothing and putting yourself and family at risk. Some of the ideas I've heard on the subject are good. Some not so much.

The one thing that I would always advocate for is to give at arm's length when possible. Find ways to give, *and do it*, but do it in a way where the person does not know where your stores are, does not know where your family is, and/or understands that you are well-defended.

I've heard of one survival community that has decided their protocol is going to be to set up a "charity roadblock." They've found a hairpin turn near their community where they're going to make a maze of cars so people have to travel slowly through it. They'll give pre-prepped packages of goods to these people, take their pictures and names so that they can't come back through for more supplies, and then send them on their way.

Pre-prepped packages? Ok, that's a viable idea. Logging who came through and telling them this is their only handout? Ok, I think that's viable as well. I round a corner or come down the road and see a road block manned by apparent thugs with guns though, and I'm either going to open fire or go the other way (maybe both). So, I think that part of the plan is stupid. Wouldn't that be a nice way to die? Peppered with bullet holes, bleeding out with all your friends, surrounded by boxes full of goodies that you fully intended to just give away, but you were stupid with your delivery system. *"We were just trying to help!"*

I've heard of other groups giving a survival handout tailored to their geographical region. The handout lists some common edibles found in their area, and gives directions to a pond a few miles away where many of these can be found. That's an interesting idea, but it's the delivery that I think you have to be most worried about. I see no problem with giving, but you have to find ways to do it without getting yourself shot.

James Wesley Rawles repeatedly gives the scenario of a young mother with two children showing up at your door. You open the door to help her and are struck in the head by a bullet from the man on the far hillside. You could easily think of similar scenarios. We've all heard the stories about the unlucky, well-meaning man who stops to help the young women with car trouble on the side of the road and ends up getting mugged by men in the ditch who then steal his car. The women were faking the whole time. Or take hitchhikers, for example. Nobody picks them up anymore because of the sheer number of times that they've turned out to be sketchy (at best). There are plenty of scenarios where well-meaning individuals are taken advantage of. Going back to Rawles' example, I think the best, and only way to give post-disaster - when people are desperate, starving, scared, and nuts – is to give on your own terms.

Why not direct the woman to the back of the house and then throw something out the second story window? Why do you have to open the front door where you're meeting her on her own terms? Why do you have to open the front door alone? Why can't there be sentries placed strategically around the property that not only provide backup, but will be able to have a better chance of catching any mischief before it happens?

What if you didn't give anything at all other than directions? "See that mountain? At the top you'll see a gnarled apple tree. There's a cache of supplies there under a rock with a spray painted cross, and it's all yours if you get there." Having several caches like this scattered throughout the area, and sending refugees to different sites would be a way to ensure the refugees 1) do receive supplies to help them; 2) that the refugees are far away; and 3) that you aren't sending them all to the same site to kill each other over the same cache.

Charity boxes are an option that some have resorted to. Say you had a charity box at the bottom of your driveway that you refilled daily. A sign could be posted warning people off from your property, but at least you would be doing *something*. Some local hiking stores that I venture out to every now and then do this for the Appalachian Trail through-hikers. They've had great success with it. People can come and pick up a thing or two that they might need, and *usually* people don't take advantage of the system. These people aren't placed in life-or-death situations though. Who knows if somebody isn't just camping out and taking all the supplies for themselves? Just something to ponder over. But it is an option that would keep you from having to open your door and place your family at risk.

If you have the space and ability, a charity route may be something to consider as well. With a charity route, there's a designated path to where you dispense charity (whether at your door or via a charity box) that is clearly marked. Signs are posted at all other approaches to your house telling people to use the charity route, and that all other approaches to your house will be viewed and responded to as a hostile action.

Probably my personal favorite plan would be to give via 3rd parties. If you had a church, storefront, warehouse, or something within walking distance of your home that was under constant supervision, *and* guarded by nearby community members who worked varying, rotating shifts, then you can not only engage in charity by helping to stock the 'giving site,' but you can keep your family out of harm's way much more readily.

With the 3rd party option, anybody that comes your way could easily be sent to the "giving site."

"I've given a lot of supplies to Berean Baptist Church. They're 3 blocks that way. If you head there, I know they'll set you up real nice. They've got warm clothes, hot meals, plenty of water, and a nurse is on-site 24/7 patching people up. If you want supplies, they're your best bet."

Where I grew up, the local churches noticed a pattern of certain community members calling like clockwork every month saying they were having trouble paying their electric bill, mortgage, car payment, whatever. The church would listen to the spiel for often a good 30 minutes, and would then give money. Once pastors in the area started talking with other pastors though, they realized that the exact same people were systematically calling all the different churches in the area asking for money for the *exact same reason*. As you can imagine, if you call 22 different churches for a $115 electric bill and even if only half of them give the money, you now have $1,265 coming in a month and all it took was a few phone calls!

To stop this, some kids from my high school started an organization within the community where churches could direct all their local giving. "You need help with your mortgage this month or they'll kick you out? You need to call XYZ. They're who we direct all of our giving through, and if they determine you're truly in need, they'll help you out."

The organization worked wonderfully. It kept very detailed records about who exactly was asking for what. When suspicious patterns were noticed or system abusers were found, things could be addressed. The abusers were stopped, churches were no longer being duped, and the people actually needing the money could get help.

This exact same type of system could be set up with a 3rd party option post-disaster. A record and picture could be taken of who is coming and what they are taking on what date and time, to ensure that nobody is taking advantage of the system.

Are there potential cons to this system? Well, sure. You can think of cons for anything. What if the giving site ends up being overrun? Then all your supplies are lost. (Do you still find ways to give?) Obviously, keeping the giving site well-guarded is a way to help prevent this, but what if that's not enough? What if two truckloads of shotgun-toting thugs show up and you lose everything?

What if the stereotypical single-mother-with-her-children shows up to your door when it's freezing rain outside? Do you still send her on her way? What if someone injured shows up at your door? You can always think of what-ifs all day long, but this option has the fewest problems to contend with.

Whatever you end up deciding on, I'd argue that you should think about it well before-hand. The military utilizes Standard Operating Procedures (SOPs) for troops because it eliminates difficult decision making on the troops' part (among other reasons). What does the SOP dictate? What is done in a particular situation. Does all your charity flow through a 3rd party? Do you give to everyone regardless, and at your door? Do you give via charity box alone, or do you get people to work for the supplies you are going to give them by weeding the garden, chopping wood, hauling hay, etc. Thinking through SOPs beforehand can save you a lot of hassle in the long run.

I think one of the main things that you've always got to remember in these types of situations is that in a post-disaster world, charity has much higher stakes. Your very life is potentially at risk every time that you help somebody here. During "normal" society, neighbors usually don't pull a gun on you after asking for help with feeding their children. Post-disaster that's a very real possibility.

Chapter 5
What about Barter?

Offering people jobs is a way to be a blessing. Though I do have things about my employer that I don't like (who doesn't?), I'm still grateful that they were willing to give me a job doing something I love with great benefits. God used them to bless me in that way. Nobody forced them to give me a job.

You can do the same thing post-disaster with others, and this may be a way to help quell any fears that you may have with just outright giving supplies. If somebody shows up and says they need warm clothes, maybe you can work out a trade. Get help chopping firewood, loading hay, cleaning horse stalls, whatever. This way you both are able to get something out of the deal, and the person has earned it, which is actually a feeling that a lot of people need.

Good people don't like to think they're at other people's mercy. We like to feel that we are able to provide for our families by the sweat of our own brow and the strength of our hands. Giving somebody the opportunity to work does that for them.

Simultaneously, you can help weed out potential free-loaders in this way. I don't think there's anything wrong with giving somebody something that they need without an expectation of repayment. If somebody's house just burned down and they show up at my door, I'm going to give them what they need to make it through the night scot-free. What I do think is that there are people out there who will take advantage of you one way or the other. If they know that you are the guy who just gives out free food, they may show up at your place day after day expecting yet another free meal, even though they no longer have need of your charity. They just like using you so that they don't have to use their own resources, time, or energy. In cases like these, the requisite to do some physical labor acts as a deterrent.

You've undoubtedly seen this same principle at work in the lives of others around you. When a 23-year old man is told that he can no longer live in his parent's basement rent-free, his ability to find a suitable job to support himself greatly increases. He quits working 12 hours a week as a lifeguard, and finds a full-time position somewhere with benefits. That same principle applies post-disaster. When people know you're going to make them work for what you're going to give them, the people who really need it are going to be the ones who show up. If they're not *willing* (not able, *willing*) to work, then I'd let them be.

Paul made it clear when he said if you don't work, you don't eat (2 Thessalonians 3:10).

Christopher Coyne beautifully illustrated these principles in his fantastic book *Doing Bad by Doing Good*. In the book, he delves into the Samaritan's Dilemma: aid can have a dependency effect, decreasing people's drive to work, and increasing peoples' reliance on that aid.[1] Sometimes, despite our good intentions, we can end up making matters worse. As the saying goes, the road to hell is paved with good intentions. It appears that this can easily be the case with charity as well. I have heard the stories of people in Africa/the Middle East/wherever who hate Christians. Not because of anything Christians believe. They're not even upset with Jesus' teachings. What they can't stand is how the Christians show up with their cargo planes and just dump several tons of goods on the ground and start distributing them to all the local people. The shoes start flying in, and suddenly, the shoe man is out of business.

> *"The people of the area are great farmers....but because there is this relief food, they did not farm for three years. I could see the difficulty. It was spoiling people. They just sleep and have food. It is very bad."*
>
> **– Yousif Kowa on the impact of U.N. aid on farmers in South Sudan[2]**

In Iraq, large amounts of trash quickly grew to be an issue. It was collecting everywhere. The US decided that we needed to do something about it. So, we started paying absurdly high rates for people who would go out there and gather trash to be disposed of. The result was that more trash was actually *created*. Why not turn the stuff around you into money? People are resourceful when it comes to making money. People grow orchards to sell fruit. In Iraq, people were growing trash to reap the harvest.[3] What's to keep me from trucking in garbage if I know I can make money from turning it in?

Again, this same principle was seen at work in North Korea. The North Korean government finally admitted that it needed U.N. assistance. However, when the U.N. arrived, they found that they were restricted to only the "good" areas of North Korea. The regions that were devastated were off-limits. This made North Korea look good to the world, since things weren't perceived to be as bad as they truly were. The U.N. was unwittingly acting as a piece within North Korean propaganda.[4]

Do I say all this to say that you should never engage in acts of direct charity? By no means. I think the Bible makes it clear that direct charity is what is needed, something Christians are to be engaged in. When the New Testament church was going through hard times with famine, what was the response? Barnabas and Saul raised money from the other churches so that the famine-afflicted regions would be able to buy food that had been shipped in (Acts 11:27-30). That's direct charity.

What I am saying is that we need to be wise with how we dispense our charity. We need to keep our heart attached to our brain. At some point you are simply contributing to the problem, as seen in the above examples. Nathan Nunn and Nancy Qian, both economists, found that US food aid typically increases civil war incidence and time when it is given due to "aid stealing," where armed groups continue to fund their conflict by stealing the aid.[5] Furthermore, journalist Linda Polman recorded numerous instances of corrupt politicians and warlords *deliberately creating* humanitarian crises and harming citizens so that there would be an increased flow of humanitarian aid shipped to the area. The resources would then be used for either private gain or to further fund an agenda.[6]

We also know that free aid can cause people to engage in overly risky behavior that they normally wouldn't engage in. You can see this with government-provided flood insurance. When it's just given to people, they're more likely to build their home in flood prone areas.[2] Without the flood insurance, they would probably think twice about building a house right by an area that faces devastating floods every couple of years. But with free insurance? Heck, who cares!

So, what do we do knowing information like that?

I've spoken with several friends of mine on the issue who have the opinion that they are to just give regardless. That Jesus has the responsibility of "separating the tare from the wheat", not them. That their personal duty as a Christian is to just give without discretion. I disagree with this opinion though. Discretion is something that we're constantly instructed to use throughout the Bible, and if you are knowingly contributing to the problem, then you're contributing to the problem! *That* is most certainly *not* your Christian duty. Why would I want to assist in the perpetuation of the cycle of substance abuse for somebody? People don't give money to homeless people as much as they used to, instead tending to give actual goods and foodstuffs. The reasoning being is that when you give the foodstuffs and actual goods, you are not only helping that person, but you are able to keep them from furthering the bad habit that put them there in the first place. Nobody would willingly give a drug addict fuel for their habit. At least, you would hope not. How do you give drug money to somebody in Jesus' name?

On the flip side of this though, I think that we can also let the pendulum swing too far the other way. We can't become so afraid to give to the wrong person (the person that doesn't deserve it), that we fail to give at all the time. Neither of these options are what we want.

You must do something. Sometimes you have to take a risk. But to contribute to the problem is to be a curse.

This reminds me of what I think is one of the funnier verses in the Bible; Proverbs 27:14.

He who blesses his friend with a loud voice, rising early in the morning, it will be counted a curse to him.

I actually knew a guy in college who demonstrated this verse perfectly. He wanted to pray for all the guys on the hall early every morning. I had nothing against that, and I was thankful to know that somebody was praying for me on a daily basis. The way this guy chose to do this though was by standing out front of every individual door on the hall and praying very loudly for its occupants somewhere between 5:00AM-6:00AM.

When you're working till 1AM at a nursing home, staying up late studying for chemistry exams, and busting your butt in the gym running treadmill stress tests for people all day long, you *do not* want somebody to wake you up after 4-5 hours of sleep. It's funny, a lot of the other guys on the hall thought the same thing. What this one guy intended to be a blessing, was actually annoying.

I believe the same principle can be applied to humanitarian aid. For example, we know that if a government announces its intention to provide humanitarian aid after any type of disaster, and people trust their government enough (for whatever reason) to believe that the promised aid will actually come, then people will *choose* to sit and wait for the aid to come instead of *choosing* to be proactive and take steps to better their situations of their own accord.[2]

The point is, when people think the government is going to take care of them, or just some other *person*, they tend to believe that they can now just sit back on their butt and do nothing. In real life though, that's just not how things work.

We saw this with Hurricane Katrina. State-led humanitarian aid post-Katrina often stymied recovery efforts by private individuals or non-government groups.[7] Shoot, does anybody else out there remember the Cajun Navy? After Hurricane Harvey hit Texas and Louisiana, men and women who owned boats for fishing started touring their neighborhoods looking for people whom they could *rescue*. They saved people from nursing homes, from house roofs, and other places. It was an informal, volunteer-led group of civilians that got together and decided to make a difference.

Then the government stepped in and decided they needed to regulate the Cajun Navy by ensuring that the volunteers were properly trained and had paid a fee in order *to help other people*.[8,9]

Commerce is something that should not be avoided, particularly post-collapse. As Coyne states, "it is a mistake for those who are truly concerned with the human condition to dismiss the importance of economic freedom" and again, "Innovation and exchange under private property is the most effective means to achieve the end of permanently improving the human condition".[18]

A proper understanding of commerce, and the beneficence of it, can allow one to do much more good than they could by simply being a humanitarian aid center.

Chapter 6
Community Post-Disaster

There's strength in numbers. Even the Bible makes this clear.

Ecclesiastes (my favorite book of the Bible – which I've been told makes me weird) has something to say about this:

Two are better than one, because they have a good reward for their labor. For if they fall, one will lift up his companion. – Ecclesiastes 4:9-10

If you're going through hard times, having other people around can insulate you from the cold, hard ground. They're able to help you get back on your feet, make sure you're okay, and walk with you along the way. I think there are some pretty visible parallels here with charity in the Christian church. If we know somebody in our church, a Christian brother, is struggling with feeding his family this week, then we're to help him!

This same principle espoused in the above verse can be applied to a post-disaster situation. You ever moved a generator without wheels by yourself up a hill? Unless you're Paul Bunyan, it's pretty hard. Have you ever tried to tack down a tarp over the hole in your roof on a windy day by yourself? If so, you probably got a taste of how parachutes work. There are countless other examples that you could think of. The point is many hands do indeed make light work.

Let's see what else Ecclesiastes has to say:

Though one may be overpowered by another, two can withstand him. And a threefold cord is not quickly broken. – Ecclesiastes 4:12

Nobody's questioning that post-disaster things can get pretty hairy pretty quickly. As we've mentioned, when people are cold, hungry, and scared they can quickly act barbaric. Desperate people do desperate things. Sometimes it's not even that though. Sociologists and psychologists often study mob behavior. Why is it that people do things within the environment of a riot that they normally wouldn't do outside of that environment? During riots people flip cars, burn buildings, break windows, beat people to death, and the like.

You never see people in normal society attempting to burn a police car by themselves. Yet in groups people do things like this all the time. Why? I believe (and many sociologists do as well) that it's because during a riot people have a belief that they won't be caught. It's anarchy (perceived or real), and even though arrests might be made later on, people still believe that in a mob they're invisible and therefore immune to consequences.

Did you ever read H.G. Well's *The Invisible Man*? I love Well's sci-fi. In *The Invisible Man*, the scientist quickly learns the extent of his power. Because he's invisible he's capable of doing quite literally anything he wants. If punishment is the main deterrent for criminals, how do you punish somebody who you have zero chance of catching? The scientist learns this and quickly becomes a terror to his community.

The same mindset applies post-disaster. When EMS personnel are tied up, when there's simply too many people who need help for your neighborhood to be reached within a reasonable amount of time, the fear of getting caught quickly disappears.

We saw this with Hurricane Katrina. People weren't only looting food and water from grocery stores. They were breaking into peoples' homes and stealing their flat screen TVs, Xboxes, PlayStations, and other valuables. Things that had monetary value, but zero survival value.

Why? Because they believed they were invisible. And post-disaster, these same people may have the same mindset as they try to break into your home. But as the above verse in Ecclesiastes (4:12) states, it's easier to fight off evil when you're not going it alone. Some guy three times your size may be able to kick down your door and knock you out, but if you have a friend, or many friends, that guy would soon look like Swiss cheese.

Rawles discusses this in his Rawlesian Philosophy.[1] A base with 20 people all working it and creating a vibrant, functioning community is much easier to defend than a base that's squeaking by with just two people. Think about it: you have to eat, you have to sleep, and you have to poop. By yourself, you are not going to be able to have a constant state of watch going on, and as the saying goes, you don't want to get caught with your pants down. Community makes you safer. You've got other people who are watching your back and working as a team!

This principle can be seen with Neighborhood Watch programs. Neighborhoods that incorporate such a program often have more than a 75% decreased risk of crime.[2] Community after disaster equals safety.

Okay, well what if you get sick or injured?

If you're the sole provider for your family, and they depend on you for their very survival, what's your next course of action should the axe accidentally slip and hit you in the shin? What's your next course of action should you get bit by a rattlesnake, come down with the flu, or sprain your ankle? Could they make it without you? It's interesting how as preppers, we have no problem with getting ready for power outages, floods, tornadoes, civil unrest, etc., but when it comes to other potential scenarios that quite literally happen hundreds of times *a day* in your own community we like to overlook that. You're not invincible. Obviously, if you are as intentional as possible with taking care of yourself you greatly decrease your risk of anything bad happening, but bad things *still* happen. Injuries still happen. People still get sick. We understand this when it comes to stocking medical supplies, but we need to understand it from a personnel backup standpoint as well. The prepper principle of two is one, and one is none, should apply to our *community* post-disaster as well.

Even if you set the defense aspect aside, community is still a vital part of making it through everything okay. As you've probably gleaned from now, not everything in post-disaster situations is blatantly black and white. It can be pretty hard to not only know what the proper action is, but how far along that path we need to go.

Proverbs, written by Solomon – the wisest man who ever lived – had a lot to say about this. He repeatedly harped on the importance of having people whose opinions he could count on.

Where there is no counsel, the people fall; but in the multitude of counselors there is safety. – Proverbs 11:14

Without counsel, plans go awry, but in the multitude of counselors they are established. – Proverbs 15:22

For by wise counsel you will wage your own war, and in a multitude of counselors there is safety. – Proverbs 24:6

So, if Solomon says that a number of people to bounce ideas and plans off of is wise, then it's probably a good idea. I mean, I like to pretend I'm wise, and if Solomon, who really was wise, needed people to talk through things with, then I most certainly do as well.

How do you decide who to let in with you? How do you decide who to give to? How do you work as efficiently as possible? These are all decisions that others' input is valuable to consider. Other perspectives can guard us, keep us on the right path, strengthen us, and show us our weaknesses not only on a personal level but on a community level as well. This is why successful businesses routinely ask their own employees for input on how things are run. Because other people may have ideas that may blow the current process out of the water with new levels of efficiency.

In Len Fisher's fascinating book *The Perfect Swarm,* he broaches the subject of community intelligence. When it comes to finding solutions, groups virtually *always* have an advantage over individuals. The reasons being that there is greater cumulative knowledge in a group, groups have a greater number of perspectives from which to analyze any given issue, groups include a greater number of ways of interpreting what the problem even is, different people have different ways of generating solutions to problems, and different people will have different ways of inferring cause and effect.[3]

Here is an interesting concept. What should you do if you're in an unfamiliar crowded setting (e.g. a concert in a different city, a rival school during a basketball game, a hotel, etc.) when something bad happens such as a fire, explosion, or shooting? Is there a way that we can use swarm intelligence to our advantage? According to Len Fisher in *The Perfect Swarm*, if placed in a dangerous situation in a crowd, and you have zero knowledge of the escape routes, go with the crowd 60% of the time, and make your own decisions 40% of the time.

Acting in such a manner ensures that you get the advantage of the crowd's intelligence (surely somebody is familiar with the area and knows a safe way out), and that you are simultaneously not falling for pure swarming, where everybody may choose the wrong exit because they're following everybody else.[4]

According to the mathematics of complexity, when given the same problem with a correct answer, the group will outperform the individual essentially *every* time. Let's look at the math of this. If there's 100 people in a room, and each of these people have a 60% chance of getting the exact same question correct, the group has a greater than 99% chance of choosing the correct answer![5]

Plans are established by counsel; by wise counsel wage war. – Proverbs 20:18

Obviously the exception is if there is an expert on the subject available. If the question is how to perform brain surgery on the cerebellum, you're much better off going with the brain surgeon's opinion than putting the procedure to a group vote. In instances where there is no expert though, there is safety in a multitude of counselors.

The group members must think individually through the problem, however. If there is a very charismatic leader pushing for everyone to choose his or her answer, then the group's average opinion becomes skewed. In mathematical models, the best way to ensure that you get the correct answer within a group setting is to ensure that everybody can think through the situation for themselves, and to submit their ideas without fear of peer approval or unacceptance.[5]

It makes me wonder if this is what Solomon had in mind when he wrote Proverbs 18:1,

"A man who isolates himself seeks his own desire; he rages against all wise judgment."

And then he goes on in Proverbs 12:15,

"The way of a fool is right in his own eyes, but he who heeds counsel is wise."

Is Solomon implying that left to his own devices and opinions, men tend to do pretty stupid things? If that is the case, in a post-collapse survival situation being a lone wolf can lead to making some poor decisions. I'm just conjecturing here, but it is something to think about.

> ***Listen to counsel and receive instruction, that you may be wise in your latter days. – Proverbs 19:20***

Community doesn't have to be a specific size. Even having just one other person can qualify as a community of sorts. And community can make you a better person. Proverbs 27:17 says,

As iron sharpens iron, so a man sharpens the countenance of his friend.

Prior to getting married, my wife and I both went to pre-marital counseling. I confess I wasn't very enthusiastic about it. But one of the things I remember was this: the counselor looked at us and said, "You both are getting married. He is going to assist in *your* (pointing to my wife) sanctification greater than anybody else on earth. And she is going to assist in *your* (pointing to me) sanctification greater than anybody else on earth." I've found that to be true. In a proper marriage, the husband and wife communicate deeply with each other, letting each other know the ins and outs of what it is that they're thinking about, praying for, aspiring toward, and worried about. If both husband and wife are steadily growing in their relationship with Christ, then they are going to be the ones with the greatest access to each other's heart.

That said, I don't think that you can dismiss the ability of a friend to do so as well.

Having others around with whom we can talk over and through things greatly increases our sharpness.

We Have Different Gifts
One final reason that community is important is because we are all good at different things. No one knows everything, but everyone knows something. To fully grasp certain fields and subjects takes *time*. I'm pretty good at raising chickens and growing food. I'm terrible at anything engine-related. It's just not something I'm good at or interested in.

My neighbor is fantastic at mechanic work, however. He makes a good bit of side money fixing small engines like lawnmowers, ATVs, weed eaters, and all that. But he doesn't do any gardening at all. For this reason, we would be stronger together than we would be apart.

Why Build Community *Now?*
What's one of the best ways to ensure that you already have the beginnings of community in place? Getting to know your neighbors *now*. Knowing who you are surrounded by helps you to know who you can turn to for what when things go wrong. Some might say otherwise.

"Why do I need to worry about getting to know my neighbors and cultivating relationships with others around me? When the collapse happens, I'm out of here anyway!"

Let's examine that viewpoint with history as our guide. We know that in most *foreseeable* disasters, evacuations are often imposed. Think incoming flood, hurricane, wildfire, or whatever. When something is creeping up on your locale, some government official is eventually going to tell people that they need to get the heck out of there. This leads to massive gridlock as an entire geographical region flees for their lives. Let me know how that goes.

We also know that most disasters are local. If that's the case, then who's going to be of more help to you, the close friend 150 miles away, or your neighbor? You can see this even with the minor mishaps of life that occur on a daily basis. It is much easier for me to ask my neighbor for help, rather than my brother 1.5 hours away, when a chicken gets stuck in a tree.

> *Better is a neighbor nearby than a brother far away.*
> **– Proverbs 27:10c**

Let's say that you eventually manage to inch away from your house and to other areas that have been deemed as safe. Do you stay in a hotel? In many cases, you won't be able to. They'll have all been booked up from all the other thousands of people who had the exact same thought you did. Bugging out could be an option for you if the people with you are able, but what if they aren't? What if you have a kid with special needs, have medical situations yourself, or have older parents with you? Good luck getting a pregnant, frightened wife to sleep out in the cold, wet, woods when she's 7 months pregnant.

You'll need a place to stay. An actual shelter. If you've built a community prior, then hopefully you have somebody that you can stay with. A friend, a relative, someone. The fact of the matter is that communities tend to be what make it through disasters. The "united we stand and divided we fall" concept holds true.

Most this strength appears to come from the enhanced resources that we find at our fingertips when we have developed a community with others. Even weak connections that we've made with others provide us with connections to the tangibles and services we need.[6] In the movie *The Shawshank Redemption*, Morgan Freeman's character is known as the guy who can get you whatever you need. Is it because he can produce those items out of thin air? No. It's because if you're the guy who knows everybody else, you know what they may have to offer. If you know what they have to offer, you'll know where to turn when you're up a creek without a paddle.

This is one of the conclusions researchers have come to on why people who are part of a church community generally fare better health-wise and in general wellbeing when compared to those who don't regularly attend church. There are studies on this.[7,8,9,10,11] A few factors are frequently floated, and I'm by no means diminishing the role of a relationship with Christ on one's well-being, but it does seem that the relationships we build with a body of believers within *our* community plays a role in helping us know to whom we should go when we need help with a particular issue.

God designed us to be social creatures. For the most part, anyway. Some of us need to be around people 24/7 to survive, and others prefer alone time. Regardless, we weren't meant to live in solitary confinement.

This principle of community bettering us is supported within the disaster planning (who knew that was a scientific field?!) scientific literature as well. It's the communities with strong social networks, where people know the people around them, that not only are able to produce concrete resources, but better weather disasters as well.[12]

Patrice Lewis wrote about her experiences with this on her blog rural-revolution.com.[14] She noted how her neighbor's husband was serving overseas in the military. Patrice wanted to show Christ's love to that neighbor. She was raising kids all alone at that time, and Patrice wanted her to know that she had people around her who cared, people she could turn to in times of help. So, they invited that neighbor to dinner. At the end of the dinner, the neighbor said she would cook next week.

Thus, the local neighborhood dinner was started. It grew overtime to include more and more people. People came and people left. But the important thing was that *community* was built. And as a result, when Patrice has problems with calving at 2AM, she's able to call neighbors for advice. When the power went out in their area due to a bad storm, everyone supported one another.

It was cool to see the relationships she had built and cultivated over the years turn into a form protection for all of them. It wasn't anything that was done for selfish gain. *"I need to be friends with you so you can help me when things get crazy."* No, it wasn't that at all. It all started out of showing Christ's love with a neighbor.

In my favorite book on permaculture, *The Resilient Farm and Homestead*, Ben Falk discusses resilience. According to Falk,

$$Resilience = Diversity \ x \ Redundancy \ x \ Connectivity \ x \ Manageability.[15]$$

The connectivity with other cogs in the machine is a vital factor in determining how resilient something is going to be.

Research has proven this as well. How do we determine which communities are resilient enough to survive disaster? Well, we put things through this algorithm:

A resilient community = social capital (the networks that have been built) + community competence (the problem-solving skills available in the community) + information and communications + a strong economy.[16]

When we can get a community to mesh with those factors within the algorithm, we know that they'll have a much higher chance of weathering any storm that comes their way that compared with lesser communities.

Putnam's theory of social capital states that the more people connect, the more they trust each other. Note however, that part of this definition, the "know who to turn to for help" part, necessitates that members of the community actually have different skills. When people have skillsets, they are useful. This is why underwater welders make more money than fast food burger flippers. Welding is a rarer skill. People are willing to pay more for something that is harder to get.

The next part of the algorithm is information. A community needs proper data to ensure that they are making proper choices. This can be done via listening to radio announcements, communicating with HAM radio operators near/outside the disaster site, utilizing the internet, and talking with other locals. Information helps the community to know what to expect.

Lastly, a strong economy is a significant factor in the resilience of a community. If the entire community lives paycheck to paycheck, it doesn't take much to tip the scales in a dangerous direction. Strong economies are much more resilient than weak economies. It's common sense.

Steps to Building Community

So, what can we do to build a preparedness-minded community around us? Then, how do we get that community to realize the importance of being prepared for disaster while simultaneously maintaining proper OPSEC, *and* without coming across as the neighborhood loon?

People operate within different stages of community readiness. If we have a basic idea of where our neighbors are at mentally in regards to prepping, then we can better know what steps we need to take in order to goad them further along the path to preparedness.

The stages look like this:

1) No Awareness
2) Denial/Resistance
3) Vague Awareness
4) Preplanning
5) Preparation
6) Initiation[18]

In Stage One, the person is oblivious to the potential threats that exist. They just don't know. Your goal at this stage is education. You just want to raise awareness. Just the simple act of educating people in a non-condescending, conversational way is a great way to get the gears turning. After the gears are turning, some people may take it from there. For others, they'll just move to stage 2: Denial/Resistance.

Stage Two is the most frustrating stage. At this point, the person is actively resisting anything you have to say. "No, that could never happen here." "The likelihood of anything like that ever happening is slim." "Yeah, that'll never happen." These are all some of the responses you'll hear. It can be frustrating. Not only can threats be ignored or denied, but the person may actively criticize any concerns you express.

Typically, within a public health perspective, the main goal here would be to use low intensity, but readily visible media to gradually change people's minds on the issue. This would include articles, fliers, handouts, billboards, and maybe even this book! These things, if done patiently and consistently, increase the number of times that the person will consider the issue. If they keep hearing a particular issue being raised from a number of different sources on a regular basis, they're more likely to believe the threat is credible.

This is a tool that marketers employ called top of mind awareness (TOMA). This is why soft drink companies plaster their logo all over creation, because doing so prompts you to think of their product first when you're thirsty. This, naturally, increases the odds you will seek out their product to quench your thirst.

On the personal level, you have to tailor this a bit. Perhaps you just raise the issue on a regular basis with the people you're "targeting" without coming across as annoying. Maybe you lend them books, movies, or other reading material on the subject. Any of these methods may work. I've even heard of people mailing out anonymous educational handouts to all the people in their neighborhood, informing them about the potential threats their area faces (power outages, earthquakes, tornadoes, flooding, hurricanes, etc.), urging them to do what they can to prepare, and then giving some advice on next steps to take. I'm not really sure about how I feel about that method, you don't want to be seen as Chicken Little saying the sky is falling, but it is certainly a method that could get people to think about the issue in an anonymous way.

Stage Three of community readiness is Vague Awareness. By this point, the person has seen the fliers, they've been informed about the issues, maybe they've read a book given to them (*Lights Out* by Ted Koppel is a good choice), and they have a general understanding that, yeah, this is something they should probably do something about. It may be an issue that's put on the backburner for them, but it is something that they'd like to get to eventually, when they have the time, energy, money, or what have you. Within a public health setting, what you would see would be informational events. This could come in the form of local seminars, talks, workshops or whatever to get a lot of people in the area to learn more about the practical, immediate steps that they can take.

An idea I've bounced around for a while is to start a local

homesteading club. Where I live, there's a local woodworkers' guild that meets once a month. It's basically a bunch of old men who all live around the area and meet at somebody's workshop for a show-and-tell of what they've made lately, give information on good tools and woods for sale locally, and exhibit a how-to session. I love it.

A homesteading club that meets once a month could easily accomplish the goal of fostering a prepared community. If you placed fliers up at local farm stores, got a meeting room at the local library reserved, and had a set number of topics to talk about at the first meeting, I think not only would you have a lot of people show up, but it'd be a fantastic way to start building a community of like-minded people, or at least of getting others more preparedness-minded.

Events like these, when kept informal, conversational, and open to anyone, would be a great way to increase local autonomy.

Stage Four is Preplanning. Right now, the person knows they want to do something to prepare their family for threats. They know they need to. But they don't know what to do next. It's like a kid in high school who has an exam coming up, and he knows that he needs to study, but he hasn't sat down and actually done any of the work needed to be "protected" from a bad grade.

At this point, increased media exposure, and identifying the outcomes of previous disasters is what needs to take place. This could be accomplished by again bringing the subject up in conversation, or by the increased word of mouth that a homestead club is up and running. Let's say you're worried about wildfires in your area. Keeping tabs on the news, and talking with others about the wildfire that just ravaged the West Coast and what the people in the line of fire did to escape would be a way to get people thinking of actionable steps they could take if they were in the same situation.

Stage Five is Preparation. Now the person is researching what it takes to better prepare themselves and their families for potential disasters. They're reading books, searching online, watching movies/ documentaries, and scoping out potential sources of the gear they're looking for. Public health officials would use key leaders' voices to advocate for preparedness to move people to the next stage of action. People have certain individuals that they look up to or respect. If that role model says you need to buy flashlights and batteries for when the power goes out, then people at this stage are more likely to follow their advice.

Growing up, my pastor illustrated this point beautifully. It was during the time of the Y2K scare. People respected his opinion. They still do. But people were also aware that Y2K had the potential to cause a lot of havoc and misery. During this time of anxiety, my pastor had the church purchase MRE-style meals that they then sold to the congregation. He talked about the importance of storing food and water, and how, should the entire grid go down, our congregation would be in a much better place physically as a result. What ended up happening? People bought the MREs and stored water. It was cool to go over to friends' houses and see the basements full of 2-liter soda bottles filled with water lining the walls, and know my pastor influenced their ability to survive a potential catastrophe.

Stage Six, the final stage, is Initiation. The target audience is now taking actual steps to ensure that they are better prepared to survive disaster. They're storing food and water. They're learning skills. They're getting finances in order. In short, they're doing what they need to do. The only goal for us at this point in the game is to increase their networking opportunities. Introduce them to people that could help them. Invite them to a homesteading club. Get them connected with others that could improve their survival position.

These stages aren't always crystal clear, and people can jump back and forth between stages. However, they do give you a general idea as to what steps *you* can take to help ensure that your community is well prepared for any type of disaster situation.

Though I hesitate to add this, I think it needs to be said. Humans are emotional creatures. Sometimes an appeal to emotions can give the kick start needed to take proper precautions. Doctors and other public health workers will often resort to this to get the desired reaction. A doctor may tell you that if you don't lose weight, you're going to have a stroke, and then tell you about what life is like for stroke patients. Anti-smoking commercials do this all the time. They show you a person who's rail thin, has tubes attached all over them, and has to speak with that little electric razor robot-voice thing held to their throat. Why do they do this? Because it works. People are afraid of bad consequences. They will do more to avoid pain than they will to gain pleasure.

Now I'm not saying that we need to go around being fearmongers or anything like that. But what I am saying is that when people calculate risk, particularly when there are high stakes. We tend to rely on feeling over fact.[19] I'm not going to run around and tell all my friends about how if they don't prepare for a hurricane, they're going to be stuck wading through waist-high sewage water in order to find food, accidentally step on a nail, and then end up with an infected foot that quickly turns into gangrene, which runs up their leg leading to death from infection and their kids getting shipped to foster care or to some physically abusive relative before ending up getting pregnant as a teenager and committing suicide shortly after the birth because they can't deal with all the pain.

That's not only stupid, but counter-productive.

What I think is okay though, is to let people know that the reason you bought a tornado shelter is because you heard the stories of parents who watched as their kids were sucked out of windows during the tornado in Alabama, and you didn't want that to happen to you. I think there are ways to express concern in a way that appeals to emotions, without resorting to being a doomsayer fearmonger. Discernment and wisdom will guide you.

That said, a little competition can go a long way in getting people to prep as well. There's theories that the Golden Horde concept will first start with the *Personal* Golden Horde – the people that you know – showing up at your door and looking for help or a handout. By getting your community more prepared, you can lessen the "burden" that they may place on you or others post-disaster. Like it or not, disaster plans need to be made with neighbors in mind.[20] An interesting way that I've heard of utilizing competition to this effect is to have a prepping contest with an end prize that people compete for.

This could be an iPad, a cow, cash, a gun, or some other cool prize that will get people participating in a competition that will help them become more resilient toward disasters in the process. Perhaps having a point scale, where somebody will get 10,000 points for being the first household to have two rain barrels installed. Whichever household gets to 200,000 points first wins. When we utilize the emotional experience, and get people involved in competition, we see increased levels of preparedness.[21]

A modern way to incorporate these into your prepping may be through an app where you can visually track your progress. A software that gives virtual badges, allows you to 'level up,' and so on when you log your recent prepping additions.

One of the things I've realized from working in personal training, is that people need to see small goals being met if they're ever going to reach the big goal. The person may be 400 pounds with the big goal of dropping 200 pounds so they can get their knee replaced. But to try to tackle 200 pounds all at once is overwhelming for people, and when they stare at the forest with their axe, rather than just chopping down one tree at a time, they quit. It's too overwhelming.

There's an old saying I really like that this reminds me of.
Mile by mile
Life's a trial.

Yard by yard
Life is hard.
But inch by inch
Life's a cinch![22]

I've found that little poem to be incredibly true, across a broad spectrum of situations. When we focus on small goals, accomplishing them gives us the fuel needed to move on toward the next. We're ultimately moving toward the finish line all along the way, but because we're focusing on the individual trees rather than the forest, it becomes doable.

When I can get a client to focus on just getting to the gym 2x/week to start, without any other changes, they have a small goal they can accomplish that will set them up for the next one. Then we'll start eating on a schedule. Then we'll start cutting junk food from their diet. Then we'll increase gym frequency, and so on.

The same concept applies to prepping. Small task achievements keep motivation going.[23] If we can move in incremental steps from storing just 3 gallons of water first, then storing a bucket of rice and beans, then reading one of Rawles' books, and so on, we can ultimately end up reaching the long-term goal of being prepared. These smaller steps are needed to begin with.

Drinking from a faucet is actually enjoyable, and we leave refreshed and no longer thirsty. If I attempt to drink from a firehose, not only is it an incredibly unpleasant experience, but I probably won't stick around for very long either. Information works that way. When we're faced with information overload about anything, especially with preparedness advice, we tend to have a just screw it mentality.[24]

We need those small steps.

Chapter 7
Do You Let Them Stay?

There's a concept known as the Golden Horde, and the term refers to the masses of people post-disaster who spread outward from cities in search of food, shelter, medicine, safety, and supplies. Some people believe that the notion of mass exodus from cities post-collapse is nothing more than a myth made up by trigger-happy Rambos. I'm not so sure.

There's a lot of debate on the Golden Horde concept, and whether it even happens at all. The term was coined by James Wesley Rawles' father, and has since taken off from there.[1] There are several arguments for and against it on both sides of the issue, but here are just a few to give you a taste of what's out there.

AGAINST
1) People have learned helplessness thanks to entitlement programs, and will wait for the government to help them. By the time they realize that the government ain't coming, they'll be starving, and too weak to travel far as a result.
2) People today are too fat and out of shape to travel by foot any length of time.
3) Cities today are so large that it would often be a multi-day trip just to get out of the city. The chances that people would have the supplies to last a multi-day trip out of a city are slim.
4) How far can unprepared people walk in extreme temperatures? What if the Event takes place in the dead of winter, or in the July heat?
5) History has shown that cities are where people find safety. That's why Spanish missions were built a day's travel apart, so that people wouldn't be exposed to the wild for too long. People will choose to stay in cities, or will actually travel *to* them in a disaster, because that's what the trend of history has shown.

FOR

1) As long as cars work, there's going to be people who will attempt to escape by vehicle. We see this with hurricane evacuation routes, earthquakes, wildfires, and the like. Why assume that everybody is going to flee on foot?

2) Even if most people in a city such as New York decide to stay, or can't physically leave, if only 10% make it out of a city with 1,000,000 people, that's still 100,000 people that are going to be leaving the area in search of supplies and shelter elsewhere.

3) The massive Syrian migration of late, The Dust Bowl migration, the 40,000 Yazidi religion members who fled ISIS, the fleeing of Rwandan civilians from ethnic genocide, the WW2 fleeing of European Jews from the Holocaust, the Vietnamese Boat People who fled Vietnam during the war by boat, and the evacuation of New Orleans during Hurricane Katrina all give credence to the Golden Horde concept. It clearly happened before, so why not again?

More than 1 million people were displaced by Katrina alone.[2] These people had to go somewhere. Where did they go? Pretty much anywhere in a fanlike motion away from the affected areas. And what do you do if all the hotels that you're showing up at are booked, there's no power at the gas station and you're out of gas, or you straight up don't have the cash to book a hotel? You end up camping out where the car stops. And that *may* be where your neighborhood is. What do you do if people start camping out on your lawn? What do you do if they start knocking on your door? Who do you let stay, if any?

Speaking of the Golden Horde, I think the potential for it raises a few thought-provoking questions. I've read several posts by preppers who claim that post-collapse, when the Horde is going to be moving en masse, they're going to place signs around their community indicating that government aid and free resources are readily available 15 miles in the opposite direction.

Hoo boy. That's a loaded question right there.

How do you know if the people coming to your door are people you should let stay or not? This needs to be examined on a case-by-case basis. There's a survival card game called Conflicted where you are faced with a series of survival/post-disaster tough decisions. One of them talks about how you find a group of orphans in an alleyway sifting through a dumpster. Do you take them in? I don't really see how you can send them on their way.

The Bible is very clear that we are to take care of both widows and orphans. God believes in taking care of the helpless (Remember, that's what we *are* without Him. No chance at Heaven without Him.), and from a human standpoint, it's hard to get much more weak, defenseless, and helpless than a widow or an orphan. Typically speaking, widows are older women who may have some health issues, and can't do everything necessary to provide for themselves or their place (a lack of know-how, strength, or stamina). They need help. Genuinely.

> *Pure and undefiled religion before God and the Father is this: to visit orphans and widows in their trouble, and to keep oneself unspotted from the world.* – James 1:27
>
> *Honor widows who are really widows. But if any widow has children or grandchildren, let them first learn to show piety at home and to repay their parents; for this is good and acceptable before God.* – 1 Timothy 5:3
>
> *Learn to do good; seek justice, rebuke the oppressor; defend the fatherless, plead for the widow.* – Isaiah 1:17

Think about orphans. How's a kid with no parent going to make it out there? Think about you when you were that young? If you're like me, you can think back to how much of an idiot you were! You had no clue about the real world, were extremely susceptible to danger, and were essentially clueless when it came to providing for yourself. Age brings wisdom, and as an older, wiser Christian you *will* be able to give that kid advice on growing up that they wouldn't have had access to otherwise.

To add to that point, remember the current state of society. We live in an age of technology where many kids no longer have chores, spend most of their time indoors, and spend most that time looking at a screen. How's a kid like *that* going to make it out in real life on their own self? They're either going to end up dead or being taken advantage of in ways that involve some pretty dark sins.

Should these kids be able to anticipate the same type of *pre-disaster* existence they had living under my roof *post-disaster*? Heck no, Pablo! They're going to have to help! They're going to have to gather eggs, weed gardens, and wash dishes. But they won't do it alone. I'll be right there with them. I'd talk with them, laugh, listen to their stories, teach them what I know. They'd have warm beds, hot meals, water when they're thirsty, medicine for when they're sick. I'd take care of them. And I think God would be pleased by that.

What about the others though? What about family, friends, friends of friends, or just the random strangers who show up at your front door viewing you as their last resort?

There is no easy answer here.

I know that if you're on a life raft after a cruise ship explosion, you can't save everybody in the water around you. If you overload the raft, it fills with water, sinks, and then *everybody* drowns. At some point, you must say no. I'm sure there were captains at Dunkirk who would have loved to take the entire army off that beach in WW2, but just couldn't. They weren't physically able, and as a result, at some point they had to say no. If, as an employer, you refuse to fire the 4 people you need to let go due to budget reasons, then the company becomes unprofitable, and then *everybody* loses their jobs. Is it the same thing with a homestead or retreat after an EMP, pandemic, or what have you? Something to think about.

As I mentioned before, I'd have no problem deciding for family and close friends. They're in. I want to take care of my own. It's the rest that I'm more hesitant toward.

There is advice that may help. In James Rawles' *Patriots* series, his characters bring the person in for an interview.[3] The person is grilled with questions, who they are, where'd they come from, what's their story, what was their prior job, etc. After examining all the facts, the group then comes to a decision about whether they should include the new person or not.

What are potential ways that the new person could help around your home? Can they fix cars? Do they have medical background? Are they a fantastic cook? Do they have their own supplies? Even those such as the widows and motorized scooter guy could have skills that benefit you. Somebody to can vegetables, babysit kids, help purify water, wash dishes, watch the front gate, etc.

I'm not saying that the ability to do a job is the one factor that decides whether somebody gets to stay with you or not. If that was the case, then a quadriplegic that rolls up your way is going to be straight out of luck even though you're probably the only one that can help them. There may be "dead weight" around where you're at, but I do think that God would bless you for it, and that even though you may not have much in the way of supplies, that He would still find ways to provide for where you're at. Aren't there numerous examples of this in Scripture?

Jim Cobb, a prepper who's written several books on prepping and survivalism, has some basic rules that he lays down as to who should be let in.

1) If they own property in your territory, let 'em in.
2) If they're family of a current resident, and that resident takes responsibility for 'em, let 'em in.
3) If they have desirable skills, let 'em in.[4]

Obviously, you don't have a right to keep people from accessing their own property. They paid for it, they paid the taxes on it, and they put the sweat equity into it. Not you. To keep them from accessing their property is essentially theft. You're robbing them of the ability to utilize their earned resources. The only exception that I can think of with this is if we're talking about a pandemic style situation, and the person is visibly sick with whatever is going around. If that's the case, you probably don't want to let somebody with an airborne virus into your community.

Wrapping It Up
Answering the question regarding who you let into your retreat/home, and who you say no to is a very tricky situation. There are many factors that you need to consider. Hopefully, this chapter has helped to shine some light on what can lead to some uncomfortable decision making.

Chapter 8
Caring for People Post-Disaster

Anytime there is a disaster, there is the capacity for people to enter a strange mental state. I don't think anybody would deny that. When your hometown was just obliterated by a hurricane, nobody expects you to behave "normal." The fact of the matter is that when things around us get crazy, we tend to get stressed, and potentially a little crazy.

Stress has a physical component that *can't* be denied or ignored. You wouldn't tell anyone lost at sea, buried under earthquake rubble, starving, being held at gunpoint, or in a physically abusive relationship that because they're stressed at that moment they lack faith.

So what would you say if I told you that despite this truth - that physical stressors exist - that there is something that we can do for it?

Well, the truth is that there are things you can do to help other people out emotionally, mentally, and spiritually post-disaster, and there's actual research behind it.

Post-disaster, people are going to be hyped-up on adrenaline. They're going to be having a lot of thoughts running through their head. They may be dealing with unnatural guilt, excessive sorrow, loss, depression, or who knows what else.

We know there are physical responses post-disaster. Increased heart rate, increased blood pressure, difficulty breathing, hyperventilation, chest pain, muscle tension, fatigue, increased perspiration, dizziness, headaches, and stomach pains are all common after a disaster.[1] These are all psychosomatic factors that occur because of what's going on in the heads and hearts of the people around you! So, what can we do to minister to these peoples' needs post-disaster?

There's a field of research called crisis theory. According to crisis theory, one of the first things that we can do is to normalize these people's feelings and experiences. Feelings of guilt, sorrow, anger, and so on are going to be normal after such a situation, and people need to know that what they're feeling is not something off the wall.

The second step in crisis theory is to provide information on what to expect with grief. In our example, somebody may have just lost several family members to the bioterrorist attack. Maybe even their home was viewed as contaminated and condemned. People need to know that they are going to take a while to get over this.

The third step is referral. Referral should be made to help the people that are going through the grieving process. Ideally, post-small scale disaster, these people would be referred to an actual counselor or therapist. But in our example, what if the bioterrorist attack followed an EMP, and devastated the nation? There's probably not going to be a lot of counselors and therapists around. In a case like this, what you have access to is what you have access to. People who have gone through similar experiences, who have the spiritual gifts of giving wisdom and advice, who have gone through counseling training in the past, are your best bet. Let's say that it's just your 23-home neighborhood that's still standing. If you know the people in the house down the road lost a child to disease several years ago, they may be able to help others through the grieving process.

The fourth step in crisis theory is to offer immediate assistance with problem solving. In our EMP/bioterrorism example, if the person needed help figuring out how to get in touch with their father in the next state over, giving them the contact information of a local HAM operator who EMP-proofed his supplies may be something that could help. Two heads can be better than one, and you may be the cooler mind during this time. Your reason may be able to peer through the darkness which their emotions can't penetrate.

The fifth step of crisis theory is to listen intently and emphatically. The person needs to know that people truly care, that they aren't going through this alone, and that they have somebody they can turn to. Think back on your own experiences here. What did you glean from the person who said they were there to help, but clearly had their mind elsewhere and weren't interested in what you had to say? Was it frustrating? Did you desire to tell them more of what was going on?

And finally, the last step of crisis theory is to help the person with their basic physical needs.[2] If the person needs food, blankets, shelter, clothing, or fuel, helping them get these basic physical needs can help them to know that things are going to turn out okay.

It's interesting to read different psychologists and counselors discuss disaster, because they tend to overlap with each other in their theories. Material resources can be one of the first things that can cause stress that we need to help with. This is Maslow's Hierarchy of Needs. If a guy is stressed out because his family has no water, providing water can eliminate that source of stress. However, socialization and spiritual resources are two other ways that we can help to combat post-disaster stress in people.[3]

The socialization aspect can be seen in Step Five of crisis theory. When people know there are others around them empathetic to what they are going through, they have increased resilience. They're less likely to crack. I've often wondered about this in regards to the nature of the church. A church is a place where a local body of believers gets together, builds community, and relationships. When people at my church are going through tough times, there are people around them who can give the hand needed to keep them from falling over the ledge. A local church body provides ready access to a body of like-minded believers who support each other through the trials and joys of life. It's comforting to see how God provided for us by creating an institution that He knew would offer the assistance needed.

Lastly, when people have gone through a disaster, they can go through spiritual distress as well. Questions can be raised regarding the nature of God, the brevity of life, what happens after death, and so on. Spiritual duress is just a part of disaster for many people. Ninety percent of those surveyed post-9/11 responded that one of the primary ways they coped with everything was through their faith.[4]

What an opportunity for Christians to step in and share the love of Christ!

Crisis theory steps into play well after the crisis has already taken place. What do you do immediately after a bomb explodes, a school shooter has just achieved his goal, or a terrorist has just flown a plane into another building? In these cases, something called Psychological First Aid (PFA) is useful. There are 5 elements to it, and though I am by no means a counselor, nor do I pretend to be, having a general idea of PFAs may be useful to you.

1. **Promote a Sense of Safety**
Let the people around you know that they are safe with you, if that is actually the case. If you've removed the person from the disaster scene, then you can reasonably assure them that they are safe. People will often operate under a herd mentality. There's the perception that numbers equates to safety. This can be seen when kids play hide and seek in the dark. Little kids don't like to hide by themselves. They like to hide with a friend. They feel more at ease than when they are alone. Just the simple fact that you are there with them can help the person feel safer, particularly if you are still in the midst of disaster.

2. **Promote Calming**
You must get the person to calm down, particularly if they're freaking out. Speak calmly and reassure them.

3. Promote Self/Collective Efficacy

"You can do this. You're a kindergarten teacher. If you can successfully manage a room full of public school tyrants, then I assure you, you can get through this." You need to help people find their strength. This may not even be on an individual level. It may be on a collective level. A "we can do this" rather than a "you can do this." If you've got an entire high school football team with you that's stranded in the mountains after a bus crash, reassuring them that they, *as a unit*, can get through this can help immensely.

4. Promote Connectedness

Separation from friends and family can be incredibly stressful during a time of crisis. People not only want to know that their loved ones are safe, but they want their loved ones to know that they are safe as well. By helping kids to find their parents post-earthquake, or parents to find their kids, you help to promote the connectedness that can help to eliminate a significant amount of psychological duress.

5. Promote Hope[5]

I was surprised when I saw this listed as the 5th step of PFA during my research. It's just something that comes naturally to a Christian. This is an area where a Christian could really shine. Why? Because what better source of hope is there than God Himself? What better source of hope can we have than to know that there is an omnipotent, omniscient, omnipresent, good, loving, and caring God who is *on our side*? (Psalms 139; John 3:16; Matthew 19:26)

Don't make overreaching promises on your behalf, though. Hope needs to be based in truth for it to have any credence. If you're telling somebody who just lost everything, "Don't worry, we're going to get you another house," then you're overstepping your boundaries (and unless you are going to get that person another house).[6]

Among other factors about PFA that I found interesting was that you should ask *how* you can help, *not* if they need it. We already know the survivor needs help.. Asking *what* you can do to help is a much better way to ensure that the person actually accepts your help in the first place.

And though it seems trivial, you must give them your full attention. You can tell when somebody isn't mentally present when you're talking. Guess what? Others can too. If you're not truly listening, you're not going to be able to build the rapport with the person you're trying to help.

Normalizing stress reactions is a part of PFA as well.[6] I saw a good illustration of this on TV once. I was watching a documentary on the war on drugs throughout Mexico. Apparently, kidnapping is a great way for cartels to make extra money. They hold the kidnapped person for ransom, and if the family doesn't pay, the hostage dies. Mexico has a special task force whose sole goal is to rescue these hostages. The documentary showed video of the hostage rescue team busting through the doors of some dilapidated stone building deep within a favela somewhere. When they got through the last door, they entered a dark room with no light and found a dirty, sweaty, bloody, and terrified hostage tied to a chair. They released him, ungagged him, and then one of the rescue team members grabbed the man in a bear hug and told him over and over again, "It's okay. We have rescued you. You're safe now. It's okay to cry. We rescued you. You're safe." The man was in complete shock at first and looked as if he didn't know what to do. Then he wept.

Don't Forget Your Own Well-being

We'll dig into more of the nuts and bolts on this one with the chapter *Dealing with the Stress*, but some of this needs to be addressed now. It's vitally important that you make sure you're physically protecting yourself as you protect others. You don't know what's in that other person's bodily fluids. The person you're attempting to stop a bleed on could very well be exposing you to blood-borne pathogens. I recommend keeping surgical gloves stocked in your house, car, and in your everyday carry (EDC) kit. If you just saved somebody else's life, but contracted AIDS, hepatitis, or some other STD, you harmed yourself, and put others at risk, in the process.

Aside from bodily fluids, do what you can to ensure that the disaster scene is relatively safe before entering. Obviously, in some circumstances there is no "safe." If terrorists are shooting up a movie theater, there is no "safe." But if an earthquake has just draped live power lines all over a car with people in it, grabbing the door handle with your bare hand isn't a wise course of action. In CPR classes, they teach this concept as "ensuring the scene is safe." If you don't do this before administering assistance, you could end up becoming a victim yourself.

Lastly, if you're the one having trouble coping mentally after a disaster, seek help. If it's a situation where society hasn't collapsed completely, then there's going to be counselors, therapists, and psychiatrists who you can talk to who can help. If it's a "the end of the world as we know it" (TEOTWAWKI) situation, just having other people around who you can talk to can help. I guarantee you you're not going through the same thoughts alone. There's a reason that support groups for alcoholism, PTSD, divorce, depression, single parenting, and the like are so popular. They help.

Chapter 9
Caring for Those Who Need More Care

It'd be great if everybody under the umbrella of your responsibility was in great shape, had zero health problems, could take care of themselves, and were productive as well. Unfortunately, that's often just not reality.

What do you do if your parents are elderly, your spouse has severe health issues, and your child is too young to be of any help? When life slaps you upside the face like that, things become much more real. So where do you even start? It'd be nice to have some sort of stepping stone that lights the way for which path we are to follow here, wouldn't it? Fortunately, that stepping stone comes from the Bible within the New Testament.

But if anyone does not provide for his own, and especially for those of his household, he has denied the faith and is worse than an unbeliever. – 1 Timothy 5:8

Failing to provide for our families to the best of our abilities is morally wrong. How can you say that you love your family if you don't do what *you* can to make sure they're taken care of? What if they need particular items to *live*? What's the best way to ensure families who may need extra help are taken care of during an emergency? To prep for them too.

What does this look like? Well, if you have a son with a severe allergy to bee stings, then you would most likely want to have more than one Epi-pen available in your preps. Isn't that an example of love? Of course, this is just a simple example, but it gives you a general idea of what we're talking about here.

That said, there are instances where individualized needs must be met for various groups. Who are some of the groups that are going to need more care? And what can we do to ensure that we *are* taking care of them to the best of our ability? Let's take a look.

Kids

When it comes to vulnerability, kids are about as vulnerable as they come. They can't fend for themselves, they don't know what they need to do to take care of themselves, they're weak, and they're easy prey for wicked people looking for victims after a disaster.

Because children are small and weak, they have difficulties escaping danger or seeking safety. Part of this is because they aren't very good at making decisions at this stage.[1] Shoot, even after college I still had trouble making wise decisions, not knowing anything about what to do in different situations. Hang around kids long enough and you'll realize that the decision-making skills just aren't there. I ran into barbed wire fences, rode bikes into rose bushes, sledded through blackberry bushes, swam through a pond in the middle of January, and almost got hit by a semi-truck when I ran across the interstate for the heck of it. And most of that was before high school! What's a kid to do when he's separated from his family, he just watched his dog die, he has no food, it's raining, and things in the world are only getting worse?

They're going to need help.

> Kid's brains aren't fully developed. Until the age of 25, people process information with the amygdala, the emotional part of the brain. This is why teens are notorious for doing stuff that's just straight up dumb. Adults process information with the prefrontal cortex, the rational part of the brain.[2] Of course, this doesn't mean that the consequences of poor decision making on a kid's/teen's part should be removed. What it does mean is that as an adult, you will be able to provide a level of thought to situations that kids cannot.
>
> I heard the story of a 17-year-old in my community who ended up getting a girl pregnant. His response? "This is going to ruin my senior year of soccer!" Really, bud? That's what you're worried about here? *High school soccer games*!? Kids don't think through things as well as an adult does. So the question is: post-disaster, does that lead to increased responsibility on your part? I'm not saying that you need to run through the streets gathering everybody you find who's not an adult. I'm simply posing a question that you must answer: if you see a kid struggling post-collapse, what do you do?

According to the Disaster Medical Assistance Team (DMAT), a group of medical professionals who are deployed by the government to the scene of large-scale national disasters, about 30% of all post-disaster patients are kids, so it's safe to say that kids are going to be a very large percentage of the population running around after any disaster.[3]

Kids have an increased risk of dehydration and hypothermia when exposed to the elements for any period of time.[4] So you need to make sure that you have fluids, shelter, clothing, and sources of warmth to help them during this time.

Because their bones aren't fully developed, kids are more prone to serious, potentially life-threatening injuries of internal organs. Most of an adult's internal organs are protected by the rib cage. A child's rib cage is not fully developed yet though. Should there be some type of physical trauma or crushing injury to a child's torso, there is a very high likelihood that the kid is going to have multi-organ trauma.[4] These types of injuries are outside of the scope of treatment for anyone other than a doctor, and need to be addressed as quickly as possible.

If you lived through a traumatic event as a child, whether that be a divorce, house fire, tornado that leveled your town, or the death of a loved one, then you know how sometimes those events can cause issues that can be difficult to process.

A kid's mental health is especially vulnerable during disasters, and this can lead to life-long consequences. Drug abuse, alcoholism, high school dropout, depression, anxiety related disorders, PTSD, poor social adjustment, long-term displacement, and poor academic achievement are all some of the bad outcomes that kids are at an increased risk of post-disaster.[5] This is where prepping is prevention! By not only having prepped supplies, but by having prepped your soul and mind with faith, biblical knowledge, a relationship with Christ, and skills, you can help to prevent some of this suffering for not only the kid, but for that kid's family from ever happening in the first place. Don't give those weeds room to grow!

> Why did I mention the kid's family suffering? Aren't we talking about the kid here? Yeah, but don't pretend that a kid's problems don't cause suffering on the part of the parents as well. If you're a good parent, you hurt when your kid hurts.

One summer I worked in the same building as my community's pediatric psych ward. On my lunch breaks, I would go outside to eat in a gazebo on the front lawn. I can't tell you how much it broke my heart every time I saw some a child, maybe 6-8 years old walking in the building to deal with what had already occurred in their short little lives. I'm not sure what happened to them, but if I had the opportunity to have prevented it, I would have.

Post-disaster, that opportunity just may float your way. As a God-fearing, knowledgeable adult, you'll be able to act as the shield that casts aside all the arrows of mental torment aimed at that kid's mind, because kids *are* really susceptible to mental issues post-disaster.

KIDS' RESPONSES TO DISASTERS	
1-5 year old	Bed wetting, crying, trembling, clinginess, nightmares
5-11 year old	Thumb sucking, clinginess, whining, depression, fear development
11-14 year old	Sleep/appetite problems, psychosomatic problems (vague pains/headaches/etc.), rebellion, no interest in social activities
14-18 year old	Confusion, poor concentration, aggression, headaches, apathy, withdrawal, irresponsible behavior (6)

As a parent, you are your kid's chief role model. Kids emulate their parents' behavior. Proverbs 17:6 tells us that parents are the pride of their children. Our kids look up to us. Within the context of disaster, this has far larger consequences. If the parent responds calmly to the disaster, or at least reasonably, the child will model this behavior from his parents.[6,7]

> Though children tend to model their parents' response post-disaster, teenagers tend to model their peers' response instead.[7] Teenagers tend to have a reputation for rebelling against their parents and listening to their friends. I think it's important to assist in building a strong peer group for them that is well-grounded in a faith in God. My church did this for me via Awana-esque programs. My peers and I would meet 1-2x/week for a Bible study and then play basketball, capture the flag, beach volleyball, or the like. We enjoyed the opportunity to hang out with each other, but we were also shepherded along the way by adults who loved us and taught us about Christ.

If the parent changes how they parent, if rules change after the disaster, if the parent themselves change after the disaster, then the kid is at an increased risk of developing PTSD.[8] I don't tell you that to lay further burden on you after a tornado has just robbed you of all your earthly possessions. Not at all. I am saying it so you understand, or at least can help others to understand, that you sometimes have to be strong for the sake of your kids. This isn't to say that every kid after a disaster is going to end up developing PTSD. Post-traumatic stress disorder is the exception, not the norm.[9] Still, that doesn't mean that just because the odds seem to be in our favor that we ignore the issue (or risk) entirely.

An acquaintance told me the story of a study done on orangutans. An orangutan was locked in a small cage, and then the cage was shaken around and jostled. The lone orangutan freaked out, jumping all around, thrashing, and screaming. When they put two orangutans in the same cage and did the exact same thing, the two orangutans just went up to each other and held onto each other tight without nearly as much fuss.[11] We want to know that somebody is there with us. It's comforting.

Kids also have a tendency to blame themselves whenever a disaster strikes.[6] As an adult, we look on their self-induced guilt in wonder. How on earth could the kid think that the loss of their favorite dog in a house fire was *their* fault? How on earth could the kid think that their parent's death from a terrorist attack was *their* fault? I don't really know why kids do this, but they do. This is an incredibly common thing to see after parents divorce. The kid thinks that if only *they* had done XYZ, then their parents would still be together. If given the opportunity, your job is to help disprove this. Kids need to know that not only are they not responsible for what happened, but that what did happen was outside the realm of their control. When kids know this, it helps them to heal. It helps them to not walk around with such a heavy burden of false guilt.

Guilt is a burden that can throttle us. Satan uses it as a tool to destroy our lives, to play us like a puppet. If you can step into the darkness and cut holes through the blanket of guilt that Satan's using to smother that person, allowing them to see the light, to finally be able to breathe again, then you have done something worthwhile. Something Christ would be proud of.

Proverbs 16:24 says, "Pleasant words are like a honeycomb, sweetness to the soul and health to the bones."

I don't think that this necessarily means everything that you say during these types of situations has to be all flowery and unicorns. If anything, that would just tick me off even more. To give good *counsel* though, to let people know that they did nothing wrong, and to help guard them from the budding weed of unnecessary guilt through your words though is something that I think can easily qualify as "pleasant words."

> There's something psychologists refer to as the "pile on effect." When bad thing after bad thing happens to a person, it can result in *cumulative* stress. Kids in particular are vulnerable to this, and it puts them at an increased risk of developing mental health issues.[12]

I don't want to leave you with the impression that children are glass vases. Kids are actually quite resilient, but you have to make sure that they have their basic needs met first.[12]

Sometimes things will still happen despite your best preparations. When loss happens despite your best efforts (and it will) memorials and rituals after the fact can help kids to cope.[13] Poems written to the lost house, a particular ice cream ordered on the anniversary of every disaster, and similar little rituals, regardless of how silly they may seem, can greatly help a kid to be able to process the grief that they are experiencing.

Above all else, remember that your relationship with Christ during this time is going to be examined under a microscope by these kids. Your relationship with Him will help to determine how your outward behavior that is viewable by others will be. This is going to be what kids are watching. Proverbs 15:13 says:

A merry heart makes a cheerful countenance, but by sorrow of the heart the spirit is broken.

Proverbs 14:30a says:

A sound heart is life to the body

Proverbs 16:20b says:

...whoever trusts in the Lord, happy is he.

And finally, Proverbs 17:22 says:

A merry heart does good, like medicine, but a broken spirit dries the bones.

So, we can see that having a sound and merry heart does us a world of good. Research shows that those who view things through an optimistic lens, who are happier, tend to just live better than those who are constantly sad and depressed.[14] And what is the key to a sound and merry heart? The answer comes as no surprise to a Christian. The key, if you really want to have a heart that is filled with joy, and a soul filled with peace, is to have a relationship with Jesus which you cultivate daily.

That is the *only* way that you'll be able to weather life's storms in a way that doesn't lead to your destruction, or aid in the destruction of the other lives in contact with yours.

The Elderly

Older adults are going to need extra help after a disaster. They're typically not as strong or energetic as *most* younger people, and they often have health issues that require special care. Even outside of disasters, older adults are one of the most vulnerable social groups in society.[15]

This can be seen when we take a closer look at just Hurricane Katrina; 1,330 people died as a result of that hurricane. Most those people were older. Sixty-eight people were found dead in nursing homes post-Katrina.[16] Some of these died at St. Rita's, a nursing home in Louisiana where 35 patients just drowned because they either could not get to the roof or weren't taken up there, depending on whose side of the story you believe. Of those elders who were evacuated out of New Orleans, many were taken to sites that were couldn't meet the level of care the patient required. Many were taken to the Katrina Superdome. Around 8,000-9,000 people ended up getting stuffed into that sweat bowl. A lot of kids, elderly, and *sick* people as well.[17] A recipe for disaster.

Now, I don't think that you can complain too much about "level of care" when somebody just saved your life by evacuating you and the entire Gulf coast is trying to get the heck away as well, but the point remains: older people often have special needs.

According to statistics, 80% of US adults aged 65 or older have at least *one* chronic health condition.[16] And after working in healthcare for quite some time, let me tell you, there's a lot of people out there that have waaaay more than just one.

So what are you supposed to do in these cases?

Well, if you have older adults out there that rely on you, parents, grandparents, friends, church members, or whatever, then stock up on the supplies they would need perchance a disaster came your way. The below list of things to prep and remember should help.

1. Keep Prescription Drugs Handy

If you have somebody in your family that is under your care who regularly needs certain drugs for medical conditions, you need to ensure that you have a ready stock of them. At first glance, this is a daunting proposition. I mean, how can you stockpile prescription medications when the pharmacist is only willing to give you a month's worth? After the month, you're screwed!

If your doctor is sympathetic to your reasoning though, you may be able to get an extra bottle of whatever drug it is that you need by asking for a twice daily prescription rather than a one-a-day prescription.

Honestly, this is going to be the hardest part of the process for you. No doctor's going to be willing to give you an extra prescription of oxycodone or other commonly abused drugs. If it's something more like nitroglycerin for chest pain, a statin for monitoring cholesterol, or even anti-psychotic drugs for those with schizophrenia/ Alzheimer's/etc., then you'd probably have higher chances of succeeding here.

You want to make sure that you know the proper dosage and schedule for each of these medications as well. During my day job, I work predominantly with older clients. Even though they may have been taking the exact same medication for the past 30 years, it'll surprise you to discover how many of them either 1) have absolutely no clue what it is that they're taking, 2) consistently forget to take their medications, 3) don't know why they're taking what they're taking, and 4) will randomly stop or double-dose pills when they feel like it.

With prescription medications, you can't be apathetic like this. There can be some serious repercussions, whether that be in the form of physical health problems or with differing states of psychosis. Nobody wants to deal with Granny running around the house battling elephants because she double-dosed on her meds. Make sure people are taking what they need, in the amount they need, and when they need.

2. Stock Over-the-Counter Medications

Keeping a well-stocked supply of basic medical gear is going to be one of the best things you can do to ensure that your higher-care individuals receive the care they need. Older people are going to need pain killers, fever reducers, laxatives, anti-diarrheal medicine, cough syrup, Nyquil, Pepto-Bismol, Tums, and other medications that can help them to better weather your run-of-the-mill maladies that older people are more susceptible to. Think constipation, arthritis, diarrhea, heartburn, insomnia, and the like.

3. Have Mobility Devices

A lot of older people have severe arthritis that limits their ability to move properly. If this is the case for you, do you have a wheelchair, crutches, canes, spare wheelchair parts, and walkers to ensure that your loved ones always have what they need?

4. Keep from Getting Injured

Older people have incredibly thin skin compared to the rest of the population. And if they're on blood thinners, as many with cardiac issues are, then any type of small cut can quickly grow to be a bigger issue, as you may have an issue stopping the bleeding. If that is the case, then QuickClot may help. It's a type of powder you apply to a superficial bleed that helps stop the bleeding.

The chance of infection greatly increases anytime the integrity of the skin is compromised. That's one of the roles of skin, to protect you from the outside environment. Survival and disaster situations aren't exactly known as being incredibly hygienic circumstances. Ask any Vietnam War vet who spent any significant amount of time out in the bush. They'll tell you just how quickly a seemingly innocent wound can turn septic without proper treatment. So to avoid any of these issues, it's best to just keep from getting injured in the first place. This doesn't mean by any stretch that just because somebody is old that they can't be allowed to do anything. What it does mean is that potentially dangerous jobs should probably be reserved for the younger folk.

5. Keep in Mind What They're Going Through

Imagine you've lived in a house for the past 60 years. You raised your kids in that house. All your photographs of your parents and extended family were there. You came home to that house after your spouse of 65 years passed away suddenly from cancer. And now that house has been destroyed by a tsunami. Nothing is salvageable, and your kids have just come to pick you up and take you to a foreign place where nothing feels like *home*.

Don't forget what older people may be going through. They may have just lost their spouse, job, income, and independence, and losing items of emotional significance such as these can compound the feelings of loss.[18] Walk in their shoes. Yeah, you need them to get to do what they need to do, but do what you can to work with them with a spirit of love, understanding, and compassion.

6. Know that Elderly are Prime Victims after Disasters

People who are elderly cannot defend themselves as well as a younger adult. Sure, you hear stories now and then of little old women who blast exit wounds through the heart of a would-be assailant in their home at 3AM, but as a whole, elderly people are easy targets. That may be something to consider post-disaster. Are there older people around you who are by their selves, and should/can you do something to help protect them?

7. Can You Care for Them if You Can't Take Care for Yourself?
I mean this to say, are you doing what you can to ensure that your body still works? If you've let yourself go to 500 pounds, are you really fit to take care of others? Ask any CNA, nurse, or doctor. Taking care of older patients all day, or even just sick people, is hard physical work! If you can barely walk up a flight of steps without getting winded, are you going to be able to take care of people?

I'm not shaming anybody with terrible back pain, or some type of disease/condition that has led to them currently being where they are. But if you have no excuse, then perhaps it would be wise to do what you can to get back into a reasonable level of fitness.

What if your loved one is in a nursing home post-disaster?
This is a question that's wise to consider beforehand. Do you just keep them there and trust that the staff will take care of them? There have been cases where the staff just leaves. In Kenner, LA after Hurricane Katrina, the entire nursing home staff just left, leaving all the residents to fend for themselves. Have you ever seen the people who reside within a nursing home? These people can't make it through a *single day* in normal society on their own. How are they going to make it through a post-disaster situation? Only 4 maintenance workers in the Kenner nursing home remained behind to help the residents. For 3 days those residents lived without showers, food, or electricity with *maintenance workers* taking care of them.[19] I think that what they did was brave and worthy of our society's applause, but a nurse or CNA is going to have a much better idea of what different medications do, when to give them, and how to work with nursing home patients than a maintenance worker will.

So what do you do in such a situation?

The choice is ultimately up to you. The staff may stay and take care of them. They may not. You've no way of really knowing. If you do decide to bring your loved one home, there's a chance they may not survive the journey. The stress, extremes of temperature, or infection from potential injury could all contribute toward that loved one's early death. Is the risk of moving them worth it? And if they make it back to your place in one piece, do you have the resources needed to take care of them properly? What do you do with a relative who has severe Alzheimer's?

I'm not going to attempt to answer any of these questions for you, but I do want to raise them just to get you thinking about the issue. Because if you think about the issue, you'll be able to devise some sort of plan should you determine that the issue is worth planning for.

Pregnant Women and Infants

It's no surprise that infants will need more care post-disaster, but pregnant women are going to need extra help as well. Look at some of these facts regarding pregnant women and infants during/after disasters and you'll see why:

- Pregnant women are at an increased risk of preterm birth if there's a disaster.
- There's an increased risk of delivery complications after disaster for pregnant women.[20]
- Prenatal/maternal stress and depression are linked with negative outcomes for infant behavior, cognitive, and psychological development.
- Pregnant women are at an increased risk of sexual assault post-disaster.[21]
- Abrupt changes in infant feeding schedules leads to an increased rate of morbidity and mortality.[21]

Let's analyze these one by one.

Pregnant women are at an increased risk of preterm birth if there's a disaster.

Stress, lack of food, lack of sleep, and hormonal changes can all result in preterm birth very much becoming a reality. Even during normal times, preemies have a difficult road ahead of them filled with challenging obstacles that they can have trouble overcoming *even with* proper medical care. Now imagine it's post-disaster, and that medical care isn't readily available. When that's the case, the chances that little baby is going to be okay quickly decreases. Ensuring that you have the capability to care for a pregnant mother and to provide her with a safe environment improve the chances that her baby will make it through okay. Does this mean you need a working neonatal intensive care unit set up? Nope. But a safe haven, and plenty of food and water go a long way.

There's an increased risk of delivery complications after disaster for pregnant women.

Though we often deny it, there's a very strong link between the mental and physical world. Constant stress and fear can play a number on our health, and this is easily seen with pregnancies post-disaster. We want the mom to be as comfortable, well-nourished, well-rested, and safe as possible when she is delivering. When these factors are met, we can help to ensure that both she and the baby make it through the delivery safely.

Prenatal/maternal stress and depression are linked with negative outcomes for infant behavior, cognitive, and psychological development.
Why should pregnant women not drink alcohol, smoke cigarettes, or do drugs? Because what goes through mom's bloodstream, goes through the baby's bloodstream. When the mom drinks, the baby drinks. The consequences of these behaviors are very easy to see once the child is born. However, even the hormones that are flowing through the mom's bloodstream are going to be flowing through the baby's bloodstream. Constant stress increases the levels of a hormone called cortisol. Fear releases adrenaline. Depression inhibits the release of the feel-good hormones. It's normal for a pregnant woman to act hormonally (you ever seen a pregnant woman cry because you got *regular* cheese pizza instead of *thin crust* cheese pizza?), but it's *not* normal for a pregnant woman to be exposed to severe stress and depression throughout the pregnancy.

By providing an environment for mom where she is not only well-fed and taken care of, but where she is sheltered from the elements, able to socialize, able to talk about her thoughts, and has the knowledge that she is physically safe we can further help to protect the little baby's future.

Pregnant women are at an increased risk of sexual assault post-disaster.
I'm not sure what the mindset of the guy is in this situation. Perhaps it's the knowledge that it's literally impossible for him to bear a child with the woman. Perhaps it's because he knows she won't be able to flee or fight back as hard. Perhaps it's because the perpetrator finds pregnant women attractive.

Regardless of the reasoning, it's not safe to be out on your own post-disaster if you're a pregnant woman. During the Rape of Nanking, when the Japanese soldiers invaded China during WW2, pregnant women were a favorite target of Japanese soldiers for raping.[22] Other disasters show the same results. The reason that pregnant women are at an increased risk of contracting a sexually transmitted disease (STD) post-disaster isn't because these women are going around and playing the prostitute.[20] It's because they're being raped.

Knowing this, I think it's vitally important that we as Christians do everything that we can to protect these women from wicked men.

Abrupt changes in infant feeding schedules lead to an increased rate of morbidity and mortality.

Babies need a schedule. After a disaster, this can be hard to maintain. If the mom doesn't create enough milk, if there's not enough access to formula, or if the mom has to spend a considerable time with other survival tasks (making fire, running, hiding, etc.), then the schedule goes right out the window.

Unfortunately, this can lead to health consequences for the baby. Regular breast feeding not only acts as infection protection for the baby, but also decreases the infants risk of sudden infant death syndrome (SIDS), decreases the chances the kid will develop asthma, decreases the incidence of potentially life-threatening diarrhea due to dehydration, guards the baby from untreated water used to make formula, *and* decreases the stress of the mother due to the release of the feel-good hormone oxytocin every time that she breast feeds.[23]

I think there are two key ways that we can help pregnant women: prepping and community. For starters, if you have diapers, formula, bottles, basic medicines, and other infant needs already stored, then the mother can be more at ease that her baby is going to be physically taken care of. It's hard to take care of somebody if you don't have the physical supplies they need to survive. Once again, I don't think that anybody needs to have an infant/pregnant woman supply room occupying hundreds of square feet in their basement, but a small supply of some basic needs can go a long way.

Secondly, I think that we can take care of pregnant women/infants post-disaster via community. As we mentioned, pregnant women are at an increased risk of danger post-disaster. One man can only do so much as far as protection goes, no matter how well-armed he is. As we pointed out in the chapter on community, when we have a *group* of people who are well armed, constantly vigilant, and knowledgeable, then the ability to resist violence greatly increases. There *is* safety in numbers.

Women

Though some of them out there may not like to be reminded of this, women are *inherently* different than men. They have special needs, both physically and emotionally, that a man does not, and post-disaster they *do* need different forms of help.

To start off, there is an increased risk of violence against women post-disasters.[21] Typically, women are much smaller and weaker than your average man (there are exceptions – the women from my college's basketball team could have ripped your average man in half). As a result, they are physically vulnerable to violence, particularly sexual violence post-collapse. You've got to remember that post-collapse, there's a lot of people out there who think that they can get away with anything. If perpetrators have the opportunity to force sex with somebody, with little to no fear of repercussion, they are more likely to steal it.

Women *have* to be vigilant about this post-collapse (and pre-collapse too!). This is where being trained in self-defense, having the means of self-defense, and safety in numbers can come into play.

I'll say this: women can be exceptionally strong (and strong *willed*. Haha!). We can all think of examples of single mothers who overcame tremendous odds and showed strength while going through some type of overwhelming trial. Look at the book of Esther. The girl put her life on the line to save an entire nation. *That's* strength. Look at what Rahab did. *That's* strength.

That being said, most wives will agree that their husbands (if they are good and loving men) serve as a source of strength, leadership, and stability in their lives. Ask any widow, and she'll agree that that is a part of what she lost. And those are all attributes that men are *supposed* to display all the time. Peter acknowledges in 1 Peter 3:7 that women are indeed the weaker vessel. Does this mean they're puny, insignificant, and supposed to just sit down and shut up? By no means!

Women are capable of exceptional strength. But men do occupy a special role here, and that needs to be recognized. In the long term, only middle-aged caregiver women fare worse than kids who have experienced a disaster.[24] Why is this? I believe it's because men are created with an inherent strength. It's part of what makes men *men*. When a woman is placed in a dangerous position post-disaster, where they not only have to take care of themselves, their children, and deal with the emotions after the fact solo, it quickly becomes overwhelming.

Women need to be heard, to be understood, and to convey what it is that they are feeling about different issues. When a partner or friend is willing to listen, to be empathetic, and to offer reassurance, guidance, and advice, it greatly puts a woman's mind to rest. The same as anyone else.

The Disabled and Diseased
56.4 million Americans have a disability of some sort.[25] When you add to that the number of people who have some form of non-contagious disease that needs to be addressed, you add a whole lot more people to the mix. What can you do to take care of these people?

Blind

Know that blind people are going to need help being led to safety. Imagine how terrifying it is to know that something bad is going on around you, but to have no way to escape from it. If the disaster is not readily apparent, then just understand that a blind person may be reluctant to follow a stranger.[26] Think about it; a lot of disasters are denied at first. If you saw the footage of the Las Vegas Jason Aldean concert shooting you saw people saying that the shots were fake, that it was just fireworks, and that people were being afraid over nothing. This is pretty common. People don't tend to believe the veracity of what's happening until it's readily apparent, and often too late.

If somebody's blind, this may be the case with them. If so, I would approach the individual, explain to them who you are, what is going on, and where you are going to take them. Verbal explanations of everything that is going on are going to be needed in this case.

Post-disaster, if these people are sheltering with you, just know that a walking stick and at times a physical guide are going to be necessary.

Deaf/Hearing Impaired

If you know you're going to be caring for somebody who utilizes hearing aids, I highly recommend storing extra batteries. I've met a lot of older dudes who lose their batteries on a regular basis for whatever reason. Due to the price, I really don't see storing extra hearing aids as a feasible option. They're often thousands of dollars. Storing extra batteries *is* doable though, and can help to make things a lot more enjoyable for both parties.

If caring for somebody who is deaf, keep a marker board and markers readily available, which will make things much simpler if you don't know how to speak sign language.

Chronic Illness

What do you do about those you love with diabetes, coronary artery disease, Chron's disease, Grave's disease, or other chronic conditions that necessitate regular doctor visits, medication, or procedures? My best advice would be to learn as much as you can about the disease, and to get as much of the medicine needed as you can. Other than that, it's hard to really do much. Keeping a source of transportation always at the ready can help to get you to a location that may still have your medication if a Katrina-style event wipes out your locale.

And if you have medication that needs to be refrigerated, invest in some source of backup power to keep a refrigerator running. Whether that be a generator or alternative energy, something is better than nothing. There's an interesting company called Frio that makes coolers for insulin which stay cool without electricity. The cooler looks like a little nylon wallet and keeps the insulin cool via evaporation. All you have to do is soak the Frio in water for the specified time period, and then it keeps the inside 64.4-78.8 degrees Fahrenheit (an ideal temperature for stored insulin) for up to 45 hours. It's reusable, and the only thing you have to do is soak it in water to get it to work.[27]

Those with Pets

I was blown away with some of the facts and statistics that I found while I was researching who would need special help after disaster, and what steps we could take as Christians and preppers to care for them. One of those things I discovered was that those with pets will often refuse to be rescued if you cannot rescue their pet as well.[28]

There are plenty of examples of people *dying* for their *animals* out there as well. Let's get something straight. An *animal* is not worth a *human* life. If you're reading this, I'm going to make an educated guess that you probably believe the same way as I do, but regardless, check out these stories of people who didn't think so:

- During the 2009 Black Friday Bushfires in Victoria, Australia, Dr. Chris Towie died attempting to save his *pet dogs*. Melanie and Penny Chambers died *trying* to save their *horses*.
- During the Queensland Floods of 2010, David Kelly died trying to save *cattle*.[29]
- Even recently, an Oklahoman man with a pre-existing heart condition died on his 50th birthday after trying to save a *rattlesnake* that was sunbathing in the middle of the road. It bit him twice. He died from cardiac arrest.[30]

What on earth were they thinking? You're in imminent danger, and you're going to put your life on the line because of a dog? Because of a horse? Because of cattle? In what way can they have a fraction of the impact on others that you as a human being can? And c'mon, a *rattlesnake*?

A friend of mine illustrated this point perfectly. We were discussing the rattlesnake incident when he pointed out that his friend does the same thing for turtles. They'll be barreling down the interstate at 70mph, when they'll pull over and dodge the traffic to "rescue the turtle." Why on earth would you risk the life of your children's father for a reptile? I'm still not sure, but people do it.

The point behind all this, is that it's something you need to be mentally prepared for. I honestly wouldn't prep for other people's pets. You want to join the group with your pet? *You* feed the dog. Not me. You provide the cage, the medicine, and the toys. Especially if your pet's more of a nuisance than a help. If it's your own animal (I do have an awesome dog who can herd chickens), then yeah, you may want to consider keeping extra food on hand. I try to keep 2 months' worth of chicken food on hand so that I can feed them if the local mill has issues (it occasionally does). Same for my dog. I don't do much more than that though.

Wrapping it Up

I'll wrap this chapter up with this: people, regardless of who they are, what they have, or how old they are, need to feel needed. We all have the innate desire to know that we are not only important, but that we make valuable contributions to the world around us. This doesn't change after a disaster. It doesn't change after TEOTWAWKI. And the cool thing is that there is always *something* that a member of your group can do to be beneficial.

Whether it be wielding a weapon, providing surveillance, relaying information, caregiving for those critically ill, transporting things, peeling potatoes, leading Bible studies, or even praying (I don't pretend that conversing with an omnipotent, omniscient, omnipresent God who is good and *loves* us isn't important), everybody can do *something*.

So, don't overlook the contributions that even the weak may be able to make. Don't count them out.

Chapter 10
Living with Others in Confined Circumstances

Let's say the threat has finally happened. Your area is absolutely devastated. Perhaps even your nation. You knew ahead of time that community was important, so you took the steps to cultivate a community of like-minded and preparedness-geared people within your locale. However, living within close confinement because you *have* to is much different than because you're just in the same region most of the time. Post-disaster not only are there safety aspects that need to be addressed for a community, but there are "getting along skills" that need to be honed as well, and that can be one of the most difficult parts to get right.

Let's start with the easy stuff first though.

Post-Disaster Community Safety

Waste management is one of the first things that needs to be addressed. Human beings poop and pee quite a bit throughout the day, and containing that waste is probably the single most protective environmental measure that you can take to ensure that your family stays safe.[1] If you have alternative energy sources and plenty of water to ensure your toilets are still working, then you're going to be in a pretty good situation already. But if the toilets don't work, if you're bugging out, if your church has a refugee camp set up, or basic toilet facilities just aren't available, then you need to ensure that you practice proper engineering and sanitation.

> On average, we poop 6 lbs worth of doodoo per week, and pee anywhere between 5,600 – 14,000 mL per week.[2,3] If you have a group of 5 people living at your retreat, that's 30 pounds of poop and between 28,000 – 70,000 mL of pee to dispose of on a weekly basis! Without proper engineering, you can easily see how this can spell disaster.

It's feces-contaminated water and food that causes the majority of outbreaks post-disaster. Diseases such as cholera, typhoid, and hepatitis can turn deadly post-disaster, especially if your access to healthcare is limited. And once an outbreak starts, good luck trying to stop it. It's only through communication within a community that you can stop this from ever happening in the first place. If your neighbors are peeing in the same pond that you're bathing in, then at some point somebody's going to get sick. Only by *communicating* are you able to avoid such situations, and only through *community* are you able to enforce such rules.

Having proper toilet facilities is perhaps *the* most important step that you can take to ensure you don't have an outbreak on your hands (or poop for that matter) post-disaster. Outhouses and latrines need to be somewhere separate and isolated from anywhere near where food, water, bathing, or washing is dealt with. Poop needs to be put in as deep a hole as possible as well.[4] Ideally, families should have their own family outhouse. The reason is this: families are exposed to each other closely and daily. They're more used to (rather, they're adapted to) each other's germs and bacteria than an outsider would be. Kind of like a microclimate. When various people and families share the same facilities, it increases the odds that somebody is going to be exposed to something that they don't have an adequate immune history to respond to.[5] The result? They'll get sick. Obviously, your family isn't going to be immune to "its version" of cholera. If you come in contact with cholera, you're getting cholera. But for some of the other random bugs out there, having immune history thanks to your family could be beneficial.

Before we go on any further though, just what are some of the common things that we need to be aware of? Just what is it that we are trying to avoid? Well, cholera, E.coli, typhoid, hepatitis (E and A in particular), and shigella are some of the most common post-disaster diseases.[6] Ensuring that people aren't coming into contact with poop is one of the best ways to ensure these diseases don't rear their ugly heads to begin with.

Hand Washing

Having hand washing is the next step. Nobody likes to touch the door handle in a public restroom because we've all seen the people who just used the toilet, and then touched that handle without washing their hands. Well, guess what? Post-disaster those germs don't just disappear. If anything, we need to be even more careful of them then. There needs to be a handwashing station, with plenty of water set aside for that *one* reason, or there at least needs to be plenty of hand sanitizer available. If bugging out, you need to carry plenty of hand sanitizer of a high alcohol content. Good ol' handwashing with soap is still the gold standard for cleaning your hands, but if bugging out, that may not be a convenient option and utilizing hand sanitizer is probably going to be your next best bet. You probably won't be able to spare a lot of actual water for hand washing then, but hand sanitizer can still get the job done, provided you didn't just land hands first in a big pile of poop.

Washing Food

Washing your fruits and vegetables in clean water before you eat them, or even just peeling them are other ways to ensure we don't get sick.[7] Think about this. If you wash a cucumber in contaminated water, you may have just washed off all the dirt, but you bathed the thing in cholera! People get sick this way. Make sure the food being handled has been properly washed by somebody with *clean* hands as well.

Of particular concern with cooking is typhoid. Perchance somebody in your group comes down with it, they need to be banned from any type of food preparation or gathering. The only food they should be touching is the food they are eating. A typhoid-infected person cannot cook for others for 3 months after the onset of symptoms.[8] And I would argue that they should just be done from that point on. I wouldn't risk it.

Have you ever heard the story of Typhoid Mary?[9] She was a cook back in the 1800s who contracted typhoid. As a typhoid epidemic ravaged the surrounding region where she lived, epidemiologists had a hard time figuring out the source. Eventually, it was found that most of the people who were getting sick had eaten food that Typhoid Mary had cooked. She was banned from cooking for the public ever again in order to help stop future outbreaks. Not too long later though, she started cooking for customers at a new establishment, and the typhoid outbreaks started all over again.

For real, these are diseases that you *do not* want to get. They will kill you and the people that you love. What's the point of preparing for disaster if you're not going to take the steps to keep the people you love alive after it strikes?

Interpersonal Contact

What about interpersonal relations? How do we make sure we're still able to live in harmony post-disaster? Over the years that I've been married, I've been keeping notes of important verses in my Bible that I've deemed "marriage keys." Making the transition from being engaged to being married was a night and day difference between the two. I quickly found that the Bible had a lot of practical things to say regarding living in as much peace as possible with your spouse. I'm not saying that my early marriage was terrible. I'm just saying that it didn't take me long to realize that I had a lot to learn. I now joke that the key to a happy marriage is working kitchen appliances. Newlyweds should name all pets "Marriage

Problem." I was also now accountable to somebody else with how I spent money. These biblical marriage keys I note have helped me tremendously, and they still apply to situations where you're "stuck" with a large community of people post-disaster.

1. Speak the Truth in Love (Ephesians 4:15)

Not speaking the truth helps no one. People *need* to know the truth (in most cases). However, for some reason, as human beings we sometimes relish doing this in as harsh a manner as possible. We want to do it in a way that serves as ammunition for us - our ace in the hole - during a heated argument. It's fine to speak the truth, but if you're going to do it, do it in love. Don't come across as some self-righteous, prideful idiot who just wants to prove somebody wrong. You need to do it with a loving aura, and in a loving manner. Doing so is key to avoiding slow-healing wounds.

2. Nip it in the Bud (Ephesians 4:26b/Proverbs 17:14)

Do not let the sun go down on your wrath, nor give place to the devil. – Ephesians 4:26b

The beginning of strife is like releasing water; therefore stop contention before a quarrel starts. – Proverbs 17:14

If you've got an issue, you need to deal with it. Don't just let resentment fester and build until an explosion occurs. Do your best to nip it in the bud. Proverbs 18:19 says, "A brother offended is harder to win than a strong city, and contentions are like the bars of a castle." Why not do preventative maintenance on your relationships by stopping the small stuff before it becomes big stuff? That way we avoid letting a small issue become a big one. This doesn't mean that every problem out there is capable of being solved overnight. Anybody who's been married knows that's not the case. There are some situations where the problem is going to take a while to deal with. Some won't ever be resolved. But to the best of your ability, do what you can to ensure that you aren't letting Satan chisel away at what he shouldn't have a handle on in the first place.

3. Don't be a Jerk (Ephesians 4:32/Matthew 7:12a)

And be kind to on another, tenderhearted, forgiving one another, even as God in Christ forgave you. – Ephesians 4:32

Therefore, whatever you want men to do to you, do also to them… - Matthew 7:12a

It's funny how easy it is to forget this one. For goodness' sake, be kind to each other. The Golden Rule still applies here.

4. Overlook the Small Stuff (Proverbs 19:11)

The discretion of a man makes him slow to anger, and his glory is to overlook a transgression. – Proverbs 19:11

This is something I've tried my best to pound into my head throughout most of my adult life. It's to a wise man's glory to overlook an offense. This is part of being slow to anger. Newsflash: people ain't Jesus. They aren't even close. People are going to say and do stupid, thoughtless, selfish things, and a lot of times it's going to be incredibly blatant. I'm not saying that you must correct somebody if they're doing stupid things or making people miserable. I'm not saying that you need to ignore everything either. Not by a long shot. Some things do need to be addressed. But I *am* saying that you learn the wisdom to know what needs to be addressed, how it needs to be addressed, and when. Be willing to overlook the small stuff.

5. Forgive (Proverbs 17:9/Matthew 18:21-35/Ephesians 4:32/Mark 11:25/Luke 6:37/Colossians 3:13/and so many other parts of the Bible that I'm only going to focus on this one verse from Proverbs.)

He who covers a transgression seeks love, but he who repeats a matter separates friends. – Proverbs 17:9

You've said things that were hurtful, done things that were wrong, and straight up screwed up before, haven't you? Of course you have. It's part of being human. We're in a fallen state. We're the ones who had God come to earth and *die* for us, to pay the penalty of *our* sins. Jesus took the bullet for us. He didn't deserve it, but He had to do it if we were to have any chance of ever having a restored relationship with Him and getting to spend eternity with Him in Heaven.

And yet despite that ultimate gift, despite all the numerous *other* times we did things purposefully (and ignorantly) that defied or hurt Him, He *still* forgave us.

And then He turns back around and tells us that we're to be like Him. To be slow to anger. To forgive. The point is that people are going to let you down. They're going to mess up. But we are to be willing to forgive them just like Christ was willing to forgive us.

Does this mean that we make ourselves a human doormat? By no means! If a group of raiders shoots my friend, and then tries to burst into my house to harm my family and steal my stuff, it doesn't mean that you're to just turn the other cheek and let them have their way. Doing what we can to stop evil is part of our job. What I am saying though is that we can't live a life of holding grudges. Of bitterness. Of anger. Forgiveness is the key that God gives us to unlock those chains, to move on, and to live *fully* once again.

6. Gentle Words Break Stone (Proverbs 25:15)

By long forbearance a ruler is persuaded, and a gentle tongue breaks a bone. – Proverbs 25:15

If there's something that you really, really think needs to change or be done, and the rest of the group doesn't think it's a good idea for whatever reason, just know that persistence and a gentle tongue can break bone. You don't want to be a nag, and you don't want to be hostile. But by persistently and gently giving the opinion you have without coming across as bitter or sarcastic, you can help persuade even the stoutest opponent that your option may be the best bet.

Obviously, sometimes your opinion is going to be flat out wrong. And in these instances, humility and accepting being outvoted is really the noblest option. The hard part is knowing where that line lies. You must be able to keep an open mind (as much as I hate that phrase), and understand that sometimes you are wrong.

> *"If you're too open minded, then your brains'll fall out."* – Humbletip (a Christian rapper)[10]

But for the times that you aren't, gentle persuasion can often be the key.

7. Just Shut Up (Proverbs 29:11/21:23)

A fool vents all his feelings, but a wise man holds them back. – Proverbs 29:11

Whoever guards his mouth and tongue keeps his soul from troubles. – Proverbs 21:23

People have a hard time with this one. Sometimes it's best to keep your mouth zipped. You don't always have to have the last say, and sometimes it's best to not say anything at all. The wise man is able to give just the right amount of information. He's not necessarily going to blast you with everything he thinks on the matter. A wise man uses discretion, even with what he vents.

8. Read *Crucial Conversations*[11]

Yeah, I know *Crucial Conversations* isn't a Christian book, but I'm sticking to my guns. This is hands down the best book on communicating in a reasonable, civil, and loving manner that I have found yet. My wife had to use it as a textbook for a Communication 101 class that she was taking while was working on her Bachelor's. The book interested me, and so I read it in my free time.

I was blown away by how good it was. Communication seems like something that should come naturally to people. But for some reason, to be effective at it, there are some things that we often need to work on that we haven't quite mastered. This book will point out what those things are, and it offers practical, well-thought advice to help you understand what you need to do to ensure you're able to paddle through any whitewater in a relationship.

9. Foster Unity (1 Peter 3:8-9)

Finally, all of you be of one mind, having compassion for one another; love as brothers, be tenderhearted, be courteous; not returning evil for evil or reviling for reviling, but on the contrary blessing, knowing that you were called to this, that you may inherit a blessing. – 1 Peter 3:8-9

Are you always going to agree with those around you? Heck, no. Do you necessarily have to? Heck, no. But that doesn't mean you can't have the common goal of fostering unity with those around you through compassion, showing love, stopping the cycle of tit-for-tat, and doing what you can to bless one another.

10. If it Ain't Your Fight, Keep Out (Proverbs 26:17)

He who passes by and meddles in a quarrel not his own is like one who takes a dog by the ears. – Proverbs 26:17

If there's no reason for you to get involved, then mind your own business! You only make things worse by butting in on these situations. What happens if you grab a dog on the street very gruffly by the ears? You now have an angry animal with very sharp teeth in your grasp. If you let go, he bites you, and your only other recourse, hanging on, isn't ideal either. Better to just avoid grabbing the dog by the ears to begin with.

Obviously, sometimes stepping in is the right thing to do (e.g. someone needs a drug addiction intervention), but utilize discretion to know what you can overlook.

11. Roll the Dice (Proverbs 18:18)

Casting lots causes contentions to cease, and keeps the mighty apart. – Proverbs 18:18

I've always thought that this was a cool, practical verse. Some disputes just can't be solved through dialogue. In such cases, perhaps just rolling the dice is the way to go. *"Alright, if we roll an even number, we'll do it my way, and if we roll an odd number, we'll do it your way. Because you're* odd."

My wife and I have actually used rock-paper-scissors a number of times to settle issues. Though it stinks to lose the game, each party knows that the outcome was fair, and agreed to whatever that outcome was beforehand. Obviously, this shouldn't be your first course of action, but I do see it as a potential way to blast through gridlock so that you can keep moving forward on an issue.

Conclusion

It doesn't matter if your intention is to be a lone wolf from the get-go or not, should a disaster take place, there's a very good chance you're going to end up "stuck" with people for a significant amount of time. But by following the advice laid out, you'll be able to not only live together in a safer manner, but in peace as well.

Chapter 11
Being a Witness

Look at history. Look at human nature. For some reason, disaster has the power to open the hearts and minds of even the most chained and stone-cold hearts out there. It brings us to our knees, we ask why, and we're willing to search for answers about things that we would have never been willing to talk about beforehand.

I vividly remember seeing this right after 9/11. After those evil men brought our towers down there was an outpouring of people at our church. The whole county was at was just in a state of shock. Things weren't normal. It was like we had all just been sucker punched in the gut, had our wind knocked out, and were just walking around in a daze with our mouths agape. "How could this have happened? What is this going to lead to? What am I to do? Do some things just happen? Why? I *knew* some of them. I was supposed to be there!"

Questions and statements like these kept circulating, and churches lacked empty pews. Disaster not only united our nation in the following months, but it opened hearts as well. Does this mean that we pray for disaster? No. But I do think that we are to take full advantage of the opportunity when the door is opened to us there.

The apostle Paul said to make the most of every opportunity, because the days are evil. Disaster fulfils both of these qualifiers. Not only is it an opportunity, but it most certainly shows us that the days are evil as well.

> **See then that you walk circumspectly, not as fools, but as wise, redeeming the time, because the days are evil. – Ephesians 5:15-16**

So, what is the Christian prepper's response here?

Well, it's interesting to note throughout the New Testament how often charity was tied in with witnessing. Doesn't James talk about this? How can you tell somebody about Christ, to go in peace, and for God to be with them, and to then leave them starving? (James 2:14-17) It's really hard to think of anything other than food when you haven't eaten in a while. Maslow's hierarchy of needs may play a role here as well. According to it, once the basic needs are met, then we are able to think about other things. Whether that applies to spiritual things completely, that's up for debate. It is something to think over though.

If you're just telling people about the Gospel and wishing them the best but aren't willing to do anything to actually *help* them with their current situation, I think a lot of times that can just lead to bitterness and the development of a belief that Christians are just those people who apply Band-Aids to bullet holes. *"The house is filled with 3 feet of water, everything is lost, my family has zero food, my mother doesn't have her blood thinner, and here this guy is telling me that I just need to trust in God, that He has a reason, and that he's going to pray with me. I know he's ok. He has supplies. He told me so. It's really hard to really want to believe anything that he has to say right now."*

Wouldn't that be the mindset of an unbeliever in these times? "Uh, excuse me. I have better things to be doing with my time right now than to listen to your useless lecture."

How many times did Jesus meet the physical needs of the people that He was talking to? He used these times as opportunities for ministry! Jesus never ignored the physical needs of the people around Him, and He liked to use those opportunities to tell that person He had just cared for more about Himself. Think about this.

In Mark 5, a demon-possessed man who lives in the mountains continually cutting himself and screaming is not only exorcised by Jesus, but then told by Jesus who He is (5:1-20). Later in Mark 5, a woman with a chronic bleeding problem is healed by Jesus (I dare anybody to tell me that Jesus didn't know that He was going to heal her) and He tells her that it was her faith in Him that healed her (v. 32-24). Then at the end of Mark 5 he brings a little girl *back to life* (v. 40-43). In Mark 6, Jesus feeds the 5,000 after teaching them (v. 34-44). In Mark 8, He feeds the 4,000. He heals a deaf-mute, heals the blind, and heals a little boy! And that's all just in the book of Mark, the shortest gospel book that there is!

If you look further in the other Gospels, Jesus provides wine for a wedding, heals *multitudes* in Matthew 4:23-25, heals lepers and centurion's servants, casts out demons, raises Lazarus from the dead, and more. And if you look through the Gospels, you'll find that He often uses these instances to tell the people around Him more about who He is, what He has done for them, and why they should love and trust Him.

We as followers of Christ, Christians, should do the same.

Because the fact remains: It's hard to listen to Christ with a hungry stomach. And I'm not talking about fasting here. I'm talking about physical hunger because you *have* no food.

Did you know that the Mormon church has a rather resilient disaster network in place? They all store plenty of food and water, and do what they can to remain somewhat self-sufficient. They have storage sites filled with necessary goods strategically located throughout the country. Now knowing that after disaster people are more spiritually open, and knowing that fulfilling physical needs can be a powerful way to open doors to people's hearts, there are opportunities here for nonbelievers.

I like what Will Smith's character had to say on the issue in the movie *I Am Legend* (I thought the book was kind of lewd). He's being questioned by another survivor on why he's been working on a cure for so long, so consistently. Smith's reply is that evil doesn't take a day off, so how can he?

What happens if some other religion does a better job of loving people than the body of Christ does? Do you think that the world won't recognize that?

Jerry Falwell said, "If it's Christian, it ought to be better."[1] I think that the same principle applies even to disaster response from Christians versus disaster response from others.

One of the things I've learned within the past few years is that God can use people. He can use people to get His message across to somebody He loves. Yeah, I know that may be a simple concept. It may be something that you learned long ago, but it's a profound, simple, truth that I've somehow overlooked for years.

God used Nathan to tell David that he had sinned with Bathsheba (2 Samuel 12). He used Moses to lead the Israelites out of Egypt. He used Ehud to deliver the Israelites from the Moabites (Judges 4:12-30). He used Esther to save the Israelites from Haman's deceptions. He used Nehemiah to rebuild the walls of Jerusalem to protect the Israelites. The list could go on and on.

I've seen this principle at work in my own life as well. There have been countless examples where I was in desperate need of some tangible, physical thing or some type of advice and counseling that I couldn't get by my own accord. In those instances, God used people to get the thing or message through to me, whether it be through the mouth of my wife, Dad, Granny, or a friend at work.

So again though, what's the Christian prepper's response to be?

Well, I'll start by saying that it's hard to be effective if you're terrible at taking care of your own family. How many times have we had a deacon/pastor/Bible study leader attempt to tell you about spiritual things and you instantly question what right this person has to tell you any of that stuff? They're spiteful to their wife, yet they give you marriage advice. Their kids hate them for very reasonable reasons, yet they give you parenting advice. They just foreclosed on their house, yet they give you financial advice.

That all comes across as hypocritical. I don't want you to glean from this that you must have your life absolutely perfect before you tell people about Jesus. I think Satan actually uses that idea as a tool to keep us from sharing God's word. It ends up being a case of false humility and an excuse. "Well I can't tell them anything about Jesus because I'm such a mess myself."

Isn't that pretty clear in Scripture? We're all messed up. We've all got junk going on. We're all humans desperately in need of Jesus.

However, a Christian should have *some* things in place.

Even from a physical standpoint, it's hard to be charitable, to be able to give to other people and open doors, if you can't feed your own family. Post-disaster you must make sure that your own family is taken care of. 1 Timothy 5:8 makes this clear. No good father would take his son's only food and give it to a stranger, forcing his own son to go hungry. If you have some food stored up though, then you can give more (and with less household havoc) than if you didn't have anything prepped in the first place.

You can't give medical supplies to somebody that needs them if you know that you need all the bandages you've got for your own son's badly lacerated forearm. Having extra stored makes this easier. Though I'm not saying that it's the only factor at play, there is something about being the one that *can* help which will give some weight for what you have to say afterward.

Which leads me to the next point. You must say something afterward. Do actions speak louder than words? Yeah, in some instances. But it's hard for people to know what Jesus did for them if they're not told in the first place. Take advantage of the opportunity just like Jesus did. Start a conversation. Steer it if you can. And insert Truth. You don't need to have everything you want to say all planned beforehand. In many cases, I think that can be detrimental - to have a script that you're working from. People can sniff out a script from a mile away. It's why we don't like talking to Amway people and car salesmen. But a true *conversation*, where you are at ease talking about Jesus, why you're helping them, and so on, can have a much larger effect.

Perhaps one way improve your ability to witness post-disaster would be through what you include in your charity. We've already discussed how charity is a part of being a Christian, and how it is something that we are told to do again and again, but so is sharing Christ. What's an easy way to combine both into one? Well, what if New Testaments, Bibles, or other Christian reading material was included in your method of charity? If you decide to use the charity package, charity cache, or charity box route, you could include this material along with the physical necessities that the people need. That really helps cover all bases, in my opinion. If it's not safe for you to be physically present to give, then charity boxes that have Bibles and Christian literature in them are going to be great ways to help ensure you are helping spread the Gospel despite current circumstances. The church in South Korea does this for North Korea all the time. They take balloons that have Scripture written all over them and release them near the border when the wind is favorable. Are they able to directly, face-to-face witness to these people? No way. North Korea's crazy. They'd be shot on the spot most likely. However, the South Korean church has used their God-given brains to find a way around that.

Post-disaster, there's a lot of free time as well. Sure, there's plenty of things to do. There's damage to be cleaned, insurance companies to be called, supplies to gather. But there will be a lot of time spent waiting. That's why prepping with board games, books, and other non-electric forms of entertainment is so often discussed. Ask anybody of any rank in the military, and they'll tell you that the morale of the unit matters. When troops are bored out of their skull, things don't run as smoothly. When people really don't have any other alternatives for entertainment, and really nothing else they can do but wait, they'd be much more likely to read the Christian literature that you provide. And there's power in God's word. You've undoubtedly heard the same testimonies of others that I have, where people came to know Christ as their Savior after reading the Bible. If we can provide people with the opportunity to do so, why wouldn't we?

I say all this to tell you that there are fantastic opportunities post-disaster to witness to people, to share Christ with them. All it takes are open eyes, open hearts, and sometimes, a bit of creativity. Use your gifts to honor God. Be a light.

Chapter 12
Leadership Post-Disaster

Read enough on prepping and survival and you'll eventually encounter the mantra to "be a sheepdog, not a sheep. Fight off the wolves." The concept behind the statement is that most people are gullible and naïve (the sheep). Like the sheep in George Orwell's *Animal Farm*, these are the people that simply repeat what they're told. They're defenseless, stupid, and don't think for themselves.

The wolves are the evil people who prey on the sheep. They will take advantage of others to satisfy their hunger. Without protection, the sheep are easy prey for the wolf. But the sheepdog protects the sheep. They keep the sheep safe, protect them from being devoured. For many preppers, the goal is to be one of the sheepdogs. To be one of the good, upright, and virtuous individuals who protects the rest from the wolves.

We know that during an emergency, people look around to see what their peers are doing, and they tend to *copy* what everybody else is doing. They use the information they've gathered to make decisions on what appropriate behavior is.[1] When something threatens the flock, they cluster together, believing there's safety in numbers. "Hey, if the wolf comes, maybe he'll get that sheep beside me instead of me." That's the mode of thinking.

And to some extent, that thinking is wise. If a hurricane is coming your way, and you look out the window and see all the neighbors packing up and evacuating, you may gather that, hey, maybe it is a good idea to get the heck out of here. This is a concept known as swarm intelligence. With swarm intelligence, people's collective *individual* behaviors average out to help to choose the best choice.

During emergencies, most people don't know what steps to take next. Especially if it's a new, novel emergency. If somebody's lived in Oklahoma for the past 25 years, odds are that they're going to know what to do when a tornado comes through town. Take that same person, remove them from their element, and see if they know what to do when a tsunami is roaring through the Caribbean on their anniversary trip.

It's during these times - these novel emergencies - that people really look to the people around them to see what the appropriate response should be. People can get paralyzed by indecision at these times as well. They simply don't know what they should do next, and so they do nothing. What these people lack is leadership. And unfortunately, when it's not present, people often die.

Take the World Trade Center for example. After the first plane hit, people were waiting around for someone to tell them what they were supposed to do.[3] These people *wanted* leadership. They *wanted* someone that they could look up to, somebody they can follow, somebody that *could* make the hard decisions.

People need leadership in an emergency. Have you ever witnessed somebody have a heart attack or break their leg? It's a weird sight. A herd of people instantly flocks around the injured party. And then they stare. They ask "Are you alright?" ("Yeah, it's just an artery bleed. I'll be fine.") And for the first few minutes, that's about all that happens. Nobody takes control of the situation. Nobody takes leadership. It's not until somebody steps up and says, "Alright, *you're* calling 911. *You're* grabbing the AED. *You're* going to flag down the ambulance. *I'm* going to start chest compressions, and *you're* going to be my backup," that stuff starts to happen. People want to help. They really do. People want to know what to do. And when leadership is provided in these types of situations, people will pour everything that they have into the task they've been given.

What an amazing opportunity for a Christian to fill.

I believe God often utilizes *people* to accomplish *His* goals. You see this over and over in Scripture. Just think about all the prophets that went out and told people what would happen should they not change their behavior. When the Israelites were trapped in slavery in Egypt, God sent Moses, Aaron, and Miriam (Micah 6:4) to lead the people out of bondage. Jonah was sent to the people of Ninevah to accomplish *His* goal of warning them of coming judgment. Esther was sent to save the Jews from extermination (Esther 4:14). God used people to help in each of these situations.

What if God could use *you* during an emergency to help ensure that the proper steps are taken to keep others safe? What if you could save people's lives because you directed them to where they needed to go, and what they needed to do when terrorists started shooting up a hospital? Would that not be incredible? Wouldn't that be powerful?

You don't have to know *everything* about a situation to be a leader (though knowing something certainly helps). You don't have to be a member of SWAT or a former Army Ranger to take steps that would save lives in a mass shooting. You just have to *start* taking steps, and others will follow. Knowing that somebody is leading gives a tremendous surge in confidence to those around you.

That said, it is important to be a *good* leader. Going back to 9/11, many people died that didn't have to because leaders told them to go back to their offices on the upper floors and wait until they were given further directions. Many people didn't evacuate soon enough because back during the early 90s bombing of the WTC, they were docked pay for the time they were absent from work after fleeing from the explosion. That's not good leadership.

In a similar vein, one man's most memorable last image of the WTC came as he was fleeing. On the 80th floor there was a room full of people in wheelchairs and using walkers waiting for firemen to evacuate them. Every single one of them died. The plan killed them.[4]

Though there was leadership in both situations, I would argue that both lacked common sense. If a plane just flew right into a building, tell people to get the heck out. Don't make them go back to their office, don't threaten their pay. Don't make them wait on the 80th floor for people to help them evacuate. Use common sense to get people out as quickly as you can.

One of the ways that you can ensure that you are a good leader during emergency situations is to ensure that you are at least somewhat knowledgeable regarding the topic at hand. And for preppers, this shouldn't be much of an obstacle. No one is going to argue that the person who knows CPR, has evacuated injured people from the backwoods, tsunamis, school shootings, terrorism, tornadoes and the like is going to be more prepared to deal with the situation at hand than the person who is clueless on the matter.

Again, that doesn't mean you have to be an expert to be a leader, but it does mean you'll be a *better* leader. I'd argue that this is probably one of the most important preps that you can make. Sure, you can conceal carry a pistol and an extra clip around with you, but if you revert to a "What do I do? What do I do?" mentality as soon as a bad guy enters the building, you can quickly find yourself dead. Knowledge increases not only your survival, but the survival of others as well.

If there's anything the world could use more of, it's strong Christians who are willing to lead.

Chapter 13
Dealing with the Stress

Something should be said about the stress that one is going to experience after a disaster. If you are in a daily battle of *survival*, you're fighting lack of resources, lack of skills, lack of shelter, disease, mischievous animals, looters, angry gangs, and attempting to keep the people around you whom you love from killing each other, I think it's fair game to say you're going to be under a lot of stress.

Fortunately, the Bible has a lot to say about the topic, and this same advice is applicable to our daily lives as well.

For starters, let's talk about the stress of helping others. In the *initial* stages of just about any disaster, people's altruism shines bright. People are willing to help each other, share resources, listen, and so on; but doing this day in and day out for any respectable length of time can quickly lead to burn out. Those that help others *must* engage in self-care. They must take time to just be alone, to rest, and to do whatever is needed in order to recharge.

There's a strong biblical case for this as well. Look at the Creation story. God worked for 6 days and then rested. Does that mean God needs rest? I don't think so. But I often wonder if He did that as a lesson for us. If He did it because He knew how frail and fragile we truly are, and that because of our humanity and mortality we would need days of rest to recover from the chaos around us.

Look at Moses.

In Exodus 18, Moses has just been used to lead the Israelites out of captivity. His father-in-law, Jethro, comes to visit and sees how Moses is spending the great part of everyday acting as a judge for all the Israelite people. Jethro sees this for what it is – stupid - and basically asks Moses what in the world he's doing. Yeah, judging the people so that they know what is right and what is wrong is a good thing. But Moses was taking it to the extreme. We as human beings aren't invincible. We can't run 110% all day, every day for weeks at a time. And even though something may be *good*, there can still be too much of a good thing.

I can remember once back in high school listening to my dad talk on the phone with somebody at the church. The friend wanted my dad to attend the new Bible study that they were starting up, but my dad said no, he was going to pass on this one. He had a lot on his plate, and didn't need to be adding any more. I was a little perplexed by all this, and so when the conversation was over, I asked my dad why he didn't want to go to Bible study. I'd gotten the impression from growing up that not going to church every time that the doors were open was basically a sign of being a backslidden Christian.

Dad said this, "Yeah, going to Bible study is a good thing. But spending time with my family is a good thing as well. I'm already going to a Bible study on Sunday mornings and Wednesday evenings. It's not that I don't want to learn about the Bible, but I want to spend time with my family as well." Dad knew the importance of not overloading yourself with too much of a good thing. He knew about the limits of human strength and endurance.

Jethro knew this too. Moses didn't. And so, Jethro counseled Moses and told him that he needed to delegate and distribute the work among a set group of men who would act as judges on Moses' behalf. Without that counsel, Moses would have quickly burned out.

And what happens when you burnout? You're unable to help. Exhaustion, crankiness, apathy, and poor cognitive ability are all *mental* symptoms of burnout. Fatigue, insomnia, heart disease, elevated cholesterol, increased risk of stroke, obesity, increased risk of diabetes, and a vulnerability to illness are just some of the physical symptoms.[1] You must be on guard against it.

Look at Jesus.

Even He escaped into the mountains every now and then. He would spend this time alone and in prayer. Though God in flesh, He was still in a human body. Human bodies need rest. They need to recharge. Have you ever worked with people all day long? They're exhausting! They complain. They're jerks. They're lazy. They're selfish.

The bottom line is that you *must* engage in self-care if you want to be able to give care to others. Take time to rest, time to *sleep*, time to just be alone.

I learned this long ago at work. When I take time to eat and drink during my 12-hour shifts, my patients get better care than if I do not. I joke with my mom that coffee is my Jesus juice. Sometimes it's hard to be Christ-like without it. Without food, drink, and coffee, I quickly become irritable and apathetic toward patients, and that is *not* what I want to be known for.

{ *"Sometimes the most spiritual thing that you can do is take a nap." – George Muller*[2] }

Some stress we bring upon ourselves. Poor planning, refusing to delegate, disorganization, or saying "yes" too often can all be factors that lead to overloading ourselves. If we can learn to attack these problems from the source, a great part of the stress can be prevented from ever happening in the first place. A college student who waits till the last minute to write a term paper is undoubtedly going to be stressed out. It's when they plan things out beforehand and manage their time effectively that stress can be prevented. Learn what steps you can do to block stress from blossoming in the first place.

Other times, stress is going to be a result of something that we have no control over. Being stressed out because the cows keep escaping because you didn't build the fence right is one thing. You can fix it. But having flood waters get closer and closer to your house daily is something that you have zero control over. In these situations, I think that we do well to keep a couple of things in mind.

First, remember that God is still in control and *can* bring good out of bad. Think about Joseph when he was sold into Egyptian slavery by his brothers. That was something completely out of his control. The only thing that he could do in such a situation, the only thing that he could control, was his attitude. And what was the result? God used him to save thousands to millions of people.

Second, understand that we *do* live in a fallen world with fallen people, and that everything is not going to end up perfect all the time. Sometimes you have to settle for good-enough, and understanding this can be a great source of relief.

Third, talk with somebody. Bottling up your frustration doesn't serve you any good. I've gradually come to learn this in my relationship with my wife. I'm not predisposed to tell her exactly what's on my mind and heart, what I'm thinking about, stressed about, worried about. But when I do, I'm pleasantly surprised to find that not only does she often have sound advice and a fresh perspective on the issue, but that talking helps me to sort through the issue with her. In the end, I feel as if the problem is not as big as I thought it was before.

Fourth, pray. Prayer is powerful. Stress can often cause anxiety, and anxiety can lead to depression. Philippians 4:6-7 states that if we pray to God about what it is that we are going through, and lace those prayers with thanks, that the peace of God which passes all understanding will guard our hearts and minds.

Fifth, remember the big picture. Taking care of loved ones is a big deal. But if what you're stressed, it may be beneficial to remember the big picture. My uncle told a story about this once that I think illustrates this perfectly. His car randomly burst into flame on the side of the road (it was an oil leak). As he was standing on somebody's lawn watching his car go up in smoke, he began to think of all the reasons this was going to cause trouble. He'd have to buy a new car, he had no money for a new car, he'd have to pay to tow this car away, he'd have to file an insurance claim, etc. It was overwhelming him. But then he said that he began to just be thankful that he was able to get out of the car alright (his seatbelt had locked and he had to cut his way out), that his girls weren't in the car with him, and that nobody had gotten hurt.

When he could look at things through the big picture, he said he felt much more at peace, and was able to move on with what his next steps should be.

Conclusion

Stress is something that we must learn how to manage with and, in some cases, avoid. If you want to delve into a book-length discussion on stress, I recommend Steve Farrar's *Overcoming Overload*.[4] He's an excellent pastor, and a great writer. If managing stress is something you have trouble with, I think you would enjoy his book.

Chapter 14
Keeping Spirits High

The end of the world has just happened. How on earth are you supposed to ensure that your family doesn't end up slipping into a constant state of depression and self-pity? Ask any military member, police officer, EMT, or youth pastor taking kids on a backpacking trip, and they'll all tell you that good morale is crucial to not only getting things done, but keeping things safe. When morale is lacking, you end up with potentially dangerous problems.

So, what are some of the factors at play to ensure there is good morale "among the troops?"

Food

Believe it or not, something as simple as food can be key in ensuring that morale stays high when the world's hitting low. Wars have been lost because armies didn't have the proper morale from lack of food. When you're hungry, it's hard to think about much *other* than food. Just read some of the accounts of Holocaust survivors and you'll see what I mean. They dreamed about food. Glucose is the primary source of energy for your brain, and when your brain isn't being supplied with that fuel, it gets cranky.

Have you ever heard the term hangry? When you're angry as a result of being hungry, you're hangry. Odds are you know people that become hangry rather quickly. The only solution is to get that person a sandwich. This is why Snickers has been able to use the campaign slogan that "You're not you when you're hungry." Because it's true!

If you've stockpiled a years' worth of rice and beans, and TEOTWAWKI happens, guess what? You're quickly going to tire of eating rice and beans. Every college-aged guy who's ever started off on his own with a shoestring budget and zero cooking ability can tell you that eating the same food repeatedly quickly gets old. You can only eat so many Poptarts and Ramen noodle packets before you begin to detest even the packaging.

There's got to be variety.

If you're prepping for kids - if you've got a family to feed - make sure you're actually stocking food that the kids like. Kids are notoriously picky eaters. How many of them do you know that gag at the sight of vegetables? Having foods they'll eat will make their and your life easier post-disaster.

Lighting

Another simple factor that can improve morale is plenty of light. Obviously, if there's been an EMP or prolonged power outage, having access to artificial light so that you can do things other than just sit and stare into the darkness once the sun sets can greatly boost morale.

"Well, I'll just go to bed when the sun goes down!"

Yeah, okay. And you'll be going to bed at 5 something o'clock in the winter time (if not sooner), and not waking up till 9-ish? Nope, that's not going to happen. Be realistic. You need to make the most of the time you have during a disaster, and sleeping 14 hours a day isn't going to be in the cards.

Having access to candles, matches, lanterns, flashlights, and alternative energy are all great ways to ensure that you're not living in a dungeon. Being unable to see increases our feeling of vulnerability.[1] When it's pitch dark in your house, any sense of safety is gone.

Entertainment

Who enjoys sitting in a candle-lit room for hours at a time every evening with literally nothing to do? Not me! And if that same routine was repeated for weeks at a time, then you would very quickly grow to dread the fall of night. Entertainment is one of the best ways to ensure you don't end up going crazy in the evening. Books and board games are the two best forms of entertainment that I can think of post-disaster. Perchance the power is out, then movies, videogames, and the like are out. Social media will be inaccessible. Smart phones won't be recharged.

In my mind, having plenty of board games and books that are not only informative, but ones that are entertaining both have their place.

Adequate Means of Security

Knowing that you actually have a chance against an enemy works wonders for morale. Nobody likes to know that an enemy is approaching and that they literally have nothing that they can do to fight back. Who's going to be more at ease? The petite 22-year old woman who lives alone and hears breaking glass downstairs at 2AM with nothing to defend herself, or the petite 22-year old woman who keeps a loaded shotgun by her bed and has a German shepherd? Though being in danger is never a situation that will allow you to be perfectly at ease, knowing that you at least have a fighting chance breeds confidence. And confidence boosts morale.

This is just another reason why a prepper should not only have weapons, but know how to use them.

Showers

As somebody who has done quite a bit of backpacking, I can attest to the fact that when one feels grungy and dirty, morale will soon plummet. In cases such as these, showers work wonders. The knowledge that one is clean seems to rejuvenate the mind and fill one with energy. Post-collapse, having working electricity just may not be a reality. In such a case, I would utilize a camping shower. It's essentially a black bag that you fill with water and hang up so that the sun can warm it. Once the water is to your liking, you then release the water as you are taking a shower under it.

The whole thing is gravity and solar powered, and you can typically find them for around $40. Well worth the investment, if you ask me.

Scheduled Group Devotions

I hesitated to put this here for the fear that I would come across as kitschy, but lately I have been trying to be more bold with the truth, and frankly, I think this one is true regardless of what you think about it. Who doesn't leave church feeling uplifted? Doesn't community with other believers and regular Bible study help us as Christians to not only remember who it is that we serve, but give us insight into our current circumstances as well?

Bringing our trials, predicaments, and problems before God together as we worship Him together is powerful. Matthew 18:26 confirms this. "For where two or three are gathered together in My name, I am there in the midst of them." Holy smokes! If Jesus is there with us when 2-3 of us gather together in His name, think of what that is! That's the Creator of the Universe, who *loves* us, is *good*, and cares about our problems being there to listen to us worship Him and tell Him about our problems. How can that be anything but uplifting?

Conclusion

As you can see, there are practical steps that we can take to ensure that morale is where it needs to be. It doesn't have to be anything profound. You don't have to set grandiose goals. Something as simple as baking cookies can be all that it takes to help people lift their head once more. Be creative. Find the little things that will help bring joy, and you will better ensure that the people around you are keeping spirits high.

Chapter 15
When Bad Stuff Happens

It's important to note that being prepared doesn't *prevent* bad things from happening – it lessens the blow. Having auto insurance doesn't mean you'll never get in a car accident. Accidents are just a part of life.

This even applies to looking at things from a spiritual warfare perspective. Look at Ephesians 6:10-18a:

Finally, my brethren, be strong in the Lord and in the power of His might. Put on the whole armor of God, that you may be able to stand against the wiles of the devil. For we do not wrestle against flesh and blood, but against principalities, against powers, against the rulers of the darkness of this age, against spiritual hosts of wickedness in the heavenly places. Therefore take up the whole armor of God, that you may be able to withstand in the evil day, and having done all, to stand. Stand therefore, having girded your waist with truth, having put on the breastplate of righteousness, and having shod your feet with the preparation of the gospel of peace; above all, taking the shield of faith with which you will be able to quench all the fiery darts of the wicked one. And take the helmet of salvation, and the sword of the Spirit, which is the word of God; praying always with all prayer and supplication in the Spirit.

The armor of God is protection, not prevention. It doesn't mean that life is all rainbows and butterflies. Earth ain't Heaven. Bad things will happen. Doesn't the fact that the *armor* of God being discussed within the Bible's pages act as proof that unfortunate things happen? Who needs armor when nothing pointy or sharp is flying their way?

I've heard it said before that we can't overcome what we aren't prepared for. And I don't think that's necessarily the case. I think that a lot of people overcome things they aren't prepared for on a daily basis. But I do know this: being prepared for something makes overcoming it a heck of a lot easier.

That said, I believe that being a follower of Christ and having a personal relationship with Him as your Savior does make one more resilient.

In John 16:33 Jesus says,

"These things I have spoken to you, that *in Me* you may have peace. In the world you will have tribulation; but be of good cheer, I have overcome the world." (Emphasis added)

I picture Jesus saying this last part with a wink.

If in Jesus we have peace, and in the world we have trouble, then where should we run when we face trouble? Any Sunday school-aged kid can happily give you this answer: JESUS! We have a hope when bad things happen.

For many of us though, when something negative happens the temptation is to blame God and run away. I really think that's a trick Satan tries to run us through. "Oh, *God* caused that problem. *He* didn't stop it. And He *could've* too, couldn't He? You have every right to be bitter, every right to be angry. You did nothing wrong. What's the point in continuing on this walk?"

Man, writing that really punches me in the gut. I've had those times. The times when what is going on makes me want to run from God. And I've traveled down that road, running, hoping things would get better, and they never did. I would be afraid to read my Bible, afraid to pray, and so on. I believe that Satan was pushing me in that direction, doing everything he could to keep me from the one thing that could give me any form of peace. I learned that when the temptation to run takes hold, the best thing one can do is to run straight *toward* God instead.

It took me quite some time to realize the trap I was walking into there.

If you really want to see a great response to trial, look at the book of Job. It took me quite a bit of time to bring myself to reading the book of Job again after going through what I experienced. I was afraid of identifying with him. But when I did finally work up the courage to go through that book again, man, what a measure of peace it gave me. I left with the understanding that yeah, sometimes crap happens, and it doesn't really make much sense as to why.

But *part* of what it taught me is that *it's okay to lack an explanation.* God pretty much straight-up tells Job, "Listen, I am God and you are not, and there are going to be things I do that you don't understand." Job still praised God. He didn't flee from Him.

Our pastor at my church recently went through a series on overcoming trials. One of the things he said that I found interesting was that the greatest weapon we have in times of trouble is worship. He said worship is a weapon that we can use in the worst moments of our lives because it forces us outside ourselves. When we choose to worship in tragedy, we start to bounce back.

I've tossed this around for a while, and here's what I know.

My favorite verse in the Bible is Exodus 4:31.

"And when they heard that the Lord was concerned about them, and had seen their misery, they bowed down and *worshipped*." (Emphasis added.)

The ancient Israelites understood the importance of worship. We already talked about why they did this in the chapter on Fear.

And then look back at Job. Look at what he did after getting the news that he not only lost all his property, but that his kids just died as well.

"Then Job arose, tore his robe, and shaved his head; and he fell to the ground and *worshipped.*" (Emphasis added)

After seeing all of this, it appears that maybe my pastor was onto something. Maybe worship *is* one of the most powerful weapons that we have against the challenges we'll face in the world.

Despite how large a challenge we might face, remember that God is in control. I really like what Jerry Falwell said on the subject:

"Life is filled with glorious opportunities brilliantly disguised as insoluble problems."[1]

"How big is your God?" That's a quote from a sermon I wrote on the inside cover of my Bible. Is He bigger than the people that you are struggling with? Is He bigger than the circumstances you have been placed in? Is He bigger than your problems?

Uhhh, yeah. Yeah, He is. Don't forget that when trouble strikes.

And don't forget that we worship a God who hears our prayers as well. As my wife and I were going through a couple of years of challenges, I was able to find peace in the book of Psalms. Because all this garbage was going on, I was praying and praying and praying, yet nothing was changing. It starts to get you wondering if you're even being heard.

Are You Being Heard?
I cried to the Lord with my voice, and He heard me from His holy hill. – Psalm 3:4

The Lord will hear when I call to Him – Psalm 4:3b

The Lord has heard the voice of my weeping. The Lord has heard my supplication. The Lord will receive my prayer. – Psalm 6:8b-9

You have seen, for You observe trouble and grief. – Psalm 10:14a

I have called upon You, for You will hear me, O God. – Psalm 17:6a

Us: "God! HELP!"

God: I AM COMING! – Psalm 18

The response that we're given in verse 21 of when David calls for help in Psalm 22

Blessed be the Lord, because He has heard the voice of my supplications! – Psalm 28:6

I said in my haste, 'I am cut off from before Your eyes'; nevertheless You heard the voice of my supplications when I cried out to You. – Psalm 31:22

I sought the Lord, and He heard me. – Psalm 34:4b

This poor man cried out, and the Lord heard him – Psalm 34:6a

The eyes of the Lord are on the righteous, and His ears are open to their cry. – Psalm 34:15

The righteous cry out and the Lord hears – Psalm 34:17

For in You, O Lord, I hope; You will hear, O Lord my God – Psalm 38:15

I waited patiently for the Lord; and He inclined to me, and heard my cry – Psalm 40:1

Evening and morning and at noon I will pray, and cry aloud, and He shall hear my voice – Psalm 55:17

I cried out to God with my voice – to God with my voice; and He gave ear to me – Psalm 77:1

In the day of my trouble I will call upon You, for You will answer me. – Psalm 86:7

I called on the Lord in distress; The Lord answered me and set me in a broad place. – Psalm 118:5

In my distress I cried to the Lord, and He heard me. – Psalm 120:1

In the day when I cried out, You answered me, and made me bold with strength in my soul. – Psalm 138:3

He also will hear their cry and save them – Psalm 145:19b

The Lord hears your prayers. Don't ever forget that.

Chapter 16
Fear

Well before I started reading prepping websites, I remember viewing them with disgust. "I've no need to read from a bunch of fearmongers." That was my mindset. And though I now see the wisdom in being prepared for lean/hard times, I still think there are alarmists out there who tend to cause more harm than good.

The best response I've seen to date on this was from Sarah Latimer of survivalblog.com.[1]

As she points out, start with real concerns. Multiple scientists, researchers, and doctors believe that a pandemic flu or similar event is simply a matter of 'when'.[2,3,4,5] Wars happen. Riots happen. Multiple economists believe that an economic collapse is inevitable at some point, and you hear about this in the news every day. Of course, you can always find somebody out there who believes something, but when the logic is sound and the warning signs are clear, the source becomes much more veritable. We could go on and on here. Earthquakes, tornadoes, power outages, and hurricanes happen all the time.

I don't think there is anything wrong with being afraid. If you hear shattering glass downstairs in your living room at 3AM, some level of fear is to be expected. (For the bad guy. Heh heh *sound of shotgun racking*.) If you're hiking and an angry grizzly bear is staring you down from around the corner, it would be normal to be struck with fear. Where I think we take a turn for the worse is when we live in a state of fear. When that fear becomes bigger than our God, we have an issue. As Sarah Latimer states, "to live in a state of fear is not only unhealthy, emotionally, and thus physically, it is also unproductive and unfaithful."[1]

Fear puts blinders on us. It causes us to focus solely on what we're afraid of. In the case of an intruder at 3AM or an angry grizzly bear, I would say that this is acceptable. But when it comes to how you are actually living your life, if you are constantly living in a state of fear, you're doing it wrong. It will paralyze you and rob you of actually *living*.

God has a lot to say about fear throughout the entire Bible. The Bible consistently is telling us to "Fear not."[6] When it comes to living our life on a day-to-day basis, if we are in a relationship with the Creator of the Universe, Someone who not only loves us unconditionally, but is good, merciful, all-powerful, *and* has our best interest at stake, why should we fear? This isn't going to say that if you're a Christian nothing bad will ever happen to you. It isn't going to say that you may as well start running through the ghetto at night, because after all, you have nothing to fear.

No, bad things still happen to good people, and God instructs us repeatedly that we are to be wise. God is wise, and we are to be like Him. How then can we purposefully and needlessly put ourselves into dangerous situations without a care in the world?

But if we get back to talking about living a life consumed by fear, I think that we can find a few verses throughout Scripture that address this. Start with Isaiah:

Fear not, for I am with you; be not dismayed, for I am your God. I will strengthen you, yes, I will help you, I will uphold you with My righteous right hand. – Isaiah 41:10

If God's got our back, who do we need to live in fear of? I mean really, think about what Paul says, if God is for us, then who can be against us (Romans 8:31)?

What about the mind of a Christian though? Is it one to be dominated by a constant fear of everything going on around us? By no means! The Bible is very clear about this in 2 Timothy:

For God has not given us a spirit of fear, but of power and of love and of a sound mind. – 2 Timothy 1:7

If you're a Christian, you're not to be weak. God doesn't put the spirit of a wimp inside you when you invite Christ into your life. Being a wimp is not part of God's character. God didn't give us a spirit of fear. He gave us a spirit of power. We have God behind us, fighting our battles with us, and when you have the only omnipotent, omnipresent, omniscient being in the universe fighting for you, do you really stand much chance to lose?

He gave us a spirit of love as well. I think Paul is backing up his point here. Because if we look in 1 John 4:18 we see this:

There is no fear in love; but perfect love casts out fear, because fear involves torment.

So, if we are filled with the love of Christ, how can fear find a dwelling place in us? Love of God means that fear of the world should be a foreign concept to us. And if we look further at the end of 2 Timothy 1:7, we find that God gave us the spirit of a sound mind as well. We don't need to run around in mental chaos, confusion, and chest-hurting anxiety. Our God is a God of order, not chaos. He's a God of confidence, not wishy-washyness. And He's a God who cares, which I think is the biggest point of all. If we know that God cares about us, then how can we not live life with a sound mind?

My absolute favorite Bible verse out there is Exodus 4:31, which illustrates this point perfectly. To put things in context here, the Israelites have been living in slavery for centuries. Moses has been chosen by God to lead His people out of bondage, and when Moses gathered the elders of the Israelites together to tell them what God was going to do for them, check out what happened:

"...And when they heard that the Lord was concerned about them and had seen their misery, they bowed down and worshipped." (NIV)

What was their response when they saw that God had heard and seen their misery? They *bowed down and worshipped*. Why would they do that? Because they knew that they worshipped a God of action. A God who cared. A God who not only rescues, but does it with style. They knew that if *that* God had seen everything they were going through, that *He* was going to do something, and it was going to be something *big*. Knowing all of that, how can you do anything other than bow down and worship?

Further on in the Old Testament we find this:

Be strong and of good courage; do not be afraid, nor be dismayed, for the Lord your God is with you wherever you go. – Joshua 1:9

God is with us. If God is with us, how can we live in fear?

"But is God always with us?"

Well, I'm glad you asked.

Where can I go from Your Spirit? Or where can I flee from Your presence? If I ascend into heaven, You are there; if I make my bed in hell, behold, You are there, if I take the wings of the morning, and dwell in the uttermost parts of the sea, even there Your hand shall lead me, and Your right hand shall hold me. – Psalms 139:7-10

And as Psalm 139 shows, you can't be hidden from Him. He's promised to *always* be there for us. He even says this again in Matthew 28:20; that He is with us *always*. That alone is incredibly comforting.

And as far as anxiety and worry go, the Bible even addresses that.

Be anxious for nothing, but in everything by prayer and supplication, with thanksgiving, let your requests be made known to God; and the peace of God, which surpasses all understanding, will guard your hearts and minds through Jesus Christ. – Philippians 4:6-7

Sure, there are other references within the Bible about what the Christian's response should be to worry, but this is one of my favorites because it gives you the step-by-step action plan. If there's something out there that is actively worrying you, and you can't seem to shake it, what does Philippians tell us to do?

The Anxiety Action Plan

First, pray. We've got the Creator of the Universe, who is all-knowing, all-powerful, and ever-present willing to listen to us. He *cares* about us deeply! Tell Him what's going on. Tell Him what you're worried about, why, and what's on your heart.

Next, ask for His help. Matthew 7:7-11 says:

Ask, and it will be given to you; seek, and you will find; knock, and it will be opened to you. For everyone who asks receives, and he who seeks finds, and to him who knocks it will be opened. Or what man is there among you who, if his son asks for bread, will give him a stone? Or if he asks for a fish, will he give him a serpent? If you then, being evil, know how to give good gifts to your children, how much more will your Father who is in heaven give good things to those who ask Him!

Check this out. Jesus here is saying, "Listen up, I love you, and I *want* to give you good things. Why not ask?" I have a notecard pinned to the corkboard in my office, and on it is a quote I wrote down from a client on the show *Fixer Upper*. The quote says, "One of the greatest joys as a parent is to give good gifts to your children."

I find there's a lot of parallels in our daily relationships that coincide with our relationship with Christ. If parents receive great joy from answering their children's requests, don't you think God does this as well? This isn't saying that we need to all start asking for Ferraris and brand new TVs, but it *is* saying that if we're stuck in a tight spot, God doesn't have a problem with our asking Him for help. On the contrary, He *wants* us to do so, and He gets *joy* from answering those prayers.[7]

The last part of the ingredient list that Philippians give us to battle anxiety is to be thankful. Despite all the stressors that may be going on around us, if you take the time to sit down and tell Christ what it is you're thankful for, it will help put things into perspective. You quickly realize that you actually do have many things going your way.

I learned this back in my beginning years of college. The switch to dorm life was a big one for me. My roommate hated my guts, and I can't say that the feeling wasn't mutual. I was sleeping *maybe* 4 hours a night (usually because of my guitar-playing roommate). I had zero money, ended up needing surgery for appendicitis (I could barely walk for 2 months afterwards), was working crazy hours, had incredibly difficult classes, and somehow kept running into a bunch of people saying hateful things. I was down in the dumps.

I found, though, that when I took pen and paper and began to write out a list of all the things in my life to be thankful for, I realized that even though life was currently pretty chaotic, I still had a lot going my way. My appendix didn't rupture. I was loving *most* of my classes. The library rocked. I had family nearby, awesome hall mates, was in good health, *had* a job, always had plenty of food, was learning a ton about things I was fascinated by, and so on. Whenever the woe-is-me syndrome sets in, I found that what I had to be thankful for always outweighed whatever it was that I was struggling with.

Would I tell somebody who just lost their father that they just need to sit down and be thankful? Heck no. When big events like that happen, people don't need to be told they're not being thankful. They need to be told that there are people around them who love them. But for the day to day, smaller issues, listing out what you're thankful for changes one's perspective.

Philippians 4:6-7 is the verse that I turn to the most when I'm struggling with anxiety and worry. But it is most certainly not the only passage that addresses the subject. Check out some of these others.

Do not fret – it only causes harm. – Psalm 37:8b

Then He said to His disciples, 'Therefore I say to you, do not worry about your life, what you will eat; nor about the body, what you will put on. Life is more than food, and the body is more than clothing. Consider the ravens, for they neither sow nor reap, which have neither storehouse nor barn; and God feeds them. Of how much more value are you than the birds? And which of you by worrying can add one cubit to his stature? If you then are not able to do the least, why are you anxious for the rest? Consider the lilies, how they grow: they neither toil nor spin; and yet I say to you, even Solomon in all his glory was not arrayed like one of these. If then God so clothes the grass, which today is in the field and tomorrow is thrown into the oven, how much more will He clothe you, O you of little faith? And do not seek what you should eat or what you should drink, nor have an anxious mind. – Luke 12:22-29

I have a thing for algorithms. For some reason, math was never a strong suit of mine all through high school. I hated it. But when I got to college and discovered statistics and probability, I wondered where it had been for so long. If high school math had been statistics, then I would have paid much more attention. I suppose one of the things I like about probability is the algorithms themselves, that give us the help needed to make better decisions. I've always thought those were fascinating. They were practical. A few years ago, while farting around on the internet, I came across an algorithm that I thought was great (partly because of the probability background). It had to deal with worry.

The decision tree goes as this: First, you have to decide if there's a problem. If the answer is no, then don't worry about it. If the answer is yes, then is it something you have any control over? If the answer is no, then don't worry about it. If the problem is something you have control over, then just fix the problem and be done worrying!

And don't forget, prayer is something that you can do about a problem!

Prayer

Prayer is one of the most powerful tools that the Christian has against fear and worry. I mean, just check out this verse:

The effective, fervent prayer of a righteous man avails much. – James 5:16b

Prayer is powerful.

What are some of the basics of it, though? What do we need to know about it? Well, let's see what the Bible has to say on the matter.

What God desires is a relationship with us in which we are completely His.[8] What relationship is fully whole without the other party knowing what is in our heart? I've heard it said before that the Bible is God's love letter to mankind. That it is 66 books of God saying, "This is Me, The Creator. I created you. I love you. And I want you to be like Me, because if you don't, you will never live the life that you were *meant* to."

It's hard to have a healthy and vibrant relationship full of life without both parties being willing to share their heart.

Pout out your heart before Him – Psalm 62:8b

I have to constantly remind myself of this in my own prayer time. Every once in a while, I find myself just going through the motions with prayer. I find myself repeating the same thing, in the same manner, once again. That's not what I want to do though. I don't want my prayers to just be me reciting a list, and checking that "conversation with God" off my to-do list. I can't even imagine what my relationship with my wife would be if I talked to her in the same manner. I guess I wouldn't have to imagine too much, because there wouldn't even *be* a relationship!

{
And when you pray, do not use vain repetitions as the heathen do. For they think that they will be heard for their many words. – Matthew 6:7
}

I want my prayers to be an outflowing of my heart. I want Him to know what I am dealing with, struggling with, thankful for, excited about, dreaming of, and so on. Though God already knows our hearts, He still wants us to actually *real* conversations with Him. I guess I liken it to listening to a kid talk about how school was that day. You may already know everything that child did at school that day – the teacher already told you – but it is still enjoyable to listen to what the kid has to say.

Look again toward Psalms. A good portion of all of them were written by David, "a man after God's own heart," and look at how expressive they are. In them, David repeatedly gushes out everything that's in his heart on the issue. He's *communing* with God, letting Him know what he's thinking. That's what God wants. He wants prayer to be part of the ongoing development of a relationship.

Pray with specifics and full of faith.

So I say to you, ask, and it will be given to you: seek, and you will find; knock, and it will be opened to you. For everyone who asks receives, and he who seeks finds, and to him who knocks it will be opened. – Luke 11:9-10

Therefore I say to you, whatever things you ask when you pray, believe that you receive them, and you will have them. – Mark 11:24

I don't need to reiterate here what you already know. Praying for a billion dollars to arrive in the mail tomorrow so you can pay off bills and have fun ain't gonna happen.

A potential source of fear in our lives is that we are going to make the wrong choice. Nobody *wants* to screw up. Nobody *wants* to make a decision we'll regret. Nobody *wants* to be remembered as the guy that consistently makes stupid decisions.

"Oh, yeah. That picture there is great-great-great grandpa. Tradition has it he was an idiot."

Great, that's just how I want to be remembered.

In a post-disaster situation, you may be faced with decisions where it is difficult, if not impossible, to know what is right and what is wrong. How do you choose who to help if there's a large number of wounded around you? *Everyone* may need help. You may be able to only apply pressure to one bleeding wound as you watch the person next to you die from the same type of wound. You can only do CPR on one person at a time. A lifeboat can only hold so many people. There's no right answer here.

What do you do when faced with such difficult, moral decisions that don't seem to be directly covered in Scripture? The only thing I know of is to ask God for wisdom.

If any of you lacks wisdom, let him ask of God, who gives to all liberally and without reproach, and it will be given to him. – James 1:5

They say with prayer God either says yes, no, or hold on. I have a hard time believing that He would say no to one of His children's cries for wisdom.

When faced with serious dilemmas, where you have no idea where to turn, start with prayer.

Final Thoughts

I think that Satan can use fear as a tool against us to control our lives. In the field of psychology, there's a concept referred to as self-fulfilling prophecy. The premise is that there are times when we actually bring about what it is we are terrified of; or certainty that it will happen assures that we indirectly let or make it happen.[9]

If you wake up assuming that today is going to be a terrible day, guess what? It probably will be, even if it wouldn't necessarily be different from any other day. If you assume you're going to blush when you talk to the pretty girl, guess what? You probably will.

Let's look deeper though.

Think about the man who is terrified of his wife cheating on him. Is that something to fear? Well, it's not exactly something you want to have happen. But if that wife has given the man no reason to fear her fidelity, and he continues to let his fear dominate and control his actions, he may come across as clingy, controlling, and suffocating. This in turn *could* lead to the woman searching for a man who isn't as paranoid and overbearing as her husband. And when it came time to pick a love, guess who she'd be most tempted to choose? The man who isn't making her life a living hell.

I like what Mark Twain had to say on living a life filled with fear. "I've had a lot of worries in my life, most of which never happened."[10]

What does worry accomplish? Jesus cleared that up in Matthew 6:25-34 and Luke 12:22-31, in case you're having trouble answering that one.

You need God to be the center of your life, and the center of your focus. It's when He is not, that we get distracted by the things of the world, and we begin to display for all to see what it is to live a life that is not in balance.

And let us not forget all the times of God's deliverance that we can find in the Bible alone. Think back on your own life. This is one of the reasons I really enjoy keeping a journal and a written account of my answered prayer accounts, because we're more like the ancient Israelites than we would like to admit. When you read through the book of Exodus and Judges in Sunday school, over and over again you see the Israelites have God step into their lives, and protect and provide for them in miraculous ways. And then in the *very next chapter*, they'll go back to worshipping Baal, a false god, and saying that he's who they need to worship now for help. How could they be so forgetful?

Really, I don't think that we are any different today. Humans are forgetful. It's just who we are for some reason. Yeah, we may vaguely remember the event that happened, but we tend to downplay the magnitude: where we were, the true scope of the predicament that we were in, how there seemed to be no hope. Simultaneously, we'll glorify our own past abilities; and if you keep a record of your own life, and read back through it every now and then, you'll often be blown away to see how God stepped into your life and delivered you from whatever it was that you were going through. I read those old journal entries of mine, and I think of just how forgetful I am that my God is a *big* God. Is your God bigger than your problem? I guarantee you He is.

But living a life filled with fear tends to blind us from that. What happened when Peter took his eyes off of Jesus and began to focus on the storm that was raging around him?* He began to sink. That same principle applies to us as well. It's when we too begin to focus on our problems - on our fears - that we forget who we worship. We worship a God who uses our problems as opportunities for His power and provision to be displayed.

Remember who it is we serve. The God who rescued a people from 400+ years of slavery, and it all started by keeping a little boy in a basket alive. The God who broke down the walls of a city when people *blew trumpets*. The God who helped a young kid with a rock defeat a veteran warrior *giant*. The God who rescued a man tossed overboard by utilizing the belly of a giant fish. The God who took on all sin to rescue you. The God who defeated *death*.

Chapter 17
What is the Role of the Church Post-Disaster?

When I say the word "church," I'm referring to a specific group of believers that attend a particular building every Sunday. Of course, on a larger scale, the "church" is the entire body of Christ, but that's not what I'm referring to here. I'm talking about a group of people that attend a physical church at a geographical location. After a disaster, what is the church's responsibility? Do they even *have* any responsibility post-disaster? I think these questions can be solved from both the Bible and logic.

To start, look at Acts 11:27-30:

And in these days prophets came from Jerusalem to Antioch. Then one of them, named Agabus, stood up and showed by the Spirit that there was going to be a great famine throughout all the world, which also happened in the days of Claudius Caesar. Then the disciples, each according to his ability, determined to send relief to the brethren dwelling in Judea. This they also did, and sent it to the elders by the hands of Barnabas and Saul.

What did the early church do here? They saw a famine taking place, which I think we can all agree would be a disaster, and they sent relief to help the people! They didn't just let the people starve, they actually did something! This is tied in with what we've already discussed about charity. Charity is part of the church's role, to be the hands and feet of Jesus. Once again, we can look at Jesus' own life while here on earth and see that He met people's physical needs and then attended to the spiritual. (John 5:17-26; 6:6-11; 7:1-10; 7:36-50; 8:22-25; 13:10-17; 14:1-6; 17:11-19; 18:35-43)

People's hearts were open after that. Jesus used these opportunities as an opportunity to witness. I believe the church should as well.

So, what is the role of the church post-disaster? Ultimately, that depends on the type and scope of disaster. I think that we can narrow the church's role post-disaster down to two simple rules though: 1) provide physical needs, and 2) tell others about Christ.

This can be illustrated by several different disasters that have taken place within my own community. A few years ago, we had an incredibly bad hurricane sweep through that left many of us out of power for a solid month. This is in a big community too. The church that I was attending at the time could most certainly be termed a "mega-church." There were multiple services, thousands of people attended, and the facilities were incredibly large to accommodate all of these people. Because there was no power, and nobody had prepared, there was a shortage of water in my community. Wells didn't work, and none of the grocery stores could keep water bottles stocked fast enough to supply the community.

My church had *thousands* of cases of water bottles trucked in from out of state, and gave them away to people free of charge. They advertised throughout the community on social media, word of mouth, etcetera that *they* had water and that if you just showed up any time you could have some. It was incredible. What's funny is that my community is pretty much split straight down the middle. Half of them love that church with a passion, and the other half absolutely despise it for reasons that never made much sense to me (e.g. "they've got property throughout this whole town"). Regardless of where people stood though, if they were thirsty, they were going to show up for that water.

During this same power outage (which took place in the middle of a Southern July, by the way) many of the local nursing homes lost power as well. That meant no air conditioning for a population *incredibly* vulnerable to temperature extremes. My church bought *hundreds* of cots and supplies and bussed in nursing home residents to live in their air-conditioned buildings at absolutely no charge. That church was so large (and had an attached university) that they had their own power grid. As a result, *they* had power when others did not. There's no doubt in my mind that my church saved the lives of older, vulnerable adults after that storm.

Now *that's* a church.

I mean, how can you argue with that? How can you argue with a group of believers who just saved your elderly mother's life, were able to keep her insulin refrigerated, and gave you and your kids the water you needed to stay alive for the past month? You can't! You *can't* walk away with the impression that Christians are hypocritical, self-righteous people after an experience like that.

Think of the doors these actions open afterward. With gratitude comes an open heart, and when people's hearts are open, they will listen.

Having a Crisis Plan

You should have a crisis plan, but I don't think that there's anything wrong with a church having some sort of crisis plan in place either.

"But God will take care of us. There's no need for us to have any sort of 'crisis plan.'"

Yeah, God is in control, and God will take care of us, but as we've already demonstrated in previous chapters, that by no means permits us to slack off. In a world that is increasingly growing to hate Christianity, where church shootings occur rather frequently, it only seems prudent to me to have some sort of crisis plan in place.[3]

(The odds of being involved in an American church during a shooting appear to be .0000079%, however.[4])

> **Recent church shootings**
> - **November 5, 2017 – Devin Kelley kills 26 and wounds 20 at First Baptist Church of Sutherland Springs, TX.**
> - **September 24, 2017 – Emanuel Kidega Samson kills 1 and wounds 6 at Burnette Chapel Church of Christ in Nashville, TN.**
> - **June 27, 2015 – Dylann Roof kills 9 at Emanuel African Methodist Episcopal Church in Charleston, SC.[5]**

At most of the churches where I am from, there is a security team in place that is armed and trained. Nobody knows who they are, but the congregation knows they are there. Other churches in the area actually hire security personnel during their services. Many church members just pack heat. Regardless of the church's choice, I think some sort of plan is wise here.

Churches seem to realize this need for increased security in today's world for the most part. I mean, why do so many of them now make you check in with a name badge or ID in order to pick up your children? Because they don't want some stranger to swing by and pick up your kid. They're taking precautions to enhance your child's security.

So why not have a crisis plan for an active shooter?

Wrapping It Up

Aside from immediate security concerns, has your church talked about what they would do if a storm devastates your area? Do they have resources in place to be *able* to help, or will they attempt to gather them from outside the area after the fact? Do the congregation members have the training needed to enhance their ability to help? I don't think one needs training for everything, and oftentimes I think that we do overdo it here, but it can't hurt to learn as much as you can. Learn as much as you can about as much as you can.

We know that post-disaster, people are more spiritually open. You see this all the time. Churches are packed after tornadoes, hurricanes, typhoons, terrorism, and the like. Maybe learning some tips on talking with those who are depressed would be the way your church wants to help. Maybe there are counseling classes your church can offer. I don't know. I'm just throwing ideas out here, but the point is to get you thinking about what some of your options may be.

What is the role of the church post-disaster? Ultimately, I believe it's to be the hands and feet of Jesus, wherever that may be.

Chapter 18
Disaster Denial

Why is it that some people are so vehemently opposed to the possibility that bad stuff can happen? There's actually a lot of research and discussion on this phenomenon.

Normalcy Bias

People think tomorrow will be just like today. They know there's going to be earthquakes, tornadoes, fires, or whatnot, but they just don't think that it can happen *here*. The mindset is that *those* are the kind of things that happen elsewhere. *Those* things happen to *other* people. How often have you heard a friend or somebody on the news say that? They've just had their home broken into, and their response is "I just didn't think it could happen to *me*."

I think it's important to realize that people have held normalcy bias for all human history. Well before even WW1, did anyone really think that Germany would be capable of mass genocide? Why did the Jews not flee sooner? Many of them did, but I believe that many of them didn't because they simply didn't believe the reports they were hearing trickling in through the shadows.

"That could never happen here."

Well guess what. It did. As Selco states, "Do not underestimate the power of propaganda."[1] Propaganda simply works. People are gullible. When you can convince a large segment of society that another segment is outright wicked and evil, then the potential for violence increases dramatically.

It Won't Be as Bad as They Say

On the flip side, people may understand that those same issues *will* happen, that fires, earthquakes, tornadoes, and whatever else are going to hit their hometown at some point, and they may even understand that there's a possibility they'll be affected. What they might underestimate or disregard is what the severity could be. They'll downplay the potential repercussions, and thus, any desire to prepare for disaster just isn't there.[2]

We Forget

Humans are forgetful creatures. How many times have you read or heard the story of the Israelites during the time of the judges? I can remember during Sunday school as a little kid thinking they were a bunch of morons. I mean, how can you see God visibly do something so miraculous that it could be nobody else *but* Him, and then in the short span of a few years, completely turn around and start offering child sacrifices to a wooden totem pole, or whatever?

It wasn't until I'd gotten a little older that I realized just how easy it was to fall into the same gutter that the Israelites did, over and over again. How many times have we learned our lesson, only to make the same mistake again? People are forgetful, and the same principle applies to disasters.

Odds are Slim it will Happen Again

Another reason that people don't feel the need to prepare is because they've already been through a prior disaster. "I've been through one tornado that tore up my neighborhood. The odds that it happens here twice are slim to none." Unfortunately, that's just not how probability works. Something happening in an area doesn't make it more unlikely to happen there in the future. If there's a 1 in 400 chance that a tornado will rip through your neighborhood on any given day, then there's literally a roll of the dice *every single day*. Your chances are *exactly the same* on any given day. The same principle can be illustrated with a dice roll or a coin toss. I may have rolled a '3' the past roll with the dice, but that doesn't diminish my chances of rolling a '3' again on the next roll. I may have flipped a heads on the past flip, but that doesn't diminish my chances any of flipping a heads again on the next flip. It's the same thing with disaster chances. Prior history doesn't affect the statistics.[3]

If I Prepare, it Will Happen

People may refuse to prepare because they're afraid that doing so will jinx them. If they prep, it's like admitting a disaster will definitely happen. That's a little superstitious though, isn't it? I mean, getting your will written doesn't mean you're going to die the very next day. It just makes it so that things run more smoothly for those you love when it *does* eventually happen. Buying car insurance doesn't mean that you're going to get in a car accident the very next day. What it means is that when something does happen, you'll not be screwed financially. Disasters happen on their own schedule. Not because you stored water, food, and supplies.

If it's My Time, it's My Time

This is just laziness masked as spirituality, in my opinion. Odds are, if there's a disaster in your area, you're going to survive. Not prepping only means that when that disaster *does* hit, because it will, you're going to be screwed, miserable, at risk, unable to take care of your family or others, and a burden to those around you rather than a help/blessing.

I know people that believe this stuff. They'll say "Hey, if we're nuked, we're dead anyway, so what's the point?" Yeah, well what if there's a bad snowstorm that leaves you without power or heat for 2 weeks instead? What are you going to do then? Are you just going to lay around and accept that it's "your time" as your daughter freezes to death? Odds are that the answer there is no.

The Government Will Save Me

I've heard the excuse that "the government will take care of me" as well, and I think that it's the most laughable reason out there people give to justify their inaction. It reveals naivety on how real life works. What would you think of the man who refused to save for retirement and gave you this as his reasoning?

How did the Jews fare when they trusted the German government with their firearms? Not so well. How did the people in the Pulse nightclub fare when they trusted the government to come and save them? Not so well. How did the people in the Parkland, Florida high school fare when they trusted the government's police officer to protect them when the school shooter went through? Not so well. How did Puerto Rico fare when they trusted the government to take care of them after that hurricane? Not so well.

You get the point.

When you trust in the government to take care of what is *your* responsibility, you end up with a bunch of entitled, lazy, and naive people laying around in misery. Healthcare and government *response* teams simply may *not* be able to assist.[4] Emergency personnel abandonment happens.[5] Obviously, government incompetence is a big part of this (have you *seen* their quality of work versus private contractors?), but many of these people have families too. Should disaster strike, if their friends, families, and homes are affected, there's a high likelihood they'll decide to take care of their own before they decide to take care of strangers.

Have you seen the movie *World War Z*? It stars Brad Pitt and tells the story of a world ravaged by a zombie outbreak. During one scene, Brad's character enters a grocery store with his family to get supplies. The shelves are stripped bare, and two men attempt to rape his wife while Brad is getting medicine. After foolishly waving a rifle around in the air, Pitt shoots one of them in the leg. The would-be rapists scamper away, and a police officer runs down the aisle where the whole situation just took place. Pitt thinks the officer is there to respond to the shooting. Instead, the officer runs right past him to grab infant formula.

Obviously, this is just fiction from a zombie movie, but as my screenwriter friend constantly asserts, movies can teach us things. The government officials who some trust for their safety often resort to fulfilling their own self-interests rather than the jobs that they've been entrusted with.

"But isn't that what FEMA's for? Aren't they the taxpayers' emergency safety net?

Yeah, in an emergency, FEMA does provide supplies. But who's to say that they're actually going to be accessible to you, arrive timely, or even show up at all? Typically, FEMA doesn't come until both the president has made an official declaration of disaster, *and* the state governor has requested national aid.[6] So let's say that both of those factors end up coinciding. Well, by the time they show up in your vicinity, you could be too far gone for them to be able to help. Trusting in FEMA, or any other government provided aid, is clearly not an efficient, safe, or responsible choice.

It's Not a Current Issue
Humans are more focused on the here and now than future possibilities. If we know that we live in an earthquake prone area, but our bills are due now, we tend to focus more on the immediate problems rather than far-off ones.[3] This doesn't mean that our current problems don't need to be taken care of, but it doesn't mean that we shouldn't prepare for the future ones either.

I Can't Afford To
I think this is excuse is mainly a result of marketing. People think that if they are going to prep in any sense of the word, that the first things that they need to do are buy thousands of rounds of ammunition, incorporate a pre-fabricated panic room into their house, and buy a $2,000 supply of freeze-dried food buckets from Mountain House.

That's simply not the case. Getting prepared, a) can be done on even a shoestring budget, and b) isn't something that happens all at once. Library books are free. Your tax dollars are paying for them, so you may as well take advantage of them. Knowledge is often the most vital part of any prepper's attributes, because without it, you're screwed, and a little goes a long way. No, you can't eat knowledge, but knowledge can help you eat.

Buying a 5-gallon bucket from Lowe's and filling it with bags of rice and beans is relatively cheap as well. As of right now (2018), an 8lb bag of pinto beans costs $5.88 at Walmart. A 5-gallon bucket is cheap (look for one made of food-grade plastic), and just one of those buckets can hold around 25lbs of beans. So, if I filled just one bucket up with dried pinto beans, it would cost me around $22. That's not bad at all. The Dollar Store (which I love) has a number of supplies that would work in a prepper's gear as well, and *The Patriot Nurse* has a great YouTube video demonstrating this.[8]

The point is that you don't *typically* have to be comprehensively prepared for a disaster by the end of the week. Doing what you can consistently, and staying within your budget, are the best ways to ensure that you become incrementally more resilient to disaster.

I'll Just Start a Garden, Start Hunting, and Harvest My Own Food
The person saying this is clearly out of touch, completely unaware of how hard that is to achieve. It's taken me several years to even feel like I've earned the title of *Novice* Gardener. I can't tell you how many plants I accidentally killed by placing in too sunny of a spot, placing in too shady of a spot, planting when it's too cold, planting when it's too hot, planting too late, planting too early, overwatering, not watering enough, or not weeding around. Then there are the plants decimated by bugs, deer, rabbits, birds, fungus, and so on. Just in the past year I've had peach trees split down the middle, a June bug epidemic, slugs that destroyed plants at night, chickens who love escaping and eating my blueberries while scratching up my tomatoes to take a dust bath, and chickens who had vent gleet (a nasty looking butt)!

Gardening is *hard*, and to believe that you can just pick it up like a pro after the fact is delusional.

Even if you do have the know-how, the seeds, *and* the tools properly laid aside, do you have enough food to last you until your crops *potentially* start coming in?

I mean, the Pilgrims had a pretty hard time of it the first winter they arrived, didn't they? And that was with a ship full of supplies! If you want to be able to grow your own food post-disaster, then you need to start now.

You have to be prepared for beforehand. Don't expect to learn it on the fly.

I'll be Raptured Before
Why assume that the Tribulation is the only bad thing that's ever going to happen on the planet? Nobody was raptured up prior to the past 50

natural disasters and power outages, as far as I know. A lot of people were very cold, miserable, and hungry as a result of not prepping. Once again, we have a spiritual sounding answer that's nothing more than masked laziness.

Conclusion

Humans are inherently lazy. We don't like to think about working now for future benefit. We want to focus on the now. Instant gratification. However, sometimes it's just a lack of information that is keeping people from doing what they need to do. If any of the above excuses are thrown your way by people whom you care about and want to see taken care of, then hopefully the above responses will help you be better able to respond.

Chapter 19
Beginning to Prepare

"Private sector preparedness is not a luxury; it is a cost of doing business in the post-9/11 world. It is ignored at a tremendous potential cost in lives, money and national security." – The 9/11 Commission Report

So, let's say you're new to prepping. Where do you start? What are the steps you can take now to better shield yourself and your family from disaster's consequences? Proverbs 24:27 says, "Prepare your outside work, make it fit for yourself in the field; and afterward build your house." Really, this verse is about priorities. What feeds people and provides a source of income in an agricultural society? Whatever is growing in a field. A house filled with frills is nice, but working on it before the income and food source is procured gives havoc a foot in the door.

In the same way with prepping, if you have all the latest night-vision/thermal optic systems, yet no food or water, your priorities out of whack. So, let's look at the most important factor in survival first.

Water

You can only live about 3 days without water. If you have water available, but it's not clean to drink, then you may live longer, but it's going to be a miserable time because you'll gradually be succumbing to some type of infectious disease along the way. Furthermore, most long-term storage foods tends to be dehydrated, in other words, it needs water. Have you ever tried to eat dehydrated mashed potatoes and dried beans for dinner, and then finish it off by choking down a glass of dehydrated milk? That's just water for consumption, not touching on water needed for cleaning, critical for keeping one's health in desperate times.

"I don't need to store water though. Flooding is my primary concern, and due to the nature of flooding, there'll be plenty of water around!"

Ok, but again will it be *clean* water? You've got to remember that if an area is flooded, that means that the sewers in the area are in direct contact with the water you're wading in. The cow patties that were in the field nearby are now floating with fish by your front doorstep. And they're putting germs in your water. People are peeing in your water, pooping in it, vomiting in it, bleeding in it, and other things.

"Well, I'll just boil everything!"

Yeah, but boiling doesn't remove chemicals. Gas cans, vehicles, factories, and a host of other sources are going to be leaking all kinds of chemicals directly into the water that you intend to cook with and drink. And I've got news for you, filtering and cooking aren't going to get those chemicals out. Some chemicals can bind with water and won't be filtered out by primitive methods. No, contaminated water is not something you want to mess with.

So, we know that ready access to clean water is vital to our survival. The general rule of thumb is to store a gallon of water per person per day. Thus, a 2-week supply of water would be around 14 gallons per person.[2] Following the arithmetic, a 55-gallon drum of clean water would equal 2 weeks of water for a family of four (provided they're being conservative with it).[3]

> According to Mormons - who have an excellent disaster prep program in place - storing 14 gallons of water per person is one of the steps they recommend to be prepared for disaster.[4]

If you know there's an incoming disaster on its way, there are a couple of different tricks that you can do to help to cap off your supplies. For starters, don't flush the toilets. The water in the top tank (NOT the bowl) is technically clean. It hasn't come into contact with sewage or anything. It's gone straight from the water source and into the storage tank of your toilet. By not flushing, you save yourself at least a gallon of potable water from the toilet storage tank.

Filling all the bathtubs, sinks, and available containers that you have with water can also add to the amount of water you have after the power goes out.

And lastly, according to Matthew Stein in his book *When Technology Fails*, you can actually get some water out of your hot water heater if you're desperate. First, you want to ensure that you've turned off the gas or electric power to the water heater. To harvest this water, open the top vent, and then drain the tank into containers with the bottom spigot.[3]

> Juice and milk containers don't make ideal long-term water storage containers. They're too difficult to clean, which can lead to some particularly nasty bacteria growing in them while they're sitting on your shelf.[5]

When it comes to sanitation, you've got a couple of different options. One of the lowest tech options is bleach.

Bleach
Adding 2-4 drops of household bleach per quart of water should clean and purify the water to the point that it is drinkable.[3] Now, obviously this won't do anything to get heavy metals such as lead, chemicals such as leached poisons, or visible particles of poop out of the water, but it will help to kill any bacteria that could make you sick. So obviously, you still want to make sure that the water is from as safe a source as you can find, and filter out the big particles as much as you can.

Supposedly, adding 1 lemon per liter of water is a way to help kill off any of the bad stuff as well.[6]

UV Light
This is the method of water filtration that I like best. It's pricey, but I like the added security I get from it. Ultraviolet light kills bacteria, protozoa, and viruses without any chemicals or heat whatsoever.[7] I use a product called a Steri-pen that I picked up at a Cabela's for around $100, and exclusively use it when I'm out in the backcountry.

Water Filter Pumps
Backpacking stores will sell these. It's essentially a little pump with two tubes attached to it. You put one tube in the water source, and the other tube in your water bottle. Then you start a'pumpin'. The water gets forced through an extremely fine filter that will catch *nearly* all the bad stuff that you don't want in your water.

Iodine Tablets
You can pick up small bottles of iodine tablets at pretty much any sporting goods store, and they'll treat water for you at the price of taste. Water treated with this stuff has a rather nasty taste. Most people who use iodine tablets to treat their water also carry powdered drink mixes with them to help mask the taste. There are some nasty water-borne illnesses that aren't killed by these little tablets as well.[7] I always carry them as a backup in case my Steri-pen breaks.

Collecting/Storing Water
Rain barrels are one of the first and most efficient ways that you can help ensure you always have some water stored in a space-effective way. Joel Salatin and Ben Falk both advocate the usage of ponds as a means of

water security as well. In their minds, ponds are the gold standard for water security. With a pond, not only do you have a large, attractive body of water on your property, but the increase in biodiversity can greatly benefit your property as well. Fish can be raised in the pond, which can add another source of food to your pantry as well.

The way Joel Salatin advocates using ponds is by placing them near the top of hills, and keeping what would need water at the bottom of the hill. So, my gardens, crops, cow troughs, and chicken coops would all be located at the bottom of the hill. That way all I need to do is have various hoses connected to different sides of the pond running down the hill. By simply turning on the knob to allow water to flow from the pond down the hose, I'm able to get water to where I want it solely off gravity. I don't need expensive electric pumps, or any other piece of fancy infrastructure to rely on. This approach, of course, will not work for most people. There are many options out there to fit your specific needs.

> Don't forget that it's wise to have a convenient way to transport water as well, perchance you must go on the move. Water weighs 8lbs/gallon.[8] It's heavy. If you decide to bug out, and all you have available are 55-gallon drums of water, you're out of luck. This is why it's important to have portable options for filtration in addition to stored water. Redundancy is a good thing.

Communications

When I first started getting into prepping, I couldn't understand why proper communications were stressed over and over again in the various articles and books I was reading. As time went by, and my research continued, I now understand why.

Information is needed to make proper, effective, efficient, and safe decisions. Without that information, you can't make educated decisions and develop smart plans. Data collection leads to good decision making, and without the data, the outcome of your choices will be left to chance. The morale component of working communications can't be left to the shelf either. I don't know about you, but when there's a huge storm coming my way, I do find some level of comfort in knowing where the worst of the storm is hitting, if there's been any damage, and if I need to be concerned about hail, flooding, or tornadoes. My radio fills me in on all that. That's why I listen to it during storms. It lets me know if I need to take any precautions to ensure everything at my place ends up making it through the storm okay.

The point is that people crave information. It's why we check our email 20 times a day, watch the news, listen to the radio, read bulletin boards, and check our phones for new texts every 15 seconds. We *want* to know what is going on out there, and without it we quickly grow aggravated, bored, and stir-crazy. Having proper communications is one of the best things you can do to ensure that this need is met in a post-disaster world.

Radio is by far the most reliable method of obtaining communication during a major incident.[9] Internet service can go down, TV depends on electricity, and phones simply may not be available. A radio works pretty consistently. You can even buy crank-powered radios eliminating the need for batteries. So, if the power *does* go down, odds are you'll still be able to use your off-the-grid radio to tune in to what's happening in the outside world.

Having a radio that's essentially a portable version of what came with your car is probably the lowest-grade way to ensure you have some sort of information flow coming in. However, if you need more in depth information, or need to convey information yourself, then I recommend considering a HAM radio license. The test isn't that bad, and there's plenty of online study tools that will help you study. I'm terrible with math, electronics, and electrician-esque skills, yet despite all this, I passed the test on the first try with a week's worth of study utilizing the study guides I found.

> Here's an interesting tip that I picked up from James Wesley Rawles' book *How to Survive the End of the World as We Know It.* Using 12-VDC marine band radios if you live far enough inland can essentially give you a private band to use. Think about it. If you're nowhere near the water, then nobody else is going to be using those types of radios! You now have a more secure way to talk![10]

If you do decide to get into HAM radio, I encourage you to start "chewing the rag", and developing some contacts within the HAM community as quickly as possible. Having a few strategically placed contacts throughout your geographic region could be incredibly beneficial when it comes to gathering information and making decisions post-disaster.

If you're in a post-apocalyptic scenario, however - let's say an EMP has destroyed most of the HAM radio equipment out there - then runners may be an option. In typical disaster scenarios runners (people literally running or using vehicles) are used as a last resort if all other options of communications fail.[12] Obviously, that's not an ideal situation, and you're probably going to want to take steps to avoid getting placed in such a predicament, but it *is* an option, and one that has been used throughout history with success for a very long time.

However, probably one of the most effective pieces of communications equipment that you can have doesn't cost any money at all. What is it? Having a pre-discussed plan. After a disaster is no time to start coming up with plans on where your family should all meet, what you should do, how you should get there, etc. Greater than 90% of families don't have any family communications plan in the event of a disaster.[13]

Remember when we were talking about psychological first aid (PFA), and how one of the most stressful parts of a disaster is that victims get separated from their families, and have no clue what steps to take to get into contact with them? Having a plan already laid down allows you to salt the earth where that weed would normally grow. After a disaster, that's one less thing that your family would have to worry about. They'd know where to go.

Perchance something bad happens in the middle of the day when your family is scattered throughout your county at school, work, friends' houses, grocery stores, and whatnot, and perchance there's zero possibility of your being able to communicate with each other post-disaster, then how do you all know where to go? How do you all know where to meet each other?

Make sure your family has a plan, and everyone knows it.

Every Day Carry, Car Kits, and Get Home Bags
"So, I've got my home pretty set as far as prepping goes. I should be good, right?"

That's great! Having your home all set is a good thing. However, there's a very good chance that you won't actually be anywhere near your home when disaster strikes. It's simple probability. Think about it. If you

137

spend 8+ hours a day at work, that's at least 1/3 of the day that you're not at home, and odds are that it's even greater than that. Are you happy with a 33% chance that disaster will strike in an area where you're unprepared?

Probably not.

Terrorist attacks don't happen at individual homes. They happen where the largest damage can be done. And perchance something terrible like this does happen to you or where you're at, being prepared puts you in a much better place.

When disaster strikes, whatever it may be, *individuals* are the first responders to the scene. *Individuals* are the ones who start life-saving procedures for people. That means that during those several minutes that police and rescue are in transport, you're up at bat. You're the one that can help to stop a person from bleeding out for another 12 minutes until the lifesaving crew arrives. Twelve minutes of bleeding out may be too late for them to wait for help.

You can see this at play with shootings. When victims of a shooting have to wait for police to arrive on the scene, a whole lot of people die. You end up with a mass casualty event. But when there's somebody on scene who conceal carries, they may be able to take care of the problem then and there.

Knowing this, it makes sense to have some form of prepping that goes everywhere with you.

Knowledge

I never really knew my great grandpa. I mean, I met him a couple of times, but I was maybe 4 years old, and he couldn't really say much. The only memory I have of him is his laying on a hospital stretcher in his house with oxygen tubes up his nose. He was dying from lung cancer.

But I did learn something from him. My family has kept his legacy alive by teaching the rest of us about who he was. One of the things that he used to always say was, "Learn as much as you can about as much as you can."

I think that's sound advice.

> *The heart of the prudent acquires knowledge, and the ear of the wise seeks knowledge. –*
> **Proverbs 18:15**

One of the most useful things that you can have as a prepper is knowledge. It's been said that the more you know, the less you need, and I believe this to be true. If you're competent with your bushcraft skills, then you don't *need* all the latest and greatest camping equipment to make it through a night in the wild. Your knowledge gives you what you need to use what you have around you for survival.

Increase your knowledge on the preparedness subjects most critical to you and your situation. Read books. Read blogs. Talk with people about how they do things, and how they tackled certain obstacles. If there's a field that you don't feel competent in, and want/need to, then do what you can to increase your knowledge on the subject.

Learn as much as you can about as much as you can.

Food

When most people think about beginning to prep food as a form of disaster insurance, they typically think they need to go out and buy thousands of dollars of Mountain House freeze dried meals. If you can afford to do so, and that is the best option for you, then by all means go ahead and do it.

For the rest of us, I offer good news: there are other ways.

Buying bulk bags of your own foodstuffs that will store for a reasonable period of time is a much cheaper alternative. So, what are some examples of foods that store well?

Rice, beans, corn, wheat, hardtack, coffee, and tea are a few of the dried foodstuffs that will last quite some time if kept stored within the proper environment. According to Rawles, your larder should consist of dried foods, canned foods, and supplementary foods.[15] Canned goods can store for a significant amount of time as well. Just how long depends on who you ask. If you talk to my Papa about the subject, he'll say forever. Others will say as little as 2 years. You have to apply some common sense here though. If you have cans that are dented and showing signs of being compromised, I'd throw those suckers away. The point is to have food you can live off, by which you won't be poisoned.

How Much Food do I Store?

How do you know how much to store? How much is too much? The answer is really up to you. What is it you are preparing for? How large is your family? How large of a charity/extra-relative stockpile do you want to have? How long are you anticipating having to rely on that stockpiled food?

Thinking of all these questions at once can quickly grow

overwhelming. So, let's start with baby steps. Obviously, it's better to have something rather than nothing. So you can start by buying some canned goods and laying them aside somewhere. Just a few extra cans is still a few extra cans, and in the event of a short-term emergency, will still do some good. If you're looking for something more comprehensive, I'd recommend utilizing the following steps.

1. **The first step is to determine how many pounds of food per person per day (ppppd) you're going to need.**

	PPPPD	Estimated Calories
Hot days/warm nights; short trips; not a lot of excessive exercise	1.5	2,500-3,000
Warm/cool days and nights; hiking with full packs; moderate to active workdays	1.75 - 2	3,000-3,500
Cool days/Cold nights; hiking with full packs; heavy workdays	2-2.5	3,500-4,500
Cold days/extremely cold nights; extremely strenuous workdays	2.5	4,000-5,000

(16)

Obviously, in a survival situation, you're not going to really know what it is that you need. Disasters don't really follow a timeline. They happen anytime they dang well please. Will it be the dead of winter? The middle of the July sun? The rainy season? Who knows? Thus, you're better off to be over prepared. If you live in a region with pretty extreme temperatures (Florida or Maine), then you'll probably have a better idea of what weather to expect during a disaster as well, and that will help you gauge your choices.

Don't forget to make room for error, and include what your best estimates for charity and Family Horde as well.

For example, let's say that there are 3 people in my immediate family, and I can foresee 3 other family members/friends heading my way if a collapse happens. My farm is just up and coming, so there's quite a bit of heavy work to do all day long with goats, chickens, bees, and gardening chores (among many other things). Fortunately, it doesn't drop down to below 10 degrees Fahrenheit too often where I live.

So, I'd estimate that my family would need 2-2.5 ppppd to live. A lot of those family members are men (who eat more), and I like to play it conservatively, so I'll say 2.5 ppppd just to play it safe.

2. Determine the length of time you want to have food available.
I neither have the space nor the funds to store a year's worth of food in my house. So, I'll shoot for 3 months. I feel this is a sufficient buffer time to get me through most disasters. Dave Ramsey advocates for at least 3 months' worth of living expenses to be stored up in the form of cash, so I apply the same principle to food.

Number of people x number of days to survive x ppppd[17]

So, with 6 family members at 2.5 ppppd for 90 days, that would be 1,350 pounds of food that I would need to store. Obviously, there would be some variation here. At what point in the disaster do the family members show up? What if they don't show up at all? What if they bring friends? Stuff like that. But for the most part, this should give you a pretty close estimate. It's a number to *work* from.

3. Utilize food multipliers.
After you calculate those numbers, the National Outdoor Leadership School (NOLS) uses something called category multipliers to help them adjust just how much food you'd actually need to survive. Keep in mind that they make these lists predominantly for outdoor athletes such as backpackers, mountaineers, kayakers, and the like, so some of these food items may not be what your average Joe would consider ideal. Regardless, it gives us a frame of reference, and if you plan on bugging out at all, I would argue that there's no better source to determine how much food you'll actually need than the NOLS.

Food Category	1.5 ppppd	1.75 ppppd	2 ppppd	2.25 ppppd	2.5 ppppd
Breakfast	.24	.28	.33	.35	.38
Dinner	.27	.32	.35	.37	.40
Cheese	.19	.22	.24	.26	.28
Trail foods	.32	.35	.37	.45	.49
Flour and baking*	.11	.13	.16	.09	.10
Sugar and fruit drinks	.10	.12	.14	.15	.18

Soups, bases, desserts	.06	.09	.13	.15	.19
Milk, eggs, margarine, cocoa	.21	.24	.28	.31	.33
Meats and substitutes**	0	0	0	.12	.15

*Colder temperatures mean that baking isn't as energy efficient, and isn't utilized as much at NOLS.

**High-fat meats are added in colder climates to assist in meeting increased caloric needs.[18]

Using the above chart, calculate the total pounds of each food category needed for the duration you've decided to prep. Let's calculate dinner as an example.

The formula is:

Food multiplier at appropriate ppppd x desired food storage days x number of people.

Remember, I have 6 people for 90 days at 2.5 ppppd.

For dinner, 2.5 ppppd is .40, so that's my food multiplier that I'll plug into the formula. Then I just plug in the rest of the numbers.

.40 x 90 days x 6 people = 216 pounds of *dinner* needed for 6 people to last 90 days with daily heavy labor.

The Mormons have a system in place for storing a year's worth of food that doesn't require as much math, should that be a bane of yours. Keep in mind that you'll be pretty hungry prepping this meagerly, but it's most certainly better than nothing. The Mormon church asks that members store:

- 400 pounds of grain per person
- 60 pounds of beans per person
- 20 pounds of meat per person
- 60 pounds of honey per person
- 90 pounds of fruits and vegetables per person
- 8 pounds of salt per person
- 16 pounds of powdered milk per person
- 10 quarts of cooking oil per person

To fine tune these numbers, the Mormons use the following calculations: for the average adult female, multiply the weight of the food item by 0.75 to determine actual needed supply. Adults involved in regular manual labor should multiply the food weight by 1.25 – 1.50. Kids aged 1-3 should multiply the weight by 0.3, aged 4-6 should multiply it by 0.5, and aged 7-9 should multiply it by 0.75.[19]

What does this look like? Well, let me give you a little taste. Two 5-gallon buckets will hold approximately 75 pounds of grain (e.g. rice/wheat/etc.). That means you would need 11 buckets of grain per family member to store the necessary amount of grain to last you a year. One 5-gallon bucket will hold around 25 pounds of beans. So, this would mean you'd need about 2.5 buckets of beans per family member to store for a year's supply.[19]

Aside from buckets of beans and rice, two other things that you may want to think about are vitamins and spices. Odds are that your stored food is not as high in the variety of vitamins and minerals that your body needs on a daily basis in order to thrive. Storing a couple bottles of vitamins can be one of the things you can do to ensure you're still getting the nutrients your body needs when you're subsisting off of MREs and who knows what else.

In a similar vein, what do you do if your wife gets pregnant? Though women have had babies for millennia without vitamin supplements, and women in eastern Europe and Africa still have healthy babies all the time without taking vitamins, it is still a wise decision to take them if you have them available, as pregnant women have an increased need for particular vitamins such as folic acid in order to ensure that the baby develops normally.

Spices are something else that is worthwhile. Why did the East India Trading Company do so well back during the Colonial Era? Because people craved variety with their foods! Eating bland mushy stuff day in and day out is boring, and we quickly can suffer from something called "appetite fatigue" when that happens. Having spices can ensure that this doesn't happen. Less appetite fatigue means that people will eat more, ensuring that they are taking the nutrients they need to survive and do the hard, manual labor one is likely to face in a post-collapse civilization. Morale is vitally important in a survival situation as well. As they say, "variety is the spice of life.,"

Medical Supplies

Do you have a very basic supply of medicines at your house? I learned in college that it was much better to have the medicines available in my dorm *before* I was sick. Nobody likes walking across town to Walmart when they have diarrhea. This is what I try to keep at the house:

- Pepto-Bismol – for indigestion
- Tums – for heart burn
- Nyquil
- Tecnu – the greatest poison ivy rash preventer that I know of
- Aspirin – it thins the blood. I keep it in case anyone nearby ever has a heart attack.
- Tylenol – the only pain medication we use. Ibuprofen may have a link to male infertility.[20]
- Hydrocortisone cream – for when I don't get to Tecnu fast enough
- Hydrogen peroxide
- Neosporin
- 91% Isopropyl alcohol
- Disposable gloves – to avoid dangerous contact
- First aid kit – This gives me the gauze, bandages, and other supplies that I need to counter a wide variety of small injuries.
- Various splints and braces that I've collected over the years – Knee braces, elbow braces, and wrist braces are but a few of them. I hang on to them even when I don't need them anymore.

Obviously, there are going to be a lot of other potential medications that you're going to probably want to add to your list. The above is just a *very* basic rundown. If you're looking for medical reference books, here are a few of the ones that I like/keep on hand:

- *KNACK First Aid* by Buck Tilton
- *Emergency War Surgery* from PrepperPress
- *NOLS Wilderness Medicine* by Tod Schimelpfenig
- *Where There is No Doctor* by Jane Maxwell[21]

One of the things to keep in mind with medical supplies is this: you're not a doctor. (Unless you're a doctor prepper, I suppose.) Having a stockpile of medicine and medical texts is great, but it's also great to know your limitations and utilize professional help when needed. As Patrice Lewis points out, it is sometimes best to know our limitations.[22] Don't expect to read a book and know how to do brain surgery. You're not a brain surgeon. With a lot of medical treatments, if you don't have the proper skills, you're only going to end up making things worse. Have the wisdom to know what you can probably treat (e.g. a small cut) with what you can't (e.g. broken bones).

Defense/Safety

Safety post-disaster is interpreted in different ways. Some believe that they need a retreat somewhere in the Rocky Mountains only accessible by underwater cave. Others believe the need own an arsenal. Look at what the potential risks are in your area, what you want to be defended from, and then make your decisions based upon that.

As far as guns go, know how to shoot, clean, and assemble your firearms flawlessly. And whether you're brand new to guns or not, I recommend Steve Markwith's Survival Guns series. I've only read *The Beginner's Guide* (Book 1), *Shotguns* (Book 2), and *Centerfire Rifles* (Book 5), but they have all been superb.[23] To date, they are the best books on guns that I have ever read, and the informed me on a lot that I didn't know, despite being around guns my entire life. Book 1 in the series does the best job of helping a newbie determine what weapons they should work on acquiring first though. If what type of ammunition is a concern for you, according to Rawles in *How to Survive the End of the World as We Know It*, #4 buckshot is the best home defense load for when over-penetration is an issue.[24] So, if you live in an apartment, or are concerned that your bullets could go through drywall and hit your kids, just know that that type of shell is probably going to be your best bet.

Other than that, I try to buy hollow points when I can. They cause a lot more damage than your typical round, and if I'm shooting somebody bigger than me, I don't want to just make them angry, I want them dead.

There's more to defense and safety than just guns, however. As Patrice Lewis points out, situational awareness (keeping your head on a swivel), property security, communications, and community are all factors that increase your safety.[25]

An acquaintance of mine who lives in Africa utilizes massive dogs to assist in his family's security. He doesn't live in the safest part of the world, and he has three very large, very territorial dogs that he keeps fenced in on his land. They're free to run around wherever, and instantly bark at and congregate toward anything that moves. The dogs are great around his small kids, but woe to the thief who tries to break in late at night.

Perimeter fences, thorn bushes, cameras, deadbolts, reinforced doors, door brace bars, motion sensor lighting, automatic light timers, and other techniques can all be used to increase the security of your home as well.

Chapter 20
Using Technology to Help Prepare

Doing everything by analog is great, but not always convenient. Sure, if the power goes down, if there's an EMP strike, if you run out of batteries, having analog backups will help ensure that everything still runs smoothly. That being said, technology still has a place. Technology still can be incredibly beneficial, and there are a lot of very practical uses for it. In particular, technology can be vital in the gathering of information. Proper information allows you to make proper decisions. This is why militaries send out scouts and spies. Because without the information that they need, their soldiers could very easily waltz right into the most heavily defended enemy area and get slaughtered. Information keeps you alive.

Obviously, you do the best with what you have, and you'll never know all that there is to know on any particular issue, but when you have the best information out there available to you it leads to increased safety, increased confidence, increased morale, increased reward for success, and decreased risk. In the big scheme of things, tracking what's happening and gathering information equals less loss of life.

So what are some of the technological tools that can help us to better prepare our families for disaster? Well, I'm glad you asked.

Records of Important Documents and Physical Possessions
To start with, keeping a record of the things that you own *and* picture proof of what those things are can save you a lot of headache down the road. A few years ago, there was a really bad tornado that hit the area near where I live. Several people lost everything. Their homes were just devastated. And the pleasant surprise that they received during the recovery phase was that their homeowner's insurance companies didn't want to pay for barely anything! Sure, they would cover the house, but when it came to the household goods that were *inside* that home, the family heirloom furniture, the computers, the jewelry, etc., the insurance companies repeatedly denied payment. Their reasoning was that the homeowners had no *proof* that they actually owned the items they said they did.

Taking pictures of valuable items you have can be one of the main things you can do to ensure that your family is prepared for rebuilding after a disaster. Sure, keeping physical copies of those pictures at your house may not be the most ideal situation. When houses burn down, pictures burn too. But that doesn't mean that there aren't alternative means to using technology to protect your records.

If you feel so inclined, uploading your images to a cloud may be an option. The cloud can then be accessed at any time or place (assuming electricity), keeping your virtual images safe. I like utilizing Shutterfly in this manner. I know that my pictures are with them. However, if you don't feel comfortable knowing that some outside entity has access to everything you own, why not print physical pictures and then bury them in a cache somewhere readily accessible? Should a disaster strike happen, you'll be able to dig up proof of all the items that you own for a fair insurance check to come your way. Potentially, multiple caches with a small stash of pictures and post-disaster supplies may be a good idea perchance one of them gets ruined by water damage, fire, or somehow manages to disappear.

I'm big into geocaching, and have hidden a number of my own caches for fellow geocachers to find. I'm constantly amazed by how caches can either be vandalized, disappear, or be destroyed by construction even when I hide them in the middle of nowhere. Granted, you're not allowed to bury geocaches, but that still doesn't mean finding a random ammo box hidden in a 400-acre wilderness should be easy! The point is that stuff can happen to your cache, even when you place it in an area that you would never imagine could be tampered with. Hiding multiple caches adds extra layers of security.

Red Cross "Safe and Well" App

One of the largest sources of stress after any disaster can be the separation that occurs between families and friends. Take the Las Vegas shooting at the Jason Aldean concert, for example. Let's say that you were there when everything went down. You take off running to you're not really sure where, you just know that you need to put distance between yourself and the bullets. Your friends may have been in the bathroom when it all happened, and took off as well. Simultaneously, your parents know that you're at the concert, and are terrified about whether you're okay or not.

It may not have been the case with that incident, but there are plenty of examples of times when it's hard to call or text people to let them know that you are safe. There are disasters where all phone lines are busy, but cell coverage is still intact.[1] Apps such as this can help during these times.

Clicking that you are ok on the 'Safe and Well' app let's everybody who has the same app know *simultaneously* that you made it through the crisis okay. That in and of itself is a huge relief. Imagine being a parent, and having the reassurance that your kid made it through a school shooting okay. Finding each other can be dealt with later via other methods, but at least with this app everyone knows who is safe.

Social Media
There's been a lot in the news of late regarding the snooping and tracking of social media into our everyday lives. I try to avoid Facebook as much as I can because of this. I haven't gotten around to deleting it yet because it's still such a great marketing tool, and I still have to make money to pay bills and eat.

Despite its privacy and censorship faults, social media can make a pretty effective tool to communicate with people while you're amid a disaster. I use Twitter. I like the real-time news that I get from it. We had a bad tornado tearing through our city just a few weeks ago. During the storm, I was able to monitor Twitter to see exactly where the twister was going, and where it had already been. It was tremendous peace of mind to know that it wasn't heading my way, and it let me know which of my friends may need help after everything had settled down. Radio wasn't really giving me any updates other than that there *was* a tornado out there *somewhere*. But it wasn't telling me where! Various local news websites weren't giving any updates. The only real source of information that I had out there was Twitter. And so, I keep it on my phone. I don't ever use it on a day-to-day basis, but I like having it just in case there's a local disaster taking place that I need to keep tabs on.

The "Know Your Plan" App
Ideally, you'll have talked over with your family what the plan for your family is should XYZ take place. If there's a shooter at the local hospital where your wife works, where will you meet? If there's a shooter at your kid's school, where will you meet? If there's a natural disaster and you can't reach home, where do you go? You get the idea.

In the heat of the situation though, it can be very easy to forget what the details were for those disaster plans. It can be pretty hard to remember the numbers on just how much bleach to use to purify your water or similar statistics. Likewise, if your family doesn't really "get" the whole prepper thing, having them download the app with your plans already updated onto it and just telling them to click on the app should anything bad happen so that they know what to do, then the app can still serve its purpose.

Basically, with these apps, after a disaster strikes your family will have everything laid out for them in an easy-to-read and detailed format so that they know exactly what steps to take. That way your family is all on the same page. Practically everyone carries their smartphone with them all the time in present-day society, so this is a way to ensure that your family has the information that they need readily at hand all the time as well.

Shelter App/Shelter Map

Let's say that for some reason you're away from home when a disaster strikes, and you don't have an adequate bug out bag or Get Out of Dodge (GOOD) bag with you. Maybe you do have a bug out bag with you, but your kid has bad asthma and dropped his inhaler into a rapidly moving body of water. The inhaler's gone, but your kid is going to need one to survive.

My point is that in some situations, you may *have* to resort to some type of humanitarian aid/shelter where supplies will be. What if you're out of the country on vacation when a hurricane strikes? This happened to my pastor. He was vacationing in the Caribbean with his wife for their 25th wedding anniversary when a hurricane destroyed the island that they were on. If the people around you don't speak English, what do you do? Knowing where proper help is can save your life in these situations, and the Shelter App or Shelter Map App can let you know where it is that you need to go to get the supplies, information, or help that you need.

Obviously, avoiding *having* to utilize government shelters in the first place is ideal, but in scenarios where that's just not an option, this app serves a purpose.

Amateur Radio Emergency Services (ARES)

If you have a HAM radio license, this may be a way that you can not only stay up to date on how things are going where you're, but a way to help others during the disaster as well. Basically, ARES transmits information to those who may need it in a rapid manner. Information is key in any disaster, and should one strike your area, being a member of ARES will allow you to use your HAM radio skills to assist local responders in making informed decisions.

You will be able to give updates on the status of things in your area as well as relay information that may not be received in a timely manner otherwise. Just *some* of the more noteworthy disasters that ARES members have assisted in lately include:

- The 2011 Houston, Texas flooding which knocked out telephone poles

- Hurricane Katrina
- 2011 tornado outbreak in the South[2]

SKYWARN

SKYWARN is a HAM radio operated system that consists of trained volunteers who alert people about and monitor dangerous weather (particularly tornadoes). Though radar can detect a very sizable portion of dangerous weather, it cannot detect everything, and somebody on the scene of a weather-related disaster will be able to fill gaps in the data, allowing meteorologists to make life-saving alerts. If you live in an area that's regularly hit by such weather, then this may be a way that you can ensure that you have the information you need to make the decisions required to keep your family safe.

Drones

I actually think drones could have a lot of potential from a prepper's perspective. Aside from being incredibly cool to fly, think of all the things that you could do safely and from the comfort of your own home with a drone. Reconnaissance of potentially hazardous areas, delivery of messages, searching for survivors after an earthquake, perimeter patrol of a home base, delivery of small supplies, and checking on the status of fencing/animal waterers/herds without having to really go anywhere are all just a few of the many applications that a drone could have for a prepper. I know there's a lot of negative press surrounding drones, and understandably when placed within the wrong hands, but when placed in the hands of somebody good and responsible, a drone could be a great, underappreciated asset to any homestead or prepper.

Chapter 21
Increasing Your Resilience

As I mentioned earlier, Ben Falk gives an excellent description of what resilience is in his book *The Resilient Farm and Homestead*. Inside its pages, Falk gives the following equation:

Resilience = diversity x redundancy x connectivity x manageability[1]

The ultimate resilience level of any system relies upon the product of these different variables. If we want to increase the resilience of something, then we need to better understand how to improve some of the factors involved.

Let's start with talking about diversity, and no, I don't mean in the same way that your day job's company does. Diversity saves lives. This can easily be seen when we look at the history of food crops throughout the world. When we have a variety of different resources that we can fall back on, then we end up much more resilient in the long run. Why was the Irish Potato Famine so bad? Because the Irish people had grown to rely on not only *one* food crop (potatoes), but on *one* variety of potatoes, the Irish Lumper.[2] When those potatoes were killed off by blight, the people had no other food to resort to.

The same concept can be found in the novel *The Death of Grass*.[3] It was the people who could rely on food sources other than grain (non-herbivore meats, non-grass crops such as potatoes) who were able to survive. This is one of the reasons that the current state of the food industry is so precarious within the US. Most our farmland is comprised of corn and soybeans. What happens if the corn or soybean crops fail? To put it simply, we starve. Monocultures are destructive. When all you have is hundreds of acres of one crop, the diseases and pests that thrive off that one crop multiply exponentially. This results in farmers having to spray more dangerous chemicals, and develop more tampered-with strains.

Even for businesses, it's diversity that keeps them resilient. Let's say you have a small farm that produces just corn. If your corn crop fails, you do too. However, if you also sell milk, honey, have a small orchard, produce blueberries, grow mushrooms, and raise flowers for bouquets, you still have other sources of income that you can rely on.

Increased diversity equals increased resilience. Putting all your eggs in one basket means you have no eggs should something cause you to drop that basket. Ecclesiastes 11:6 illustrates this.

In the morning sow your seed, and in the evening do not withhold your hand; for you do not know which will prosper, whether this or that, or whether both alike will be good.

Redundancy increases resilience as well. There's a popular saying among preppers, "Two is one, and one is none." When something breaks (and it will), if you have no backup, then you may be screwed. If you have an extra timing belt laying around post-disaster after the one in your truck breaks, then you have a means of getting back on track.

Aside from wine and cheese, things don't get better with age (though my dad would claim he's the exception to the rule). They decay. You can't beat the laws of thermodynamics or Murphy's Law. So, you may as well be prepared for it by having a backup (or perhaps multiple backups) in place.

For example, I have a well that uses an electric pump to get water to my house. When the power goes out though, how am I supposed to get water to my animals? A rain barrel collecting water off my shed, and a 330-gallon water container collecting water off my chicken coop (it's a big chicken coop) help to give me the redundancy I need to ensure that there is plenty of water for the animals should the power go out.

We've talked about the connectivity aspect in the community section, but we haven't touched on manageability yet. The simpler things are to run, the easier it is to fix them when they break. If you're relying upon an incredibly complicated piece of equipment to do a job, when that piece of equipment malfunctions or breaks – because it will – it is exponentially harder to get everything back up and running again than it is for a simpler system. With a simple system that utilizes maybe 3 pieces, you can more easily discover which piece is busted, and can better come up with a solution. Often, that solution may be just swapping out the part with the backup that you already have stored.

As other authors have noted, resilience is the capacity of a system to absorb disturbance and to reorganize while undergoing change so as to still function normally. One of my favorite examples that I've ever heard illustrating this is the elastic in your underwear. When the resilience of the elastic fails, your underwear falls down, leaving you susceptible to a potentially embarrassing social situation.[4] When the resilience of your household, community, or self begins to plummet, worse outcomes are possible.

There are 5 early warning signs of a loss of resilience that can alert us to the presence of a problem if we are willing to keep our eyes open.

1) Increasing occurrence of extreme states
2) Fluctuations between different states
3) Critical slowing down
4) Changes in spatial patterns

5) Increasing skewness in the distribution of states[5]

Increasing Occurrence of Extreme States
We see this within the animal population when we see rapid changes year-to-year in the population of any given species. In relationships, you may see this in immature high schoolers. Those that are dating one week and not the next are showing signs of increasing fluctuations of extreme states. Both examples show indications of a loss of resilience, and in both cases the outcome doesn't look good. They're not going to make it.

Fluctuations Between Different States
This one's similar to the above point. The only difference is that it doesn't necessarily entail extremes. If we're seeing unordinary variance, we have a hint that resilience has taken a hit.

Critical Slowing Down
This is when nothing is being achieved. Things have slowed down to the point where any progress is either not permitted or impossible.

Changes in Spatial Patterns
There are patterns all around us if we just look. When we begin to see drastic changes to the traditional pattern though, that is when we know change is on the horizon, and that the old pattern probably does not have much time left.

Increasing Skewness in Distribution of States
This would be visible when a small town suddenly loses an important factory. The unemployment rate rises, and the distribution between employed and unemployed is now skewed in a bad direction. If another similar factory goes under, the entire locale could soon become a ghost town as people leave to find new jobs elsewhere.

Thoughts on the 5 Warning Signs
When we see any of the above 5 warning signs, we know that the resilience of whatever we are observing is decreasing. We've seen a rise in the number of mass shootings, crimes against police officers, riots in large cities, and talk of civil violence has increased. You could nail all five those warning signs down in there.

Here's an interesting tangent though: I would argue that Christians are more resilient than non-believers when it comes to facing the storms of life. Doesn't the Bible talk about this reasoning over and over? What happens to the man who builds his house on the sand? When the storm comes, his house crumbles. And the man who builds his house on the rock? When the storms come, his house is still left standing.

A relationship with Christ is the *only* thing that allows us the capability to make it through the storms of life in one piece. Without Christ, life is hollow, and a hollow life often follows transient "pleasures" that only end up leading one down the path of further destruction.

Now here's an idea that I'd like to throw out there: does a decrease in Christianity lead to a loss of resilience in a nation? I'd argue unequivocally yes. Just look at the past 30 years and what we've seen happen to our country. Traditional marriage is viewed as worthless. Homosexuality is not just accepted, it's championed. Transgenders are fighting for equal bathroom rights. Parents who spank their children are reported to social services. Pornography is widespread. Pedophiles are now seeking societal acceptance. Praying in public schools has been banned. The judicial system is doing everything it can to remove any semblance of God or Christianity from the public sector. And there's much more going on out there that you can probably think of.

Steps to Increase Resilience

If we want to increase our resilience, one of the first things that we can do is to create a checklist (mental or physical) of just what we actually have in front of us. That makes sense. It's good to know what we have resource-wise. Proverbs 27:23-24 says,

"Be diligent to know the state of your flocks, and attend to your herds; for riches are not forever, nor does a crown endure to all generations."

If you don't know what you have, then you don't know what you can do without! If I don't know how much money I have in the bank, then I could write checks for more than I'm worth and end up with my butt in jail.

Public health officials do this to assess community disaster resilience. They'll take an estimated inventory of the cash, land, tools, food, jobs, energy sources, access to credit, transportation, and so forth for a community and use that list to help them to determine where they'll probably need to focus their efforts in the event of a disaster.[6]

In Len Fisher's book *Crashes, Crises, and Calamities*, he explores the concept of whether we can predict when future disasters will happen. The book runs on the premise that "long before its actual occurrence, a crisis sends off a repeated and persistent trail of early warning signals".[7] Therefore, we should be able to see certain warning signs that will enable us to be aware if something is coming down the pipeline we need to be ready for. Most of the book talks about psychology and statistics, but by the last few chapters, a general alert system is laid out. The main warning signs for an upcoming sudden disaster in personal, social, economic, physical, or environmental circumstances are these:

1) An unacceptable buildup of stress
2) The concentration of stress at the weak points of a system
3) The potential for uncontrolled runaway effects
4) Loss of resilience
5) Increasing swings between different states
6) Increased occurrence of extreme states
7) Changes in the pattern[8]

Again, when we apply these factors to today's society, do we leave with the impression that things are currently going great, or that the United States (or even the world) is at risk of sudden disaster of some form or another?

On the individual level, one of the things that psychologists often use to measure disaster potential is the Social Readjustment Rating Scale. It gives a point value to a variety of different potential lifestyle sources of stress (e.g. death of loved one/divorce/etc.), and uses the sum of these points to represent an individual's exposure to stress.[9] Think of it as a form of Geiger counter for individuals. If you work in a nuclear reactor, or around nuclear medicine, then you have a set exposure level to radiation that you are permitted to keep you safe. Exposure levels to radiation outside of the mandated limits can quickly lead to vast consequences such as burns, sickness, cancer, or death.

The Social Readjustment Rating Scale is just that, but for the exposure level to stressors found in daily life instead. As these stressful life events accumulate, then the likelihood for emotional disaster increases as well.[10] In a post-collapse, TEOTWAWKI-type scenario, then everyone is going to be exposed to a very high rate of stressors on this scale. Widespread death, starvation, medical issues, loss of loved ones, extremes of temperature, fear for life, and many other factors are going to be affecting everyone.

Prepping is one of the practical things that we can do to help to limit these stressors that our family members would potentially face. It serves to increase our resilience.

Chapter 22
Financial Preparation

Search through enough preparedness websites, browse enough survival forums, and talk with enough preppers about their life philosophy and you'll quickly learn that financial preparedness is actually a big part of what they believe in. I'd argue that it's one of the most practical things that you can do on a day-to-day basis as well.

What if you get injured outside of work? You aren't eligible for worker's compensation, you are physically unable to earn money for your family, and you have plenty of bills to pay. What happens then? Do you have the savings available to help weather these storms that can send families to the brink? I'm not saying that you need a million dollars in the bank to consider yourself a proper prepper. What I am saying is that it is wise to have some savings stored up in the form of cash to be able to ride out life's storms.

Start an Emergency Fund
This is a huge thing that Dave Ramsey (a Christian financial planner) teaches, the importance of an emergency fund. The first thing he tells people to do in his various books is to save up $1,000 *cash* fast. Why? Because you never know when you may need it. This is your first line of defense emergency fund. With this $1,000 you'll be able to field the unexpected payment that sucker punches you unexpectedly without facing as much of a blow. Cash is the way to do this though. You need something that is easily accessible. Having $1,000 tied up in bonds, CDs, or tangibles is not something that is easily accessed. You need the cash and you need it now, so save that $1,000 first, and then don't touch it. Don't touch this money unless you absolutely *must*. I'm not saying if you're just having a little trouble paying bills this month. If that's the case, you probably need to budget better and pick up side jobs or extra shifts where you can. This $1,000 is reserved for true *emergencies*.

> Did you know that for every $1 spent on mitigating the risk of disaster by public health and disaster planning officials that it saves $4 in future losses?[1] Though I haven't found any research on the savings at the individual level, I don't think it's too far of a stretch to assume that the same principle applies to personal prepping.

One of the most glaring examples of this that I've seen in recent news took place in Texas. When flood waters continued to rise in toward Texas, one man set up an inflatable sandbag-esque system around his entire property.[2] The system looked like a gigantic black rubber donut that you would pump full of water. The storm hit as expected, and massive flooding resulted. The entire community was underwater. Except for that one man. If you look at pictures of the storm, his house is a literal island in an area that was several feet under water. Many of the flood victims either did not have flood insurance, or did not have enough insurance to cover the damage to their property that they experienced. I'd imagine that the cost they paid to fix their property was much more than this man's preventative system.

An ounce of prevention truly is worth a pound of cure!

The next step that Dave Ramsey recommends is to save up 3-6 months of living expenses. Obviously, the more you save up here the better, but if 3 months is all you can swing right now, then just start working on that. Once again, don't touch this. This is *emergency* money. Not vacation money, not college money, not fun money. This is money that you very well may need if you want to pay the light bill and feed your family. This is the best insurance that you have should something happen.

Odds are if you hurt your leg in a chainsaw accident on the homestead, you're going to need surgery, time to heal, and physical therapy. You won't be able to work. Having this 3-6 months available can take a load of stress off your plate.

It's often said that most fights among married couples revolve around money and sex (money is #1) .[4] If you know that money is a potential source of friction in your relationship, why not try to do something about it? This 3-6 months of savings could save you a whole lot of headache, heartache, and potentially your marriage as well.

Pay Off Debt

The next step is to pay off debt. The average American spends $1.06 for every dollar that they earn.[5] What's this mean? That most Americans out there are in debt, which is *not* a good place to be if you want to be financially prepared for disaster as well as financially independent. Once again, if you are injured or ill, you need to be able to pay bills. The mortgage doesn't care if you're hurt. It still needs to be paid. By getting out of debt as quickly as you can a couple of things happen. First, you're free. You're no longer a slave to your creditor. Because that's exactly what you were before. You were quite literally working *for* them. No, they probably weren't calling you names and flogging you, but your every waking hour spent at work was *theirs*. No debt means no slavery. You are free to do with your money as you please.

Secondly, it takes a load of stress off your plate. Just the simple act of knowing that you are no longer $54,000 in debt with student loans is a very good feeling. Debt can feel suffocating. You know that you can't do what you want because you have thousands of dollars in loans. Our first year of marriage, both my wife and I felt this way. We were loaded down with student loans, and it just didn't feel as if we could do anything fun (that cost money) because we'd feel guilty about spending money on anything other than bills! Paying off loans helps to relieve some of that burden.

Third, with the freedom to use your money in the way you want, you are also enabled to be charitable where others can't. It's the same thing as storing food. You store excess food so that when people come knocking at your door post-disaster, you are able to help them without putting your family at risk. When you are free to use your money in the way you want, you're able to financially give to people, churches, organizations, and other things that you would not have been able to do otherwise.

What about the other savings that you often hear about in prepping circles? What about bartering goods, tangibles, and precious metals?

To start with, just understand that wise investors diversify. If you put all your eggs in one basket, you lose all your eggs if you drop the basket. If you put all your money into Walmart stock, what happens if Walmart tanks? Big, invincible companies have tanked again and again throughout history. Just look at the East India Trading Company, Sears, Circuit City, RadioShack, and many others. It's when you diversify your portfolio by placing your money in different places that you stand a better chance of making it through any hardships in one piece.

Cash

It is incredibly wise in today's world to always have cash on-hand in a variety of denominations. If a massive storm, earthquake, or whatever comes through your locale it will most likely wipe out the electricity. Card readers do not work without electricity, and good luck finding a place that still has the manual knuckle-scraper style card readers. Cash is used in such instances. Cash is what gets you the groceries, medicine, and tools that you need post power outage. And what if we escalated the situation? What if it's an EMP? Then you have a whole lot of money in the bank, or credit on your card, but what good does it do you if you can't access it? You're screwed.

Keeping a supply of physical cash in various small denominations on your person at all times is a wise idea.

I believe that keeping a larger amount of physical cash in various denominations at your house is wise as well. Carrying $5,000 in-person with you at all times is foolish. People kill for much less. You open a wallet with that much money and somebody's going to take notice. Keeping some cash at home is the solution to this. At some point, you may need to make a bigger purchase, and having physical cash at your home can help with this. I'd place this money either in a high-quality safe or hidden out of sight. Nobody should be able to walk into your office and see a cardboard box full of $20 bills. If a thief breaks in, or if you *invite* a thief in (strange relatives, and such. We've all got 'em.), then you're straight out of luck. The money's gone and good luck getting it back. By placing the money in a safe, you at least keep all but the most determined thief from getting it, and by hiding it somehow, then they never know that you have it in the first place, which I'd argue is even better.

I've been reading a lot on the early titans of the American economy lately: John D. Rockefeller, JP Morgan, Andrew Carnegie, Jay Gould, Cornelius Vanderbilt, etc., and you start to notice a few patterns after a while. Aside from hating debt, working hard, and actually *investing* money, one of the things that they all did was keep large cash reserves on hand. This not only allowed them a financial buffer for when the world around them got shaky, but it allowed them to capitalize off that same storm that was hurting others. When the markets were tanking, they could buy thousands of shares of stock at a bargain price in companies that they knew would rebound. When the stocks inevitably climbed back up again, they made a lot of money.

While other people were struggling just to stay afloat, because of these men's ability to see what was coming down the line, they were able to flourish. That's not taking advantage of people, that's just wise investing.

So, as you can see, keeping some cash on yourself and at your home at all times is a wise decision.

Tangibles

The argument for tangibles is that they are things that hold *intrinsic* value. Ever since the US went off the gold standard we've been trusting that what the government tells us the green piece of paper in our hand is actually worth is true. And to make things even better, the Fed can tinker with the value of that green piece of paper any time they darn well please. A shovel always has an approximate price to it though. A bottle of wine will always bring in a certain amount. A box of bullets is always worth x price in peoples' minds.

What happens if we get hyperinflation? The paper dollars we use as value today could end up being worth nothing tomorrow. This has happened many, many times throughout history. Zimbabwe, Venezuela, and post-war Germany are but a *few* examples. During the economic collapse of Greece, Greek farmers were actually faring much better than the rest of the population despite the economic self-destruction going on all around them.[6]

Why? Because they had chickens in the yard, orchards producing fruit, goats making milk, and gardens growing vegetables. They were actually *producing* something. They were producing food, which not only meant that they weren't going to starve, but that they could barter with people! With plenty of food coming in, you can trade milk for medicine, apples for a new coat, eggs for tools, and so on. Food production places you in a much better place post-disaster.

Plus, even if the disaster that you've been planning for *doesn't* occur, if you actually are growing and eating your own food in the meantime, it's much cheaper than buying store food, and it's infinitely healthier for you as well! You're no longer eating as many preservatives, growth hormones, antibiotics, pesticides, salt, sugar, fat, and empty calories than the people that don't grow their own food.

This past year is really the first time that I've gotten the opportunity to see this principle in action. I spent the winter pouring over gardening and permaculture books, laying an emphasis on *Square Foot Gardening*.[7] I made a pretty big garden following the methods laid out in that book. For three of the square foot garden beds I planted spinach, lettuce, and mixed greens. Due to the time of the season, those are the only three beds that I've been able to harvest from so far, but the harvest has been incredible! My wife and I estimate that a gallon sized bag of organic spinach or lettuce mix is around $3 - $4. Using the lower number to be conservative (overly conservative, I might add), we've produced somewhere around 20 gallons of greens. At $3/gallon, that's $60 worth of produce! We've been eating salads every day, and I've been able to sell some at work too. So just a small little investment in some lumber, seeds, and soil has already paid off in two months.

Just the act of storing food can save you money as well. Ben Falk and Joel Salatin (a famous permaculturist and famous farmer, respectively) both advocate storing around a year's worth of food. Aside from the health benefits, one of the pros that Falk advocates is that storing food saves money. Food costs are ever increasing, and inflation has the appetite of a bonfire. By storing food now, it should save you money throughout the course of the year simply due to inflation.[8]

So really, farming and gardening are a win-win here.

"But this sounds like basic materialism at its finest. If I invest in tangibles that's all I'm doing."

I believe the main flinch-moment here revolves around the word "tangibles," as if simply because something can be touched it is inherently wrong. I don't buy this. Look around you right now. This book in your hand is tangible. The computer at your desk, car in your driveway, tools in your basement, and kitchen utensils by your stove are all tangibles. They're all physical things that can be felt. There's nothing inherently wrong about owning something. There's nothing inherently wrong about buying a few shovels, some rakes, and a hoe to make sure that you're able to properly work your garden both pre- and post-disaster. Solomon owned a thing or two. It's when we set our heart on material things rather than Him that there's an issue.[9] When we live our lives with the sole pursuit being the accumulation of more stuff rather than the furthering of our relationship with Jesus then we are being a fool.

Precious Metals

On their own, I don't think precious metals are the best investment. What I mean by that is that they most likely aren't going to make you a lot of money. The market prices can fluctuate, and they don't tend to appreciate as much as you might think.

Precious metals, in my opinion, are more of a security hedge against inflation. If there's a hyperinflation crisis in the US, then with some precious metals behind you - whether that be in the form of gold, silver, copper, or whatever - then you have a tangible that's worth something. And *tangible* is the key word here. If your investment in precious metals is backed by a contract on a piece of paper, and that precious metal isn't actually in *your* safe, do you really own it? Legally you might, but if things turn sour, can you actually access it? Physical possession is important.

James Wesley Rawles notes that precious metals are something to work on only after you've got your tangibles and other bases covered.[11] In short, don't go out and buy a whole bunch of silver dimes tomorrow when you've got student loans, no ammo for your gun, no food, no savings, and massive credit card debt. To do so would be foolish.

I don't think that post-collapse bartering gold and silver coins is going to be something that happens either. Why? For starters, according to Dave Ramsey, anytime that there is a societal collapse there's not a bunch of people running around trading silver dimes for services. What pops up is either a black market or a barter economy. People trading goods and services for other goods and services. He notes that as an investment, gold has a pretty terrible track record, with the average rate of return from as far back as Napoleon's era being around 2%/year.[12]

Most likely, the event you'll face won't be on the scale of an international pandemic. Facing a local tornado that levels your community is *more* likely. After Hurricane Katrina, I didn't hear about people trading gold and silver for services. Gold and silver doesn't fill a hungry belly. You can't eat it. Food and clean water was what people wanted, and I'd argue that in most disasters those are the two items that people want.

One of the good things about precious metals though is their portability. A Jewish refugee running for his life in pre-WW2 Germany would have no chance getting the heck out of the area with a cart full of chickens, guns, and worthless German marks. Tangibles wouldn't cut it for him. And what Allied country would be willing to respect the currency of German marks? If he attempted to trade those marks in for pounds or US dollars, wouldn't he be viewed with suspicion?

The only way for such a character to escape and move to a new location without literally losing all the money that he has would be to invest in precious metals. With high carat diamonds, gold coins, and the like, that refugee would have a highly portable and easy to hide way of moving his finances to a new country and starting over fresh post-disaster.

That's where I think precious metals come in handy.

A lot of people invest in old silver dimes, gold bars and such with the idea in mind that post-disaster they're instantly going to be reverted to as the new form of currency, but I just don't see how that would be practical from a bartering standpoint. For starters, look around. What millennial is going to know the intrinsic worth of a silver dime? "I'll give you one silver dime for 5 cans of corn." They're just going to think that's a gigantic rip-off. Unless they're heavy into numismatic stuff, then they're going to have no clue. They're just going to think that this guy is trying to fleece them with a really old dime.

Plus, how are people going to know that you're trading with the real deal? Post-disaster you don't see a bunch of people walking around with silver and gold testing kits, and even if they did, would you really be ok with them messing up your precious metal and then deciding that they really don't want to do the trade? Even pre-disaster, I don't think I know anybody out there that has precious metal testing kits. That's not to say that all my friends are foolish, unprepared sheeple who have no clue about life. Not at all. It just means that precious metals are, for the most part, an abstract concept to a lot of people. It's not something that people are super familiar with as a whole. Everybody knows the approximate value of a bullet, of medical supplies, of eggs. But a big golden coin? Good luck finding somebody who can estimate the trading value of that unless they still get the Wall Street Journal helicoptered into their house after the flood.

Once again, Dave Ramsey notes the same thing. He states that real estate, canned soup, or the knowledge of a valuable skill would be what has value should society collapse.[12] History speaks to this as well. Read through any war history and you'll see prisoners of war utilizing cigarettes and other goods as forms of currency. Look at the Wild West. The reason shot glasses got their name was because people would trade a "shot" for them, exchanging one bullet for a glass full of whiskey.[13] When money was short, barter worked. Just look at Venezuela right now. Bartering is the only way things can be bought and paid for now. The currency is worthless. People are paying for haircuts with bananas and taxi rides with cigarettes.[14] Barter economies are what happens post-disaster. Not reversions to precious metals.

If I was going to put some money into precious metals though, I think that silver would be a better bet compared against gold. It has nothing to do about the long term inflation values of the two precious metals; it's just that gold is too compact a form of currency for most daily transactions.[15] If I want to buy two gallons of water off of somebody, and all I have is gold coins, I'm screwed. I'm not paying hundreds of dollars for water bottles. What do you do in these cases? And even if you do pay in gold coins, how do you expect to get change? Nobody's going to be willing or able to cut up a gold coin into 1/8 pieces to give you the change back for the ammunition that you just bought. As Rawles notes in his book Patriots, a couple of boxes of 22LR ammunition kept for barter would be much more valuable. Likewise, according to Rawles in his book *How to Survive the End of the World as We Know It*, just 5-10% of your net worth should be in the form of precious metals, and this is primarily as a hedge against hyperinflation.[16]

Retirement Accounts

What if you did all this prepping, you had every contingency planned for, and you go through your entire life and nothing happens? Does that make you a fool? Does it make you stupid? By no means. However, to go through your entire life and to not prepare for old age *does*. The Bible makes it clear that the ant is to be admired because it gathers up stores during the summer - the time of plenty - to provide for the times of winter - the times of scarcity.

When old age comes to you, and hopefully it will, you are still going to need to eat, you are still going to have bills to pay, and you may have medical expenses to pay as well. I hope that last one doesn't happen to you, but it is a possibility.

To not have money in some form or another for this time is to plan to spend the next 30-40 years after retirement eating Alpo and wondering whether you should pay the light bill this month or buy your medication. You don't want to live like that. Why would you if you could do something to prevent it?

I understand that there's a lot of alternative views on retirement out there. People believe that they're kids will just take care of them, their garden will feed them, their house will be paid for, their energy will be off-grid, and that the stock market will crash. And while all those things may be true, stuff still happens. If your kids are going to potentially be burdened (you know what I mean) emotionally and physically with having to take care of you, do you really want them to be financially burdened as well?

I can't tell you how many clients I've worked with at my day job (cardiac rehab) who have expressed anger to me that their parents/spouse didn't have their funeral costs all squared away, and how big of a blow that was to them financially. If you think your garden will feed you the rest of your life, do you really have a proper understanding of how age works? Old people get hurt easier and they don't have as much energy. What happens if you find out you have spinal stenosis, arthritic hands, or diabetic neuropathy in your feet? How are you going to tend your garden then?

If you say your house is already paid for, what are you going to do when you need a new roof, the water heater dies, and so on? Things break down. You've got to have a way to pay for them. Even renewable energy sources such as solar, wind, and hydro need repairs now and then, and it's not cheap. Will the stock market crash? Yeah, it's crashed before. I see no reason to believe that it'll never crash again. But that doesn't mean that I don't invest in a Roth IRA or 401(k). The only thing that I'm guaranteeing will happen should I refuse to save for retirement is that I won't be prepared for retirement.

You want to be able to pay medical bills. You want to be able to buy your grandchildren gifts. You want to be able to take a once-in-a-lifetime cruise to that place you've always dreamed about. You want to leave an inheritance to your kids. There's nothing wrong with that. But if you don't save for it within the form of some type of traditional retirement account, then none of those things are going to happen.

And please, please, *please* don't cash out your retirement account to invest in tangibles. I can't tell you how close I get to throwing up whenever I hear about somebody doing that. It makes me almost physically ill to know that somebody has just shot themselves in the gut like that. It's a "what have you done?!" type moment for me. Financial suicide. Why? Because tangibles decay. Mutual funds do not.

Just look at the prices of tangibles brand new at Lowe's, and then the prices that you'll get for them at a yard sale. I can get high-quality tools at any yard sale right now for just a few bucks! Seriously, I'm talking about 75%+ discounts! People are not willing to pay top dollar for used products.

And lastly, tangibles don't increase in value. A shovel doesn't go up and magically become worth hundreds more over time. Mutual funds do. Don't cash in your retirement account. To do so is foolish.

Conclusion

Like it or not, we live in a world that requires money. You need it to make it through today's society if you want to be able to pay bills, keep your house, and take vacations. On a day-to-day basis though, this is the area that people seem to be the most unprepared. Storms don't always have to involve a physical tornado. Sometimes they can be financial. How many times have you felt like the financial blows continued to come in torrents? First the truck needed new tires, then the dishwasher died, then the dog got sick, then your kid broke his arm, and now the mortgage is due. Isn't that how it feels sometimes?

It is better to be prepared financially as well.

Chapter 23
Safety

It's no secret that disasters are unsafe environments. It's worthwhile to take the time to discuss some of the various factors that affect the level of safety one can possess post-disaster.

"All I Need is a Gun"

Occasionally, when talking with people about prepping, disasters, or similar scenarios, somebody will claim all they need is a gun and plenty of ammo, and that everything will be okay after that. What a foolish survival strategy. Nobody's arguing that guns and ammo aren't important for your safety, but you stand just about a zero chance of making it through disaster if that's your sole plan.

You can't eat ammo. You can't drink lead (Flint, Michigan may argue otherwise). A gun doesn't keep you warm at night. Sure, you could barter ammo away for food, clothing, and water, but what do you do if there's nobody around to trade with, or they don't want your ammo. What they want is gasoline for their car, and all you have to trade is 9mm ammunition. All they have is a 22LR rifle, so your ammo is useless to them. If you get stuck in a situation like that, you're screwed.

Most people who hold this mindset though tend to think that they're just going to hunt for everything they eat. Yeah, okay. You and the rest of the unprepped populace that had the exact same idea. News flash: hunting is hard. Even people who hunt everyday around where I live go through dry spells where they just can't seem to find a thing. And post-disaster, do you really stand much of a chance when a finite resource is now being sought after by the rest of the unprepped populace? That finite resource is going to make itself scarce very quickly. And even if you have the equipment to skin, butcher, prepare, and preserve your meat (which I highly doubt), then what do you do if where you try hunting is laced with desperate people who shoot at anything they see and assume it's game? What do you do if where you try hunting is guarded by angry locals who view *you* as a threat to *their* resource? Nothing. You're screwed.

This mindset operates under the assumption that the disaster that hits your area is going to be a "without rule of law" type situation. A world where you can shoot whoever the heck you want for whatever reason you want just like the Wild West, and there will be no consequences. *Most likely* that's not going to be the case. And when the law finds out what you've done, they're going to prosecute you and throw your butt in prison for a very long time, if not strap you to a chair that plugs into a wall.

> Speaking of guns and gunfights, did you know that hemorrhage is the major cause of preventable combat death?[1] As a prepper, it's probably worth your while to learn something about stopping excessive bleeding from gunshot wounds and lacerations. Tourniquets, QuickClot, and other medical market bleed stoppers may be worth a bit of your energy and research. Having the biggest and baddest rifle on the market doesn't guarantee that you or your friends and family will get through a gunfight in one piece. It'd be prudent to be prepared for the worst. Even Navy SEALS get shot.

This isn't to say that post-disaster things can't get hairy, because they most certainly can. After Hurricane Katrina devastated the Gulf Coast, Houston, San Antonio, and Phoenix all reported increased rates of murder, robbery, assault, rape, burglary, and auto theft.[2] Some of this is undoubtedly because desperate times make people desperate, and desperate people do desperate things. However, a lot of it was related to drug activity and gangs.

> *"Out of fear and hate, violence grows easy and fast..."* – Selco[3]

Post-Collapse People are Dangerous

Post-Katrina there was a drug boom in the affected areas as well as an increase in alcohol abuse.[4] These addicts looted and burglarized to fund their addictions, and many of them placed their addiction above their personal safety.[2] Do you want to get in between a druggie and their addiction? Nope. The people that do so without adequate means of protection either end up really hurt or really dead.

In fact, some FEMA money that came into the affected areas was used to finance drug activity. There was a larger drug quantity of higher quality after Katrina that found its way into the affected areas, and this resulted in cheaper prices and increased usage.[2] And did you know that there's a very large proportion of Americans that are currently on psych meds, (whether they be for depression, anxiety, bipolar disorder, schizophrenia, or other mental illnesses)? There can be severe repercussions when the people that need those pills can't get them.[5] The withdrawal symptoms can be straight up crazy.

So, if we know that substance abuse can become a particular issue of concern post-disaster, we know that people who are under the influence of various drugs can become particularly dangerous and violent, we know that people who need money to fund their addictions are particularly dangerous and violent, and we know that people who are going through withdrawal are particularly dangerous and violent, then it makes sense that we do things to protect ourselves from such people. This isn't making a mountain out of a molehill, this is just common sense.

Rape and Why You Should Carry a Knife

Rape's not exactly the most fun topic to talk about, but there are a few statistics here that may better help you survive intact should you ever be placed in a situation nobody should ever have to go through.

During cases of attempted rape, there's a 90% success rate for the rapist when the woman doesn't even attempt to resist. When she's passive about what is happening to her, or simply begs the rapist to stop, or curls up and cries, odds are she's going to get raped. If the intended victim screams as loud as she can throughout the entire attempted rape, the success rate of the rapist drops down to 50%. Screaming attracts attention, and the rapist most likely doesn't want to be caught. Why? Because if somebody does show up, not only does the rapist's chances of being locked up drastically increase, but their odds of being killed do as well. If the intended victim does everything she can to run away from the rapist, then the rapist has a 15% success rate. And lastly, should the intended victim fight back with either a knife or a gun, the rapist only has a 1% success rate.[6]

I think there are several lessons that we can learn from this. For starters, be proactive. Don't just passively accept the idea of being raped, because if you do, you're going to get raped. Scream as loud as you can, do everything you can to run away, and fight like mad. Secondly, I think that we can glean that women should carry some type of weapon with them always. Ideally, I think that people should conceal carry a pistol and be trained to use their firearm. A firearm is the great equalizer, allowing any petite woman to be able to successfully hold her own against a much larger, stronger opponent. Even carrying a knife can drastically improve one's chances. Honestly, I don't know why anybody *wouldn't* carry a knife. My wife and I absolutely love the television show *NCIS*, and one of Agent Gibb's "rules" that he's always quoting is "Always carry a knife."[7] I wholeheartedly agree.

Aside from the numerous instances of convenient use that you'll encounter daily, it also greatly increases your likelihood of surviving disaster. My uncle was trapped by his seat belt inside his car as the engine caught fire. The only reason that he's still around today is because he was able to slash his seat belt with a knife that he had within reach. The entire car ended up going up in flames. And though a knife is by no means on par with a firearm when it comes to self-defense, it still greatly increases your ability to intimidate and fight off a much larger attacker. So why not regularly carry a knife?

Infectious Diseases

Staying safe involves looking after your own health as well, something that many people overlook. When we start talking about safety, people instantly think about gunfights, rapes, and muggings. Staying safe against disease is important as well. What good is it to have all those preps in place if you end up getting sick and dying from something that could have been prevented? Post-collapse sickness is no joke!

> **During WWI, Spanish flu and pneumonia killed more American soldiers than enemy weapons did.[9]**

Post-collapse, there are several diseases that flourish among a displaced population. Cholera, diarrhea, diphtheria, hepatitis A, malaria, upper respiratory tract infections, measles, meningitis, rabies, shigella, tetanus, typhoid, and typhus are some of the most common diseases that you'll see in a post-collapse civilization.[10] There are a couple of simple rules to follow that can help you to avoid coming down with any of these diseases:

1. Wash your hands before you eat.

Not doing so is the best way I know of to ensure that you end up ingesting some type of microbe that wants to kill you. It's a simple measure, really, with a very large health impact.

2. Get your water from a safe source.

Do *you* want to drink poo poo water? Drinking that crap (no pun intended) is a prime way to ensure you end up dying an early and miserable death after a prolonged and painful struggle. Make sure you're getting your water someplace non-contaminated, and then treat it in some manner before you drink it.

3. Stay away from wild animals.

There's a reason that mankind feared rabies for so many centuries. Because once you have it, you're done for. Rabies has a 100% fatality rate if left untreated. And in a post-collapse, post-apocalyptic society, do you really have any chance of finding proper medical treatment for rabies? So, do what you can to avoid getting bit by rabid animals. Even if you do manage to strangle a rabid bobcat to death as it attacks your face, you'll still probably exit the predicament infected.[11]

4. Stay out of refugee camps (if you can).

For real, refugee camps are where you go to get infected. These places are disgusting, and disease breeding grounds. Despite the best possible engineering, people are still going to use the bathroom where they very well please, and anytime that you have a high population density of dirty people, disease outbreaks (and death) aren't too far away.

Simultaneously, there's a pretty disgusting fact that you should be aware of. The occurrence of sex crimes from humanitarian action is more common than you'd think.[12] There's a surprisingly large number of cases where people who have fled to areas where humanitarian aid was being offered, and have been either raped or sexually assaulted by the very people they have been led to believe were there to help them.

Why does this happen? It ties in with the economics of crime. The should-be-hanged may have immunity because of the situation (if they are in a different country), it is very hard to catch perpetrators in disaster situations. If you can, it's best to avoid venturing into these places to begin with.

5. Have the supplies needed to fight off infection.

In a disaster scenario, small cuts can turn into big nightmares. Having alcohol, Neosporin, hydrogen peroxide, bandages, and other disinfecting agents can keep you alive. Ask any Vietnam vet how long it took for a cut in the jungle to turn septic. Ask Henry David Thoreau's brother. He nicked his neck with a razor while shaving, and died from infection just a few days later.[13] Infections have the potential to get nasty real quick if they're not dealt with promptly. Obviously, it's best to avoid getting cut in the first place. Keep your knives sharp (they're safer than a dull knife), wear protective equipment, and don't place yourself in stupid scenarios. Just doing those three things can greatly decrease your risk of injury.

Civilization is a Veneer

Civilization is a thin veneer. It only takes a few days for things to fall apart, and most likely that number is around 3 (that being the number of days' worth of food the average American has stored within their home). What happens when the food runs out? After 72 hours without food, nice people do bad things. What happens when peoples' credit cards don't work because of long-term power outages and they can't buy anything because they didn't store any cash? What happens when supplies aren't getting trucked into an area? A lack of resources leads to violence.

Selco illustrates this point. He states, "the thing that is important for readers [to know] is that we were a modern society one day, and then in [a] few weeks it turned into carnage."[14] Once people begin to grow scared and hungry, they'll grow desperate. And desperate people are capable of desperate actions.

And even if you just place the desperate people to the backburner for a moment, don't forget that there are also people out in the world who are just *wicked*. They're always hiding in the shadows. It drives me up a wall when I watch the news, and some bad guy has just been caught who did something horrendous to a group of kids, shot up a building, or whatnot and the people around me say, "Well, he *must* be insane to do anything like that." Uh, *no*. Some people are just wicked. Quit excusing everybody with your neutered "insane" reasoning.

There's a reason that we have laws punishing rape, murder, kidnapping, and the like. When people know that there is a severe punishment for engaging in a particular action, they're much less likely to engage in it.

This is the economics of committing a crime. The cost of engaging in a crime equals the probability of being caught, and the associated punishment *if* one is actually caught.[12]

Cost of crime = probability of being caught + punishment if caught

Just like with anything else, as the price goes up, the less people will buy it. The same thing goes for crime. As the price of committing a crime increases, the willingness to engage in it decreases. So, if you lower the cost to the point that the crime is essentially free, there's no being caught and no chance of punishment, then crime instantly becomes a whole lot "cheaper" and the prevalence of it increases drastically.

We saw this in my community just a few months ago. A tornado tore through our town, absolutely destroying everything in its path. The entire storm only lasted a few minutes, but cleaning up the devastation is a process that a lot of people are *still* working through. In the immediate days following the twister though, everything was confusion and pandemonium. And we had thieves going around pretending that they were volunteers to assist in the cleanup efforts who were actually stealing peoples' things from their yards. How's that for low-life activity? Taking advantage of somebody after their house has been destroyed?

"Yeah, but these people would be pretty recognizable, so I'd know who to stay away from."

Would you though? Are they really that recognizable? Watch the news. How many interviews have you seen of murderers' and terrorists' neighbors and family members who have claimed that the bad guy "was so sweet," "really was a great guy," and so on. Normal appearing people can have dark secrets, and you don't know who they are. This doesn't mean that you go slinking around in abject fear everywhere you go, but it does mean that you need to be on the watch, not be stupid, and be able to defend yourself and family if necessary.

Know How to Use Your Weapons

Know how to use your weapon as well. If you have a Smith and Wesson 9mm Shield and an AR-15 rifle, but have never shot or handled either of them, you are not equipped to keep yourself safe. Just having the weapon isn't enough. You must know how to use it as well. I suppose you could compare this to somebody who keeps a Bible on the top shelf in the back of their bookshelf. They never read it, it's just there. But the Christian who regularly studies God's Word, and memorizes what it has to say has a much more effective weapon against Satan's attacks and the world's trials compared to the man who thinks the Bible is nothing more than a good luck charm.

You need to know how to load, clean, and fire your weapon if you are going to have any chance with it at all. Otherwise, you end up being like an acquaintance of mine. He has a shotgun in his house that a family member gave to him for self-defense purposes. But the guy has zero shells, and wouldn't know how to shoot the thing even if he did. He doesn't have a shotgun. What he has is an expensive club. You gotta know how to use what you have.

I think it's interesting to note that Selco states that a lot of accidental deaths happened during the Bosnian civil war simply because people didn't know how to use the weapon that they had. And people will choose to keep a weapon if they can obtain it.[16] Regardless of their politics, when people feel that they are at risk of physical harm, they will do what they can to protect themselves. Literally everyone stuck inside a school during a school shooting would gladly accept a firearm if you gave it to them then. Politics quickly go out the window when a potential rapist is attempting to break down your bedroom door at 3AM. People want to feel safe, and a weapon helps to provide a sense of safety.

That being said, have you ever given a clueless person a gun? Ever been shooting with somebody who'd never handled a firearm before? How many times did they strafe you or themselves with the muzzle without realizing it? Every community has experienced the tragedy of somebody dying from an accidental discharge of a firearm. A little kid finds his daddy's pistol. A newbie goes hunting with his friend. Somebody is cleaning their firearm and kills somebody in the next room. Knowing how to use a weapon before you need it is one of the best things you can do to keep your family safe.

Situational Awareness
Without a doubt, one of the most important things that we can do to keep ourselves and families safe in a post-collapse scenario is to remain aware of what is going on in our immediate environment. By keeping your head on a swivel, you have a much better chance of seeing any impending threat coming your way, giving you more time to react.

An intern of ours showed up to work one day with a pretty bad black eye. He had been grocery shopping in the bad part of town, and woke up in the parking lot with a headache, and no wallet or phone. He didn't remember what happened. Somebody had sucker punched him and stolen his stuff, and because the intern never got the chance to see who it was that attacked him, there was zero chance the thug would be caught. I don't mean to be the armchair referee, but would this have happened if he had been aware of what was going on around him? Would this have happened if he never put himself in the bad part of town to begin with?

You have to be aware not only of those approaching you, but when the place that you are in turns into a bad place to be.

For example, if I'm chilling at the playground watching my kids play on a hot July day, anybody that walks up in a large black trench coat is going to have my full attention. They don't fit the scene. Trench coats are not common garb in the middle of July. Are there clues out there that don't fit the pattern? If I'm at the beach and a guy is walking down the beach in a 3-piece suit, does that fit the pattern of where I'm at? No way.

Will I be as concerned as I would be for the trench coat guy? Probably not, but the point is to be aware of the things that are going on in your immediate vicinity that stand out and are out of place. Because odds are, there's something fishy going on.

Self-Defense

There seems to be some confusion out there on the issue of self-defense. People will cite Luke 6:29, and how they are to "turn the other cheek," and how it is therefore wrong to defend yourself from somebody who's trying to kill you. Talk about taking things to the extreme. So does this mean that if somebody breaks into my house and attempts to tie me up at 3AM, I should just let them?

Look at the Old Testament law on the subject.

If the thief is found breaking in, and he is struck so that he dies, there shall be no guilt for his bloodshed. – Exodus 22:2

Doesn't this show that self-defense is a good thing?

I see a lot of people contorting the Ten Commandments as well. They'll take Exodus 20:13, "You shall not murder," and say instead, "You shall not kill." There's a vast difference between the two words.

As Pastor Terry from survivalblog.com states, "Knowing where God permits killing and where not and being able to show one this can be the difference between a person living with guilt or not."[20]

Look at what Abram did in Genesis 14:11-16 when his nephew was kidnapped. He strapped on his weapons and headed out.

Chapter 24
OPSEC

OPSEC is a military acronym that stands for operational security, and if you do any form of prepping whatsoever it is something that you need to be vigilant about. "Loose lips sink ships." This World War 2 phrase aptly applies here.

If you've blabbed to the entire office, at every family gathering, and to all your neighbors about how much food you have stored, how much food you can produce, the battery of guns that you possess, and how you've managed to stockpile a small hospital's worth of medicine, guess where everybody is going to go when the collapse hits?

Your place.

And it won't just be the people you know. It'll be your neighbor's relatives. Your colleague's mistress. Your divorced cousin's sister-in-law. It's going to be everybody, and not everybody that shows up is going to play nice or be somebody you'd want to be trapped with for who knows how long.

I mean seriously, post-disaster do you really *want* to be known as the place with plenty of ammo, precious metals, alcohol, medicine, and food?

No way!

Is OPSEC Biblical?

I'm constantly surprised when I read hyper-spiritual comments on various survivalist/prepper forums that claim the very *idea* of OPSEC is unchristian. Because after all, we're to have an open-door policy all the time, right?

Yet this is the *exact* protocol that we're following when we don't leave the boxes to expensive gifts such as flat screen TVs, gaming consoles, etc. on the street corner after Christmas. We don't *want* people to know what our house is full of. Why? Because people may break into our house when we're gone and steal all the goodies that they know are inside!

Why do we put our newspaper subscription and mail service on hold when we go on vacation? Because we don't want the world to know we'll be gone for an extended period of time, and that our house is unoccupied!

Why do intelligent people not post for the world to see on social media that they're on vacation while they're actually still on vacation? For the exact same reason! People break into houses they know are unoccupied. It's not as messy for the thief, there's less risk for them of being shot/killed/recognized in a police lineup, and they can take their time finding what they're looking for.

Why do we not wear expensive clothes and jewelry when we're traveling through the rough part of town? Why do we not open our wallets in front of people? Why do we not leave our internet passwords posted on easily visible notes within our office cubicles? Because to do so in these cases would be stupid.

These aren't unchristian things to do, to not let burglars know what's available and when. It's a wise thing to do! Being a Christian doesn't mean you have to leave yourself vulnerable and not take the necessary precautions to ensure you're safe.

Again, think of it this way. If you've advertised to the world that you have tons of precious metals stored at your house, what happens if there's an economic collapse or crisis? People know where to go to get currency. If you've shown everybody you know, *and* taken pictures of your impressive alcohol stockpile (which you then posted online), what happens when people who are addicted to alcohol need to get their fix? They know where to go.

OPSEC from "The Man"
Even if you have the best neighbors in the world, you could still be in trouble. Your whole community could be preppers, all of your neighbors rock-solid individuals with unshakeable morals, you generally keep it a secret that you prep, and lack of proper OPSEC could still place you at risk. From who? Uncle Sam, of course.

If martial law is imposed on an area (and this has happened within the US very recently), then the army can simply walk right in and take your preps, if they know that you have them. It would be argued that the army "needs" them for redistribution of food supplies.[1,2] How wicked is that? You've bought, saved, and earned everything that you have, and some other person gets to decide that, naw, someone else needs that. Give it to the people over *here*.

This exact same thing happened during Hurricane Katrina. Martial Law was put into place and government employees went around confiscating people's firearms.[3] Aside from the unconstitutional aspect of all this, think about what this did for public safety. If you've got a problem with bad guys running around with guns, why on earth would you take away the good guy's guns that they'll need to defend themselves with? A public neutering of the *good* people is what just happened here.

Better to not let the government know that you have any supplies in the first place, isn't it?

So, as you can see, you have to be incredibly careful with who you let in to the knowledge that you are a prepper. It's not just the people around you, but the government as well that you have to be careful of. And once OPSEC is lost, it's not something that you can just pick back up again. People have long memories when they're desperate. They become resourceful. If somebody is running out of food, they'll think long and hard about where they can get some, and they'll have no problem remembering the barbecue 4 years ago where you mentioned that you were really into prepping.

Even temporary slip-ups can have big consequences. Loose lips sink ships. All it takes is one mouth to spread the information that you have supplies available at your house. We've all seen how fast gossip can spread. Have you ever told somebody a secret, only to be blindsided by the entire community seeming to know not too long later? Talking little birdies can do quite a bit of damage. So OPSEC is something that you actively maintain not only after the chaos has started, but before it even begins.

So Before the Chaos, What Does This Look Like?

1. Don't talk about it!
Other than with people you trust intimately, the world doesn't need to know what you have available. You don't want them to know.

2. Watch what you post to social media.
That information is stored indefinitely. Even posting links and sharing pages to prominent survival or prepper websites/videos can give people a hint that you are a prepper. "Hey, remember Steve? He always posted all that weird survival stuff on Facebook. I bet *he* has some food."

3. Keep your preps relatively hidden.
Entertaining guests at your house is fun. I get that. But if rifles are leaning in all corners of the room, your food barrels are prominently displayed in the basement, and cases of water are on the floor in every room, then you've just advertised to everybody that you are "into" prepping. And people talk. They'll tell all their friends about how weird or eccentric you are.

Keep preps under your bed. Lock the doors of rooms you don't want people peeking in. Utilize privacy shrubs, trees, and fences to conceal what's around you from prying eyes. Keep things in containers that don't look like what they contain. Nobody's going to think that a big box in the basement labeled "baby clothes" is going to be filled with medical supplies. Put canned foods behind books on the top shelves of book cases. Be creative.

4. Learn basic internet anonymity.

This is huge. You don't want the government knowing all your business? Then you need to learn how to remain anonymous online. Utilize a Tor browser or DuckDuckGo. Turn off location settings on your phone. Add browser extensions to block tracking services such as Ghostery. Read *The Art of Invisibility* by Kevin Mitnick.[4]

5. Utilize hidden caches.

This is burglary insurance, whether that burglar comes in the traditional form or holding a government-issued badge. A few well-placed, hidden caches stocked with supplies that you might find expedient to have should your family be overpowered/robbed is a good way to ensure that your family is provided for should disaster happen and thieves be on the loose.

After the chaos, what can you do to ensure that your home remains as safe and hidden as possible?

1. Use dark curtains.

Light is incredibly visible at night. A single candle is visible from roughly 1.7 miles at night (given the right conditions).[5] If the entire neighborhood has been out of power for weeks, and every window from your house is beaming light, you're essentially broadcasting to the neighborhood that you still have power when they don't. And if you have power, what *else* might you have? Utilizing blackout curtains, or even black plastic sheeting are both ways to ensure that you don't have unexpected/undesired visitors.

2. Be careful with generators.

For a short-term power outage, sure, generators probably aren't going to be a problem. Society still exists. But in a Without Rule Of Law (WROL) situation where society has evaporated, do you really want an incredibly loud, constant motor pinpointing your location to the world?

Nope.

Are there alternatives to generators? Really the only options that I'm aware of are to either utilize solar, hydro, or wind energy. Out of the three of these, I'm not too sold on wind energy. A 40+ feet tall wind turbine on your property doesn't exactly scream "nothing to see here." Not everybody has a wind turbine. They're not that commonplace. The people that do are *probably* into prepping of some sort or another.

> If society hasn't collapsed, you're probably going to be willing to use a loud gasoline-run generator so that the food in your fridge doesn't spoil. Nobody likes to lose $300 worth of food in the fridge, and another $200 worth in the freezer. Perchance you don't have that much food currently refrigerated or frozen though, it may be worth your time to do the math on your generator's cost-effectiveness. At what point does the gasoline in the generator begin to cost more than the food that's currently in your fridge? When that line is crossed, you may want to just deal with the lost food bill, if you can't eat or preserve it all in time.

I'd argue for the utilization of solar and hydro energy. They're both quiet, and they're both concealable. If you've got solar panels on the roof of your garage out back, not everybody's going to know they're there. Very few are going to discover the strange box next to the running stream back in the woods of your property, and even fewer are going to know what it is (a hydro generator).

If these alternative forms of energy are worth the cost is ultimately up to you, but it may be something to look into if you hope to still have electricity post-disaster.

Of course, the easiest change you can make is reducing your need for electricity in the first place. Do you have a woodstove to heat your home? Do you have a propane range that will still run? Do you have crank radios that don't require electricity or batteries? You get the idea.

3. Be freakin' quiet.
If you're running around utilizing motors, banging on things with hammers, dropping lumber, blacksmithing, or doing anything else that's going to cause a lot of noise, then you're advertising your location and

that you potentially have supplies.

4. Trash discipline.

People create a lot of trash. Post-disaster there's not going to be a garbage man available to pick up every bag you drop off at the end of your driveway. It's just going to accumulate. If trash keeps accumulating at the end of your driveway, it tells the world a few very important things about you:

- One, that you live there. Nobody assumes that your house is empty now. They know that *somebody* lives there, and that the somebody probably has things they may want.
- Two, you have supplies. If everybody else quit having the ability to produce much trash a few weeks ago, and you're still hauling trash out every morning, then they know that you actually have the supplies to *make* the trash.
- Three, they know what you have. Anybody can swipe a trash bag real quick and dig through it to see the contents. If someone digs through a full bag and sees MRE wrappers, spent batteries, empty pill bottles, and the like, then it's safe to assume that there's going to be more where that come from inside the house.

You must be careful with what you do with your trash post-disaster.

"Well, I could burn it! Then there wouldn't be any bags to go through!"

Yeah, sure. You *could* burn it, but you'd simultaneously be sending out a giant column of smoke that tells the entire world where you are. You have to have somebody man the fire as well, and you're going to have to utilize precious post-chaos water to put it out as well. Neither of those outcomes sound good to me if I understand the importance of OPSEC.

Burying it, throwing it in a deep pit, or disposing of it way back in the woods are really the only options I see that would work. Does it take manpower and calories to dig the holes/pit, or to drag garbage into the woods? Heck, yeah. But it also keeps people from seeing you have trash, that you live somewhere, and that you may have precious items inside. I'd rather spend a day sweating through a Snickers bar than patched up from a thief-given knife wound.

5. Look like others.

If you're the guy who's visibly patrolling the neighborhood in his camo-painted hummer, wearing all camouflage and a MOLLE vest strapped to the brim with pouches, people are going to assume that you are well prepared for everything going on. This is why most preppers advocate a non-military GOOD (Get Out Of Dodge), bug out, or GHB (Get Home Bag).

Practice OPSEC Even with Your Charity

If there are signs all around the neighborhood pointing their way to your house saying "This way to free relief supplies!", then you have *zero* OPSEC, and you've just placed your well-being in jeopardy. Even with your charity, you need to ensure that you are practicing proper OPSEC. If everyone knows that you're the guy with a room full of food and water in the basement, everyone's showing up at your house and they may not come invited.

That's why I like the idea of the charity cache. It is a way that keeps people from knowing what you have behind those walls, and simultaneously removes them from your location.

What if you give to a 3rd party site though? What if your church is the site, and you're one of the volunteers there? If it's a post-collapse scenario, wouldn't making multiple runs to the 3rd party to drop off supplies create the opportunity for bad guys to follow you back to your house? This could easily happen if you had acres of corn that were coming in, and you were making regular trips to the 3rd party site to drop it off for charity purposes. What if I decide I want all your corn, and I don't want to pay for it?

The bottom line is that OPSEC is about safety. However, just having a few guns and knowing how to use them isn't the sole definition of safety (though it certainly does help). In public health, we constantly use the saying that an ounce of prevention is worth a pound of cure. I've found that this principle applies to pretty much every facet of life. Particularly in a survival scenario. OPSEC is this ounce of prevention. It keeps the bad things from materializing, and consequentially, it keeps them from being things that you need to clean up after.

OPSEC During the Long Walk Home

Let's say that the worse has just happened. An EMP has hit, your car's broke down in the middle of nowhere, or civil war has just broke out in the country that you're in. You're a very long way away from home, and you need to get the heck out of where you're at. This is the survival situation known as The Long Walk Home (TLWH). Most preppers are prepared for this. It's where the concept of a Get Home Bag came into play. Trying to get home in these types of situations is going to be incredibly more dangerous than simply surviving in a shelter stocked full of food, medicine, and that provides you some degree of security.

A few notes on The Long Walk Home.

Obviously, avoiding the walk in the first place is going to be your best bet. Many preppers have survival retreats that are quite some distance from where they actually live. Should the threat happen, it's generally a whole lot safer to be able to hunker down where you're at rather than have to drive several hours to get to a retreat that has *hopefully* not been plundered. Already living where you plan to hunker down is the ideal scenario.

If you're just wandering around without a home, know that refugees can very quickly become casualties. Walls provide 24/7 security, and supplies are heavy. You're going to have a very hard time of it if you only have what you carry on your back.

"But nomadic tribes have existed for millennia!"

Yeah, but they were a community that could help each other out, they had bushcraft skills that yours come nowhere near rivaling, and they still didn't live in as safe of an environment as the people who stayed put did.

"Well what about the early pioneers!?"

From everything I've heard, most of them didn't live very long.[6,7,8]

(Though I could be wrong about this. People still lived to be pretty old even back in George Washington's time, despite what some data will lead you to believe. Could the ridiculously high infant mortality rate of the times have lowered the average life expectancy of the time?)[8]

"Well, fine then! I'll just buy an RV! I'll have a mobile retreat!"

I think this is a terrible option. During evacuations or disasters of any sort, roads quickly become parking lots. The middle of a road is not an ideal place to get stuck. Secondly,

> RVs need gas, and if the power is out or the supply trucks aren't rolling in, what are you going to do when your tank runs dry? RVs aren't exactly known for sipping gas like a British lady sips tea. RVs are easy to shoot through as well. What's to keep somebody from doing one quick strafe down the side of your RV, and then walking over your body to gather everything that's inside? And lastly, mobile RVs are hard to hide. They're bulky, shiny white metal (typically), they can't go off-road, *and* they stick out like a sore thumb.
>
> Obviously, there are going to be some scenarios you just can't control. You still have to enjoy vacations. You're still going to visit family. You're still going to have to take business trips, run errands, and travel around your geographical area. Your best bet in such situations is to have gear in your car, have an EDC kit, and just go about your business.

Being on the move in a dangerous situation is another area where OPSEC needs to be followed to a T. There's a concept known as "being the gray man." That's what you want to do in these scenarios. You want to blend into the background. To be the person that is ignored because they don't seem of particular interest. You don't want to stand out. You want to be "gray."

So, what can you do to blend in, to become the Gray Man in these scenarios?

1. Don't look like a prepper.

On most prepper websites that I see, the Get Home Bag looks like something that would be standard issue for our snipers in Iraq. If you're going to look like a soldier, you're going to stand out. Anybody walking around in a civilian environment that's decked out in solid camouflage, is wearing a MOLLE rig, and has a MOLLE military backpack does not look like somebody that blends in.

If you're in a situation where other people are going through the same disaster that you are, then you look like a juicy candidate for a robbing. Why? Because you have all the stuff! If you're in some type of civil war-type situation, you're still screwed looking like this. If soldiers are running around and being shot by other soldiers, do you really want to look like one at that moment? Nope. You don't. You want to be able to blend in. So leave the military look at home. Likewise, I don't think that keeping a gigantic expedition-style backpack with an external frame in the trunk of your car is a good option for a long walk home either.

Gigantic bags don't allow you to move quickly, are physically exhausting to carry, and don't exactly look subtle, if you know what I mean. Shoot, even in current society, any time I see somebody walking through town wearing a gigantic hiking backpack they not only stand out like a sore thumb, but I instantly assume that they have the supplies that they need in order to live outside for a while.

2. Don't run unless it's socially acceptable.
If running wouldn't look weird in your environment (e.g. others are doing it), *then* you can do it without attracting attention to yourself. The human eye is attracted to movement.[10] If you've ever been hunting, you can attest to this. A deer has perfect camouflage when it's still, but once it begins to move, you know where it's at. Remaining perfectly still within a post-collapse urban environment may not be a good idea, but the underlying premise remains: doing things out of the ordinary will draw attention. If everybody else is walking or standing, and you're sprinting like your life depends upon it, people are going to watch.

3. Be careful with who sees your stuff.
If people see you open your bag at night and pull out MREs, glow sticks, and a Mylar emergency blanket, then they know you have good things they might like to possess. Once again, this sets you up as an easy target. If somebody follows you and finds out where you're sleeping, at *best* you'll just lose your stuff, waking up without a pack. There's a solid chance you'll wake up injured or won't wake up at all though.

Remember the part about there being strength in numbers? By yourself on TLWH, you don't have anybody to stand watch throughout the night. It's just you. And being asleep when it's just you leaves you in a state of vulnerability.

Even if you decide to help somebody - if some guy comes up to you with his family and says he notices you have a bag, and was wondering if you may have anything to help him with - you need to practice OPSEC. I'd argue that you've probably already failed if people have noticed that you're prepared. What if somebody else is watching you help those people, and that somebody else isn't the most noble person in the world?

You need to be careful with who sees your stuff on the long walk home.

Life has Inherent Risks

Obviously, you can't eliminate all risk. I think it's wise as a prepper to remember that. When you try to plan through every potential bad thing that could ever happen to you, I think you end up being more paranoid than prepared. "Well, what if aliens release mutant dog monsters that only die from fire? I'll need a flamethrower in every room then! What if sun flares force all humanity 80ft underground? I'll have an advantage with my underground tower! What if a bazooka blast blows off my legs? Good thing I've stored this electronic wheelchair though I don't know anybody else that uses one!"

You get what I'm saying?

There is always going to be some risk. Sorry, that's just life. Life is not 100% safe, and to assume that you can make it so, that you can plan for every single possible contingency, no matter how small the chances, is foolish. That being said, it doesn't mean it's wrong to try to reduce your risk when possible. And just basic prepping and studying can give you what you need to get through most problems ok!

As Bishop of preparednesspro.com states,

"No matter how physically prepared a person is with know-how, supplies, strategies and tactical maneuvers, there will ALWAYS be a challenge thrown at us that simply cannot be fixed with 'things.' Being tied in to one's core values and beliefs will often be the only thing that can get a person through tough times."[11]

Conclusion

The fact of the matter is that you need to practice some degree of OPSEC if you want your family to remain safe in a disaster situation. To do so does not make you a bad person, or Christian, and to believe so is silly. Obviously, there is a separation between charity and OPSEC, and it is still possible to engage in one without compromising the other.

Chapter 25
The Ethics of Forced Quarantine

I'm going to start this one off by saying if you forcibly try to quarantine anyone while there is still a functioning society, you're going to end up in a LOT of trouble. Think jail time for a potential kidnapping charge and more.

That being said, an international deadly pandemic is one of the things that many people prep for. And let's say that a pandemic *did* happen. Let's do a little thought experiment here. And we've got to make it really bad to make it work, so bear with me.

Pretend that terrorists infected themselves with some weaponized smallpox strain and traveled throughout the country by airplane during the week of Thanksgiving, the most traveled time of the year. Maybe they were ISIS, maybe al-Qaeda, maybe just soldiers of Iran who were tired of our helping Israel. Now what if these same people were in cahoots with Russia or China? They had an agreement where they'd hit with the smallpox first, and then an EMP strike by one of the larger nations would occur about a week later before any of the symptoms begin to show.

The electricity would be gone, and there'd be a massive die off that would occur solely from that alone. But in the beginning stage when everybody is trying to help everybody else, the disease is being transmitted undetected. And then it explodes. Smallpox symptoms start popping up everywhere. Nobody's immune, and the disease is running rampant through an already devastated nation. Starvation, mass casualties, smallpox, other contagious diseases, violence, and looting have led to the destruction of any sense of society whatsoever.

Now in this situation, if you somehow managed to avoid the infection with the rest of your community, and you know that people are traveling to find supplies, is it okay to quarantine them? Are there moral qualms involved here? Are there considerations that we need to think about? Contingencies that we need to plan for? Remember, this is a world without rule of law (WROL). There are no police officers to call. No judges. No Congress, no lawyers, no president, and no politicians. There is no government. It's complete anarchy, and there are zero signs of that changing anytime soon.

From the late-night discussions that members of your community hold, and from what you hear over HAM radio, this is bad. Really bad. And things are probably going to get a lot worse too.

So, should stragglers begin to show up at your door, what do you do? Let's say that they meet all the general guidelines that we covered in the chapter *Who Do You Let Stay?* A single mother shows up with her two kids, and she's pregnant to boot. Her husband died shortly after The Pulse from pox. She owns a cabin in the woods her family used to vacation at every summer in your community. Before all the junk went down she was a veterinarian as well.

So, she's pregnant, she's got small kids, she has property within your community, and she has a valuable skill in a post-disaster world. Your group wants her as part of the team, but knowing that she's had such close exposure to smallpox, you're worried that she may still be asymptomatic. Do you forcibly quarantine her and her family before she's allowed in?

> **It's important to note that there's a difference between quarantine and isolation.**
>
> ***Quarantine*** **is the "separation of those exposed individuals who are not yet symptomatic for a period of time (usually the known incubation period of the suspected pathogen) to determine whether they will develop symptoms"**
>
> ***Isolation*** **is the keeping of symptomatic individuals away from contact with the general population.[1]**

In the current world, numerous organizations and entities, such as hospitals, the World Health Organization (WHO), and the Centers for Disease Control (CDC) have strived to answer similar questions. When you've got an Ebola outbreak ravaging Africa, and people are beginning to bring it over to Europe and the States, what do you do to stop the spread? When you've got an unidentified virus dropping people like flies, similar to the way AIDS did in the 1980s, and you're still trying to figure out just what the heck is going on, what do you do?

Here are some of the answers those entities have come up with. First, we must ask ourselves this question: With the particular disease that's going around, is quarantine justifiable ethically, and is it actually effective? Obviously, quarantine doesn't keep people from getting diabetes, so in such instances, quarantine wouldn't be justifiable. If there's a major tsunami expected to come through the area any day now, can you really justify locking somebody up in a room for 20 days as well?

These are both factors that must be further delved into on a case-by-case basis.

When quarantine has in fact been deemed necessary (the individual has actually been deemed a threat to the public), professionals follow a few basic guidelines. First, the patient must remain as autonomous as possible. Quarantined people still have the right to make choices based on the type of care that they will receive. You can't just go in and start injecting who-knows-what into them without their consent.[2] Doing so very quickly turns into a *Fire in the Sky* type scenario.

> In *Fire in the Sky*, a man is abducted by aliens who then perform experiments on him against his will.[3]

Next, the treatment provided must do more good than harm. Although treatments can often be painful (who likes long needles?), the treatment that quarantined patients receive should still be beneficial to them overall. This is often referred to as the 'harm principle' by the CDC.

According to the CDC, there are another additional 3 principles that they strive to follow during forced quarantines: the proportionality principle, the reciprocity principle, and the transparency principle.[2]

Proportionality Principle
Have you ever seen somebody use a sledgehammer to crack a nut? That's overkill, isn't it? The proportionality principle says that we need to avoid overkill when we can. The least-restrictive means of quarantine should be used at all times. This could be via voluntary quarantines, home quarantines, or quarantining somebody in an area apart from the community, but not necessarily within a hospital. If these softer measures do not show a high chance of success, then stricter measures must be taken.[1]

Reciprocity Principle
If a patient is willing to undergo quarantine, they should receive some benefit in exchange for their loss. In current society, that frequently means that the quarantined subject will receive shelter, food, water, medicine, care, and other services as needed.[2] If the person is willing to be quarantined for the public good, then the public should assist them with what they need in order to live in a reasonable amount of comfort in the interim.[1] Providing quarantined patients with reasonable monetary compensation is also viewed as necessary to this step. This doesn't mean

that the patient deserves a large cash settlement, but in ordinary times, it does mean they're reasonably compensated for lost income.[4] In a post-disaster situation, this may mean providing the patient with a reasonable amount of canned food or something if they were already a member of your community prior to the quarantine, and they contributed to the group during that prior time as well.

For an outsider wanting to come into a community, I think that just ensuring that they are well fed and cared for during the quarantine would be enough. They'd probably have been starving as vagabonds during the quarantine period anyway (in a TEOTWAWKI WROL situation), and if they want into your group quarantine may just be the membership fee.

Transparency Principle

In the event of a forced quarantine, public health officials have the obligation of telling the quarantined individual the justification for their actions. Why are they doing what they're doing? This frequently involves a process for appeal of the quarantine time as well, should the potential subject feel that to do so would not only violate their human rights, but be unjust, unnecessary, unsafe, and overly severe of a response.[1] If quarantine was something that you would have to toy with, whether you have an appeal process or not would be up to you. If somebody wanted to forgo quarantine altogether, perhaps banishment is your only option.

"Yeah, you can be excused from any form of quarantine, but you sure as heck can't come in here then. You're free to go anywhere else though. Whatever choice you desire."

Additional Thoughts

There's a reason that isolated confinement is such a severe punishment within the prison system (not saying that I disagree with it, just saying that it's severe). It's because people are social creatures. That's the way God wired us. We need human contact. Without it, we can end up pretty messed up in the head. That needs to be remembered with quarantine. If somebody is left in quarantine or isolation for several weeks without any human contact whatsoever, the person is at risk for developing some pretty serious mental illnesses and/or social disorders.[2] So we have to make sure that we're covering even the little things when it comes to this subject.

As you can see, there's a host of factors that we must consider here. You have to find the balance between the community health and individual rights. It gets pretty tricky with this particular subject though. As Ayn Rand would say, there are no public rights. Just individual rights.[5] It's the individuals who make up the public. However, if your kid gets mumps and ends up infertile because some other kid didn't get vaccinated and the viral load your kid was exposed to was so large that the immunization did nothing for him, then I have a feeling you'd be pretty upset. You can see why this gets so tricky.

Take the case of Kaci Hickox, a nurse who volunteered to work in Sierra Leone during the big Ebola epidemic that was going on there a few years ago. She came home and decided the first thing she was going to do was take a bike ride with her boyfriend in Maine. She landed in New Jersey though, which forcibly quarantined her for a number of days. She ended up suing New Jersey for violating her rights.

Now, Ebola is bad. And by this point, there had already been cases of other American healthcare workers who contracted the disease while volunteering overseas for the same epidemic.

I personally think that the right thing was done. You just got back from Ebola-ville, and you think you're gonna go on a bike ride with your boyfriend?! Heck no! Her argument was that asymptomatic Ebola infected individuals are not contagious. What if you turn symptomatic though? What if you decide to wait a couple of days for the "cold" to wear off after you turn symptomatic? What if you give it to other people? Do you really think the public is going to be ok with a nurse that's just been exposed to Ebola riding around their community without having been quarantined for at least a few days, even if she's currently asymptomatic? Nope.

So back to our original example.

We've got a pregnant woman with two small kids who's been exposed to smallpox via her husband (and potentially others) that wants to stay in our community. Society has completely disintegrated, and as a result, I don't have to worry about this lady suing me or hauling me away to prison. There are no courts and no prisons left.

Heck yeah, I'd quarantine her. We'll let you in, but we're checking you out first. We're not letting you bring smallpox in here. I'm not letting you put my kids' lives at stake.

On the flip side, if the person has had zero exposure to the infectious agent, and isn't within the period of communicability (when the disease can actually spread to other people), there's really not any good reason to quarantine somebody.[4]

What About Mass Quarantine?

Let's say that two carloads of extended family members show up at your gate post-disaster. The pandemic has hit everywhere hard, and especially the cities. The population density was so high, and the lack of the ability to produce food/clean water or dispose of human waste within the cities was so bad that the disease spread like wildfire there. And here's your family members from the city wanting to come in.

You decide that their exposure warrants quarantine. What do you do though? Are there tips that can help? Well, putting a lot of people together in a quarantine situation can actually make things worse in some cases. Increased population density can equal increased disease virulence. Why? Because the disease can now spread a whole lot easier via aerosol droplets from conversations, coughing, and sneezing. If you're forcing everybody to breathe the same air, those little droplets have a much higher chance of infecting more people, placing every member of the mass quarantine at risk of infection.[4]

So is that something that you and the group members are willing to risk?

That's something you're going to have to work through. When possible, choosing the least restrictive measures is the way to go. Voluntary isolation does seem to work in many cases. Just stuff to think about.

Typhoid Mary
You may have heard the term "typhoid Mary" tossed around in casual conversation, but do you know the story behind the woman? Mary Mallon was an Irish immigrant to America back during the early 1900s. She soon gained work as a cook for wealthier families within New York City. In 1906, George Soper, a sanitation engineer, noticed that typhoid outbreaks frequently occurred in the families that Mary Mallon had cooked for. After asking Mary for specimens of her feces (and in turn being chased away by a woman brandishing a carving fork), doctors soon discovered that Mary was actually an asymptomatic carrier of typhoid, and that she was spreading the disease through her cooking to others.[6]

She was placed in solitary confinement in a small cottage on North Brother Island near the Bronx in 1907, and not released until 1910 under the promise that she would no longer work as a cook or to prepare meals for anybody other than herself. She soon violated this agreement, being employed as a cook once more, and was promptly

captured. This time she was placed in solitary
confinement until her death from stroke
complications 23 years later.[7]

She would work as a cook for an employer
under an alias, and once a typhoid outbreak began
there, would quietly change her name and
employer, never mentioning the prior outbreaks at
her prior employers.[7] All in all, more than 50 cases
of typhoid were attributed to her (most likely more),
and 3 deaths.[6]

The Visibly Sick

I love watching movies about pandemics, and I think the reason that they
tend to do so well at the box office, the reason that zombie movies came
into vogue for so long, is that people like to ponder over the ethical
dilemmas that the survivors of those movies get placed in. It's fun to think
over what *you* would do in such a situation.

You've undoubtedly seen the same scenes that I have where a very
visibly sick patient (like the lady in *10 Cloverfield Lane*) attempts to get into
a disease-free region. What do you do then?

Well, at least in current society within the US, states can place an
infected and contagious patient under involuntary isolation if the patient
has an easily transmissible disease and refuses to isolate themselves.[8]

You can't get infected with polio, plague, smallpox, or Ebola and
expect to be able to just waltz around the United States at your leisure.
Doing so puts others' health at risk. I don't want anyone with smallpox
traveling through my town, do you?

Once again, this is where that balance comes into play; of protecting
individual rights and freedom, while simultaneously protecting the public
health. Ultimately, if you want to make the best decision that you can
here, there are a number of sources that I would refer to: The Holy Spirit,
common sense, a basic understanding of human rights, past legal
precedence, and a basic understanding of infectious diseases.

Lepers in the Bible

Even during Bible times, people had to work
around what to do with contagious individuals. In
particular, lepers.

Though "leprosy" within the Bible most
likely refers to a large number of skin/nervous
tissue disorders (as evidenced by the fact that

192

parts of the Bible refer to it being something homes or garments could come down with), the point remains that people who had it were dangerous to those who didn't.[9]

If you look through Leviticus 13-14 you'll find an entire set of instructions that were given to Moses regarding what to do with people who had leprosy.

That being said, I think it's important to note that the presence of disease doesn't necessarily mean God's judgment on an individual. Consider John 9:1-3:

Now as Jesus passed by, He saw a man who was blind from birth. And His disciples asked Him, saying, "Rabbi, who sinned, this man or his parents, that he was born blind?" Jesus answered, "Neither this man nor his parents sinned, but that the works of God should be revealed in him..."

Final Thoughts

I think it's important to note that there is no specific command throughout Scripture to prep. If you're looking for a verse that says, "And thou shalt prep, and have one year worth of food stored on your property always", you're not going to find it.

As I'm realizing with a lot of other topics, God was too smart for that.

Like gambling. You'll never find a verse throughout Scripture that outright commands you not to gamble. Because everything (I'm generalizing with a broad brush) in life is a gamble! If I'm not allowed to gamble, then as my Granny says I better not ever become a farmer. You're really rolling the dice with every seed that you put in the ground. If I'm not allowed to gamble, then I better not ever put money in the stock market. I better not ever buy a used car. I better not ever buy a power tool at a flea market.

The point is that there are no guarantees in life, and so sometimes you do have to take a gamble at it.

If God had specifically commanded us to prep in Scripture, then wouldn't every Christian who has ever languished in prison be condemned? They're not currently doing anything to ensure that they are better prepared for future disaster! Wouldn't every Christian who is injured and stuck in the hospital be condemned? They're not currently doing anything to prep!

Do you see what I mean here?

Now I know that this seems silly. I mean, you *did* just read an entire book that I wrote on Christian perspectives on prepping. And here I am now saying that there's no specific command within Scripture to actually prep.

Yeah, that is the case. But wisdom is definitely biblical. Discretion is definitely biblical. I think the entire book of Proverbs make this pretty clear. I most certainly don't want to indirectly lead to the conclusion that prepping is necessarily a Christian thing to do, because I think that legalism can quickly follow, and the last thing I want to do is to be the root that people tripped over causing them to roll down the slope of legalism.

That said, I do believe that having the food, water, medicine, and methods to keep your family safe and protected from the inevitable storms of life is most certainly wise. You don't want to be walking around as an idiot. In the same breath, I don't think that preppers should look at non-preppers as "less spiritual" than them by any means. Jesus had some pretty severe things to say to those who had a holier-than-thou attitude.

The point I'm trying to make is that if you feel that prepping is a wise course of action for your family, an action filled with discretion based on what you have seen in the world around you, then go ahead and engage in it. It is most certainly not wrong to do so.

We've touched on a lot of other topics as well. Is OPSEC wrong, is prepping a lack of faith, how can you best take care of others, etc. And I've done my best to answer them all to the best of my ability. If you have further questions on any subject within this book, I encourage you to be like the Bereans within the book of Acts who were willing to do their own investigations to determine if what was said was true. I have done my very best to load this book down with Scripture, facts, and common sense to back up everything that I have said.

I hope that this book has left you feeling both uplifted and informed.

Prepper Acronyms and Terms

GOOD – "Get out of dodge"

BOB – Bug-out bag; a pre-assembled bag that contains everything that you would need to survive out in the wilderness for a period of time. Something that you would be able to quickly grab on the go if you need to evacuate your retreat location in a hurry.

Bug Out – To clandestinely evacuate your primary dwelling and live out in the wilderness off of the land

BOV – Bug-out vehicle; a vehicle that is outfitted to either get you to a survival retreat, or to be used as a mobile survival retreat.

Black Swan – An unexpected event that could trigger catastrophic conditions

WROL – Without rule of law; a society where law and government no longer exist.

TLWH – The long walk home; what happens when society disintegrates while you are a long distance from home. Typically associated with an EMP, where you would then have to walk back to your primary residence.

EDC – Every day carry; the things that you carry on your person every day regardless of where you go. It typically consists of the things that you carry in your pockets, or that one keeps on their person in a EDC bag of some sort.

False Flag – A destructive covert government operation that gives the appearance that another party was responsible for the damage/problem.

MRE – Meals ready to eat; frequently eaten by military personnel.

OPSEC – Operational security; the art of keeping your preparations hidden.

SHTF – Poopoo* hits the fan; a term used for when the bad stuff finally happens.

TEOTWAWKI – The end of the world as we know it; a term used for when an event takes place which forever changes life as we know it.

Further Reading

The Total Money Makeover (Dave Ramsey)
Preppers: History and Cultural Phenomenon (Lynda King)
The Resilient Farm and Homestead (Ben Falk)
Gaia's Garden: A Guide to Home-scale Permaculture (Toby Hemenway)
Square Foot Gardening (Mel Bartholomew)

References

Chapter 1: What's Going on in the World?

1. Badiru, A., & Racz, L. (2013). *Handbook of Emergency Response.* Boca Raton, FL: CRC Press. pg. 274.

2. Gillespie, D. & Danso K. (2010). *Disaster Concepts and Issues.* Alexandria, VA: Council on Social Work Education. pg. xi.

3. Ibid., pg. 15.

4. MacRae, D. Thomas Malthus. In Encyclopedia Brittanica. Retrieved August 7, 2018, from https://www.britannica.com/biography/Thomas-Malthus

5. Fisher, L. (2009). *The Perfect Swarm.* NYC: Basic Books. pg. 14.

This is just one of three books in a trilogy by Len Fisher, and the trio is fascinating. I highly recommend them. The other two books are *Crises, Crashes, and Calamities* and *Rock, Paper, Scissors.* I don't condone his politics which seem to leech their way into his works (he has some very European socialist/left ideas), but the actual *science* is interesting.

By the way, if you want to get a better idea of what I think about different books, I recommend checking out my pet project shouldchristiansread.com. It gives you a filth gauge to determine what exactly is in the book in your hands, hopefully saving you time and money. The URL is what it is just to help with search engine optimization. I don't actually answer if you should read the book or not (lest you think I'm being legalistic).

6. Rawles, J. (2009). *How to Survive the End of the World as We Know It.* Westminster, MD: Plume. p. x.

7. Bissell, R., Jensen, S., & Feldmen-Jensen, S. (2013). *Preparedness and Response to Catastrophic Disasters.* Boca Raton, FL: CRC Press. pg. 304.

8. Center for Urban Education About Sustainable Agriculture (CUESA). How Far Does Your Food Travel to Get to Your Plate? Accessed August 7, 2018, from https://cuesa.org/learn/how-far-does-your-food-travel-get-your-plate

9. Rawles, J. (2009). *How to Survive the End of the World as We Know It.* Westminster, MD: Plume. p. 10.

10. Gillespie, D. & Danso K. (2010). *Disaster Concepts and Issues.* Alexandria, VA: Council on Social Work Education. pg. 226.

11. King, L. (2014). *Preppers: History and the Cultural Phenomenon.* Prepper Press. p. 162.

This book, available from Prepper Press, is highly worth your time. Not only will it give you *dozens* of examples from history of why we should prep, but the philosophy explored within the text is very interesting as well. Highly researched, and I recommend it.

12. Fox 5 KVVU-TV. (2015, January 28). Colorado Theater Shooting Fast Facts. Accessed August 7, 2018, from http://www.fox5vegas.com/story/26008026/colorado-theater-shooting-fast-facts

13. King, L. (2014). *Preppers: History and the Cultural Phenomenon.* Prepper Press. p. 164.

14. Baker, L. & Cormier, L. (2015). *Disasters and Vulnerable Populations: Evidence-Based Practice for the Helping Professions.* Danvers, MA: Springer Publishing Company. p. 22.

15. Emberlin, R. (2017, July 5). Ambushed: Dallas Police Massacre, One Year Later. Fox News. Accessed August 7, 2018, from http://www.foxnews.com/opinion/2017/07/05/ambushed-dallas-police-massacre-one-year-later.html

16. Housley, A., Jeunesse, W., Gibson, J., Herridge, C., Arroyo, M., Singman, B., et al. (2017, October 2). Las Vegas Shooting: At Least 59 Dead in Massacre Trump Calls 'Act of Pure Evil'. Fox News. Accessed August 7, 2018, from http://www.foxnews.com/us/2017/ 10/02/reports-active-shooter-near-mandalay-bay-in-las-vegas.html

17. Mercy Corps. Quick Facts: Hurricane Maria's Effect on Puerto Rico. Accessed August 7, 2018, from https://www.mercycorps.org/articles/united-states/quick-facts-hurricane-marias-effect-puerto-rico

18. Baker, L. & Cormier, L. (2015). *Disasters and Vulnerable Populations: Evidence-Based Practice for the Helping Professions.* Danvers, MA: Springer Publishing Company. p. 26.

Hands down this was *the* best resource I found out there on the topic of how to prep for those with special needs. I devote just one chapter in this book to the subject. This is an entire book on the issue. I highly recommend it if you want to get more into the nitty-gritty of taking care of those with various medical and physical needs.

19. Harrison, K. (2008). *Just in Case: How to be Self-Sufficient When the Unexpected Happens.* North Adams, MA: Storey Publishing. p. 145.

20. Baker, L. & Cormier, L. (2015). *Disasters and Vulnerable Populations: Evidence-Based Practice for the Helping Professions.* Danvers, MA: Springer Publishing Company. p. 12.

21. Landesman, L. & Weisfuse, I. (2014). *Case Studies in Public Health Preparedness and Response to Disasters.* Burlington, MA: Jones and Bartlett Learning. p. 8.

22. Baker, L. & Cormier, L. (2015). *Disasters and Vulnerable Populations: Evidence-Based Practice for the Helping Professions.* Danvers,

MA: Springer Publishing Company. p. 5.

23. The Centers for Disease Control and Prevention (CDC). (2017, June 13). Zombie Preparedness Graphic Novel. Accessed August 7, 2018, from https://www.cdc.gov/phpr/zombie/novel.htm

24. Badiru, A., & Racz, L. (2013) *Handbook of Emergency Response.* Boca Raton, FL: CRC Press. pg. 308.

25. Zwirz, E. (2017, December 26). North Korean Defector Had Anthrax Antibodies in System, Report Says. Fox News. Accessed August 7, 2018, from http://www.foxnews.com/world/2017/12/26/ north-korean-defector-had-anthrax-antibodies-in-system-report-says.html

People don't seem to understand that bioweapon research is very much alive. This story should send chills down anyone's spine. If you're looking for reading more on the subject of biowarfare/ bioterrorism, I highly recommend Richard Preston's *The Demon in the Freezer.* It's terrifying.

26. Alibeck, K., & Handelman, S. (2000). *Biohazard: The Chilling True Story of the Largest Biological Weapons Program in the World – Told from Inside by the Man Who Ran It.* Delta.

Once again, another terrifying book that should have peoples' attention. After the collapse of the Soviet Union, their bioweapons simply disappeared. Who has them now?

27. The Mold Source. Mycotoxins and Gulf War Illness. Accessed August 8, 2018, from http://www.themoldsource.com/archives/5archives.html

28. Park, C., & Dembek, Z. (2016, March 9). CBRNE – T2 Mycotoxins. Medscape. Accessed August 8, 2018, from https://emedicine.medscape.com/article/830892-overview

29. Keyes, D., Burstein, J., Schwartz, R., & Swienton, R. (2004). *Medical Response to Terrorism: Preparedness and Clinical Practice.* Baltimore, MD: Lippincott Williams and Wilkins. p. 131.

30. Novak, Matt. (2016, November 1). The Largest Bioterrorism Attack in US History was an Attempt to Swing an Election. Paleofuture Website. Accessed August 8, 2018, from https://www.gizmodo.com.au/2016/11/the-largest-bioterrorism-attack-in-us-history-was-an-attempt-to-swing-an-election/

31. Alfred, C. (2015, March 20). 20 Years Ago, A Shadowy Cult Poisoned the Tokyo Subway. The Huffington Post. Accessed August 8, 2018, from https://www.huffingtonpost.com/2015/03/20/tokyo-subway-sarin-attack_n_6896754.html

32. Rosner, D., & Markowitz, G. (2006). *Are We Ready?: Public Health Since 9/11.* Oakland, CA: University of California Press. p. 66.

33. Koppel, T. *Lights Out: A Cyberattack, a Nation Unprepared, Surviving the Aftermath.*

Forstchen, W. (2011). *One Second After.* NYC, NY: Forge Books.

Crawford, D. (2010). *Lights Out.* Halfast Publishing.

34. Johnson, S. (2017, July 8). North Korean EMP Attack: The Dark Possibility. Business Insider. Accessed August 8, 2018, from https://www.businessinsider.com/north-korean-emp-attack-the-dark-possibility-2017-7

35. Berlatsky, N. (2012). *Opposing Viewpoints: Inflation.* Farmington Hills, MI: Greenhaven Press. p. 137.

An interesting look at inflation from different economists' perspectives. There's actually a reference to James Wesley Rawle's book *Patriots* in here. I found it interesting to see just how popular his book has become, even among professional economists apparently.

36. Ibid., p. 73.

37. Ibid., p. 69.

38. Ibid., p. 136.

39. Slavo, M. (2018, July 24). SOCIALISM: Venezuela's Inflation Rate Could Hit ONE MILLION PERCENT. SHTFplan Web site. Accessed August 8, 2018, from http://www.shtfplan.com/headline-news/socialism-venezuelas-inflation-rate-could-hit-one-million-percent_07242018

40. LaPierre, W. (2010). *Safe: How to Protect Yourself, Your Family, and Your Home.* WND Books. p. 70.

41. Ibid., p. 24.

42. Lennquist, S. (2012). *Medical Response to Major Incidents and Disasters: A Practical Guide for All Medical Staff.* NYC, NY: Springer Publishing. p. 337.

43. Ibid., p. 340.

44. Stein, M. (2008). *When Technology Fails.* White River Junction, VT: Chelsea Green Publishing. p. 5.

I'd heard that this was considered a classic within prepping literature. I didn't like it. It was too much fluff and not enough information.

45. Novick, L., Morrow, C., & Mays, G. (2008). *Public Health Administration: Principles for Population-Based Management.* Sudbury, MA: Jones and Bartlett Publishers. p. 704.

46. Center for Disease Control and Prevention (CDC). National Strategy for Pandemic Influenza Implementation Plan. p. 1. Accessed August 8, 2018, from https://www.cdc.gov/flu/pandemic-resources/pdf/pandemic-influenza-implementation.pdf

47. Center for Disease Control and Prevention (CDC). (2014, January 8). First Human Avian Influenza A (H5N1) Virus Infection Reported in Americas. Accessed August 14, 2018, from https://www.cdc.gov/flu/news/first-human-h5n1-americas.htm http://www.who.int/influenza/human_animal_interface/H5N1_avian_influenza_update.pdf

48. Center for Disease Control and Prevention (CDC). Pandemic Influenza Plan: 2017 Update. p. 7. Accessed August 8, 2018, from https://www.cdc.gov/flu/pandemic-resources/pdf/pan-flu-report-2017v2.pdf

49. Center for Disease Control and Prevention (CDC). Pandemic Influenza Plan: 2017 Update. p. 7. Accessed August 8, 2018, from https://www.cdc.gov/flu/pandemic-resources/pdf/pan-flu-report-2017v2.pdf

50. Center for Disease Control and Prevention (CDC). National Strategy for Pandemic Influenza Implementation Plan. p. 6. Accessed August 8, 2018, from https://www.cdc.gov/flu/pandemic-resources/pdf/pandemic-influenza-implementation.pdf

51. Center for Disease Control and Prevention (CDC). Pandemic Influenza Plan: 2017 Update. p. 42. Accessed August 8, 2018, from https://www.cdc.gov/flu/pandemic-resources/pdf/pan-flu-report-2017v2.pdf

52. Center for Disease Control and Prevention (CDC). National Strategy for Pandemic Influenza Implementation Plan. p. 198. Accessed August 8, 2018, from https://www.cdc.gov/flu/pandemic-resources/pdf/pandemic-influenza-implementation.pdf

53. Novick, L., Morrow, C., & Mays, G. (2008). *Public Health Administration: Principles for Population-Based Management.* Sudbury, MA: Jones and Bartlett Publishers. p. 706.

54. Center for Disease Control and Prevention (CDC). Pandemic Influenza Plan: 2017 Update. p. Appendix A. Accessed August 8, 2018, from https://www.cdc.gov/flu/pandemic-resources/pdf/pan-flu-report-2017v2.pdf

55. Center for Disease Control and Prevention (CDC). Pandemic Influenza Plan: 2017 Update. p. 43. Accessed August 8, 2018, from https://www.cdc.gov/flu/pandemic-resources/pdf/pan-flu-report-2017v2.pdf

56. Center for Disease Control and Prevention (CDC). National Strategy for Pandemic Influenza Implementation Plan. p. 170. Accessed August 8, 2018, from https://www.cdc.gov/flu/pandemic-resources/pdf/pandemic-influenza-implementation.pdf

57. Center for Disease Control and Prevention (CDC). National Strategy for Pandemic Influenza Implementation Plan. p. 78. Accessed August 8, 2018, from https://www.cdc.gov/flu/pandemic-resources/pdf/pandemic-influenza-implementation.pdf

58. Center for Disease Control and Prevention (CDC). National Strategy for Pandemic Influenza Implementation Plan. p. 25. Accessed August 8, 2018, from https://www.cdc.gov/flu/pandemic-resources/pdf/pandemic-influenza-implementation.pdf

59. FluView can be found by visiting https://www.cdc.gov/flu/weekly/index.htm

Chapter 2: Is Prepping Biblical?

1. J.P. (2012, March 28). A Christian's Call to Prepare. Survivalblog. Accessed August 8, 2018, from https://survivalblog.com /a-christians-call-to-prepare-by-jp/

2. The Data Team. (2017, August 29). Weather Related Disasters are Increasing. The Economist. Accessed August 8, 2018, from https://www.economist.com/blogs/graphicdetail/2017/08/daily-chart-19

3. P.H. (2013, March 31). Pre—Trib Rapture Doctrine and Preparedness. Survivalblog. Accessed August 8, 2018, from https://survivalblog.com/pre-trib-rapture-doctrine-and-preparedness-by-ph/

Chapter 3: Is Prepping a Lack of Faith in God?

1. Kapucu, N., & Ozerdem A. (2011). *Managing Emergencies and Crises*. Burlington, MA: Jones and Bartlett Learning. p. 43.

2. Lewis, P. (2017, March 7). Are You "No Earthly Good"? Rural Revolution blog. Accessed August 8, 2018, from http://www.rural-revolution.com/2017/03/are-you-no-earthly-good.html

3. Falwell, J. (1982). *Liberty Bible Commentary: New Testament*. Nashville, TN: Thomas Nelson. p. 617.

4. Lewis, P. (2017, March 7). Are You "No Earthly Good"? Rural Revolution blog. Accessed August 8, 2018, from http://www.rural-revolution.com/2017/03/are-you-no-earthly-good.html

I love Patrice Lewis' blog, and I think that this is one of her best posts to date. It was entirely refreshing. I highly recommend following her work, and contributing to what she does by purchasing some of her e-books if you are into homesteading.

Chapter 4: Biblical Perspectives on Charity Post-Disaster

1. M., J. (2018, April 5). A Helping Hand. Survivalblog Web site. Accessed August 9, 2018, from https://survivalblog.com/helping-hand-j-m/

Survivalblog.com is one of my favorite websites, and I check it multiple times daily. I believe that it is not only the best survivalist/prepper website in existence, but that it is also one of the best "alternative" news sites available. Rawles does a superb job of keeping freedom-loving people informed about the things that are freedom-destroying, evil, and stupid in this world.

2. Lewis, P. (2015, June 2). Review: The Seven Core Areas of Preparedness. The Rural Revolution blog. Accessed August 8, 2018, from http://www.rural-revolution.com/2015/06/review-seven-core-areas-of-preparedness.html

Chapter 5: What About Barter?

1. Coyne, C. (2013). *Doing Bad by Doing Good*. Stanford, CA: Stanford Economics and Finance. p. 154.

I absolutely loved this book. I've harped to my friends for years about keeping your heart attached to your brain. This book was the research proving my point. You need to read this one. It will add a deeper layer to how you view charity.

2. Ibid., p. 155.
3. Ibid., p. 150.
4. Ibid., p. 153.
5. Ibid., p. 158.
6. Ibid., p. 157.
7. Ibid., p. 185.
8. Perry, M. (2016, August 23). Louisiana Lawmaker Wants to Subject the 'Cajun Navy' Volunteer Group to Government Red Tape, Regulations, and Fees. The AEI Ideas Web site. Accessed August 8, 2018, from https://www.aei.org/publication/louisiana-lawmaker-wants-to-subject-cajun-navy-volunteer-group-to-government-red-tape-regulations-fees/
9. Luther, D. (2016, September 7). Louisiana Officials Demand that Self-Reliant Locals Stop Surviving the Flood Without Permission. SHTF Plan Web site. Accessed August 8, 2018, from http://www.shtfplan.com/headline-news/louisiana-officials-demand-that-self-reliant-locals-stop-surviving-the-flood-without-permission_09072016
10. Domonoske, C. (2017, September 28). In Puerto Rico, Containers Full of Goods Sit Undistributed at Ports. The NPR Web site. Accessed

August 8, 2018, from https://www.npr.org/sections/ thetwo-way/2017/09/28/554297787/puerto-rico-relief-goods-sit-undistributed-at-ports

11. Rodriguez, J. (2017, September 30). 'Inept' Puerto Rican Government 'Riddled with Corruption': CEO. The New York Post Web site. Accessed August 8, 2018, from https://nypost.com/2017/09/30/inept-puerto-rican-government-riddled-with-corruption-ceo/

12. Coyne, C. (2013). *Doing Bad by Doing Good*. Stanford, CA: Stanford Economics and Finance. p. 182.

13. Rawles, J. (2009). *Patriots: A Novel of Survival in the Coming Collapse*. Berkeley, CA: Ulysses Press.

Rawles has written a number of books on the subject of survival, but I believe this is his best. You have to understand going into reading this one that it is *not* a novel; it's a *how-to* book. Rawles is telling you how to do the various survival skills via the context of a novel. The story is simply the meat on the bones.

That being said, the story's not bad either, and the entire series is worth checking out. *Liberators* and *Survivors* were my other two favorites in the series.

14. Smith, A. (2012). *The Wealth of Nations*. Arden, Warwickshire: Coda Books.

15. Quote from Montesquieu. You can find it at http://oll.libertyfund.org/quote/85

16. Coyne, C. (2013). *Doing Bad by Doing Good*. Stanford, CA: Stanford Economics and Finance. p. 181.

17. Pridemore, W. (2006). Heavy drinking and suicide in Russia. *Social Forces, 85*(1), 413-430. Accessed August 8, 2018, from https://www.ncbi.nlm.nih.gov/pmc/articles/PMC1642767/

18. Coyne, C. (2013). *Doing Bad by Doing Good*. Stanford, CA: Stanford Economics and Finance. p. 181.

Chapter 6: Community Post-Disaster

1. Rawles, J. The Precepts of Rawlesian Survivalist Philosophy. Survivalblog. Accessed August 8, 2018, from https://survivalblog.com/precepts/

2. LaPierre, W. (2010). *Safe: How to Protect Yourself, Your Family, and Your Home*. WND Books. p. 116.

3. Fisher, L. (2009). *The Perfect Swarm*. NYC: Basic Books. pg. 74.

4. Ibid., pg. 59.

5. Ibid., pg. 69.

6. Ersing, R., & Kost, K. (2011). *Surviving Disaster: The Role of Social*

Networks. Oxford, England: Oxford University Press. p. 7.

7. Bruce, M., Martins, D., Duru, K., Beech, B., Sims, M., Harawa, N., Vargas, R., et al. (2017). Church attendance, allostatic load and mortality in middle aged adults. *PLoS One, 12*(5). Accessed August 8, 2018, from http://journals.plos.org/plosone/article?id=10.1371/journal.pone.0177618

8. VanderWeele, T., Li, S., Tsai, A., et al. (2016). Association between religious service attendance and lower suicide rates among US Women. *JAMA Psychiatry, 73*(8). Accessed August 8, 2018, from https://jamanetwork.com/journals/jamapsychiatry/fullarticle/2529152

9. Li, S., Stampfer, M., & VanderWeele, T. (2016). Association of religious service attendance with mortality among women. *JAMA Internal Medicine, 176*(6), 777-785. Accessed August 8, 2018, from https://www.ncbi.nlm.nih.gov/pubmed/27183175

10. VanderWeele, T. (2016). Religious service attendance associated with lower suicide risk among women. *JAMA Psychiatry.* Accessed August 14, 2018, from https://media.jamanetwork.com/news-item/religious-service-attendance-associated-with-lower-suicide-risk-among-women/

11. Lim, C., & Putnam, R. (2010). Religion, social networks, and life satisfaction. American Sociological Review, 75(6). Accessed August 8, 2018, from http://journals.sagepub.com/doi/abs/10.1177/0003122410386686

12. Ersing, R., & Kost, K. (2011). *Surviving Disaster: The Role of Social Networks.* Oxford, England: Oxford University Press. p. 22 & 33.

13. Gillespie, D. & Danso K. (2010). *Disaster Concepts and Issues.* Alexandria, VA: Council on Social Work Education. pg. 74.

14. Lewis, P. (2018, April 7). And to Think it All Started with a Potluck. Rural Revolution blog. Accessed August 8, 2018, from http://www.rural-revolution.com/2018/04/and-to-think-it-all-started-with-potluck.html

15. Falk, B. (2013). *The Resilient Farm and Homestead.* White River Junction, VT: Chelsea Green Publishing. p. 32.

16. Kapucu, N., & Ozerdem A. (2011). *Managing Emergencies and Crises.* Burlington, MA: Jones and Bartlett Learning. p. 89.

17. Gillespie, D. & Danso K. (2010). *Disaster Concepts and Issues.* Alexandria, VA: Council on Social Work Education. pg. 145.

18. Ersing, R., & Kost, K. (2011). *Surviving Disaster: The Role of Social Networks.* Oxford, England: Oxford University Press. p. 40.

19. Bliss, L. (2015, July 21). Why You Don't Really Care About the Next 'Big One'. CityLab website. Accessed August 12, 2018, from

https://www.citylab.com/environment/2015/07/why-you-dont-really-care-about-the-next-big-one/398969/

20. Badiru, A., & Racz, L. (2013) *Handbook of Emergency Response.* Boca Raton, FL: CRC Press. pg. 286.

21. Ibid., pg. 287.

22. I can't find a source for this one anywhere, ya'll. I first heard this rhyme as a little kid, and it's stuck with me ever since.

23. Badiru, A., & Racz, L. (2013) *Handbook of Emergency Response.* Boca Raton, FL: CRC Press. pg. 288.

24. Ibid., pg. 276.

Chapter 7: Do You Let Them Stay?

1. Rawles, J. (2008, August 12). The Golden Horde and the Thin Veneer. Survivalblog. Accessed August 8, 2018, from https://survivalblog.com/the-golden-horde-and-the-thin/

2. Bissell, R., Jensen, S., & Feldmen-Jensen, S. (2013). *Preparedness and Response to Catastrophic Disasters.* Boca Raton, FL: CRC Press. pg. 187.

3. Rawles, J. (2009). *Patriots: A Novel of Survival in the Coming Collapse.* Berkeley, CA: Ulysses Press.

4. Cobb, J. (2014). *Prepper's Long-Term Survival Guide: Food, Shelter, Security, Off-the-Grid Power and More Life-Saving Strategies for Self-Sufficient Living.* Berkeley, CA: Ulysses Press. p. 160.

I read through a number of Cobb's books, and if you were brand-new to prepping, then I can see how they would be useful. If you've been into it for quite some time, then you may want to look elsewhere for new information.

Chapter 8: Caring for People Post-Disaster

1. Priscilla, D. (2009). *Crisis and Disaster Counseling.* Washington, DC: SAGE Publishing. p. 54.

2. Ibid., p. 37.

3. Kloos, B., Hill, J., Thomas, E., Wandersman, A., Dalton, J. (2011). *Community Psychology: Linking Individuals and Communities.* Belmont, CA: Wadsworth Publishing. p. 263.

4. Priscilla, D. (2009). *Crisis and Disaster Counseling.* Washington, DC: SAGE Publishing. p. 134.

5. Baker, L. & Cormier, L. (2015). *Disasters and Vulnerable Populations: Evidence-Based Practice for the Helping Professions.* Danvers, MA: Springer Publishing Company. p. 51.

6. Lennquist, S. (2012). *Medical Response to Major Incidents and Disasters: A Practical Guide for All Medical Staff.* NYC, NY: Springer

Publishing. p. 370.

7. Baker, L. & Cormier, L. (2015). *Disasters and Vulnerable Populations: Evidence-Based Practice for the Helping Professions*. Danvers, MA: Springer Publishing Company. p. 194.

Chapter 9: Caring for Those Who Need More Care

1. Baker, L. & Cormier, L. (2015). *Disasters and Vulnerable Populations: Evidence-Based Practice for the Helping Professions*. Danvers, MA: Springer Publishing Company. p. 70.

2. University of Rochester Medical Center. Understanding the Teen Brain. Health Encyclopedia. Accessed August 11, 2018, from https://www.urmc.rochester.edu/encyclopedia/content.aspx?ContentTypeID=1&ContentID=3051

3. Baker, L. & Cormier, L. (2015). *Disasters and Vulnerable Populations: Evidence-Based Practice for the Helping Professions*. Danvers, MA: Springer Publishing Company. p. 73.

4. Ibid., p. 82.

5. Gillespie, D. & Danso K. (2010). *Disaster Concepts and Issues*. Alexandria, VA: Council on Social Work Education. pg. 192.

6. Priscilla, D. (2009). *Crisis and Disaster Counseling*. Washington, DC: SAGE Publishing. p. 85-86.

7. Landesman, L. (2011). *Public Health Management of Disasters: The Practice Guide*. Washington DC: American Public Health Association. p. 207.

8. Baker, L. & Cormier, L. (2015). *Disasters and Vulnerable Populations: Evidence-Based Practice for the Helping Professions*. Danvers, MA: Springer Publishing Company. p. 81.

9. Ibid., p. 86.

10. Gillespie, D. & Danso K. (2010). *Disaster Concepts and Issues*. Alexandria, VA: Council on Social Work Education. pg. 191.

11. I can't find the source for this one anywhere, ya'll. I'm not sure where my friend got the study from.

12. Gillespie, D. & Danso K. (2010). *Disaster Concepts and Issues*. Alexandria, VA: Council on Social Work Education. pg. 193.

13. Priscilla, D. (2009). *Crisis and Disaster Counseling*. Washington, DC: SAGE Publishing. p. 88.

I found this book to be packed full of useful information for anyone that is interested in the after-effects of disasters on the *individual*. The advice given within it is well-researched, and will enable one to have the tools necessary to help those around them whom they love cope with the consequences of disaster.

14. Conversano, C., Rotondo, A., Lensi, E., Vista, O., Arpone, F., & Reda, M. (2010). Optimism and its impact on mental and physical well-being. *Clinical Practical Epidemiology in Mental Health, 6*, 25-29. Accessed August 11, 2018, from https://www.ncbi.nlm.nih.gov/pmc/ articles/ PMC2894461/

15. Kapucu, N., & Ozerdem A. (2011). *Managing Emergencies and Crises.* Burlington, MA: Jones and Bartlett Learning. p. 25.

16. Ibid., p. 26.

17. Gillespie, D. & Danso K. (2010). *Disaster Concepts and Issues.* Alexandria, VA: Council on Social Work Education. pg. 230.

18. Baker, L. & Cormier, L. (2015). *Disasters and Vulnerable Populations: Evidence-Based Practice for the Helping Professions.* Danvers, MA: Springer Publishing Company. p. 120.

19. Ibid., p. 117.

20. Ibid., p. 67.

21. Ibid., p. 69.

22. Chang, I. (2012). *The Rape of Nanking: The Forgotten Holocaust of World War II.* NYC, NY: Basic Books.

This book will help you to understand why Japan and China hate each other so much, a forgotten aspect of WW2, and what acts of evil invading troops are capable of doing to a people whom they have dehumanized.

23. Baker, L. & Cormier, L. (2015). *Disasters and Vulnerable Populations: Evidence-Based Practice for the Helping Professions.* Danvers, MA: Springer Publishing Company. p. 68.

24. Landesman, L. (2011). *Public Health Management of Disasters: The Practice Guide.* Washington DC: American Public Health Association. p. 239.

25. Ibid., p. 230.

26. Ibid., p. 241.

27. Frio. How a Frio Works. Accessed August 11, 2018, from https://friouk.com/how-a-frio-works/

28. Baker, L. & Cormier, L. (2015). *Disasters and Vulnerable Populations: Evidence-Based Practice for the Helping Professions.* Danvers, MA: Springer Publishing Company. p. 175.

29. Ibid., p. 176.

30. Farber, M. (2018, May 1). Oklahoma man, 57, dies after rattlesnake bites him twice: 'Don't mess with snakes' Fox News website. Accessed August 14, 2018, from http://www.foxnews.com/ science/2018/05/01/oklahoma-man-57-dies-after-rattlesnake-bites-him-twice-dont-mess-with-snakes.html

Chapter 10: Living with Others in Confined Circumstances

1. Landesman, L. (2011). *Public Health Management of Disasters: The Practice Guide*. Washington DC: American Public Health Association. p. 175.

2. Weisberger, M. (2018, March 21). How Much Do You Poop in Your Lifetime? The Live Science Web site. Accessed August 11, 2018, from https://www.livescience.com/61966-how-much-you-poop-in-lifetime.html

3. MedlinePlus. Urine 24-Hour Volume. Medical Encyclopedia. The Medline Plus Web site. Accessed August 11, 2018, from https://medlineplus.gov/ency/article/003425.htm

4. Harrison, K. (2008). *Just in Case: How to be Self-Sufficient When the Unexpected Happens*. North Adams, MA: Storey Publishing. p. 73.

    Another "classic" of the prepping genre. I found this one useful for the beginning prepper who just wants to be prepared for your average flood, tornado, power outage, etc. For somebody who's more concerned about EMP, pandemic, invasion, WROL, or other similar scenarios, this one's probably going to be rather tame.

    That being said, the information in this book will most certainly give one a strong foundation for beginning to prepare for more severe scenarios.

5. Novick, L., Morrow, C., & Mays, G. (2008). *Public Health Administration: Principles for Population-Based Management*. Sudbury, MA: Jones and Bartlett Publishers. p. 690.

6. Ibid., p. 694.

7. Landesman, L. (2011). *Public Health Management of Disasters: The Practice Guide*. Washington DC: American Public Health Association. p. 189.

8. Landesman, L. (2011). *Public Health Management of Disasters: The Practice Guide*. Washington DC: American Public Health Association. p. 191.

9. Check out the citations from Chapter 26 on Typhoid Mary. Number 7.

10. Lyrics from Humbletip's "Liberty University Anthem"

11. Patterson, K., Grenny, J., McMillan, R., & Switzler, A. (2011). *Crucial Conversations: Tools for Talking When Stakes are High*. Groveport, OH: McGraw Hill Education.

    Hands down, the best book on communication that I have ever read. I truly think that every married couple needs to read this book. I wish I had read it earlier on within my marriage. I had read Gary Chapman's *The 5 Love Languages*, and Clayton King's *12 Questions to Ask*

Before You Marry, which were both good, but nobody prepares you for learning how to communicate in an efficient way without hurting others feelings like this book does.

"But that's something that comes naturally!"

Yeah, okay. I've found the people who say such things, haven't been married (or if so, aren't successful at it). Marriage takes *work*. As a man, you have to learn how to fight for your marriage. Satan doesn't want you to succeed with it. And this book will help you to be an effective "marriage mechanic,"

Chapter 11: Being a Witness

1. Bible, M. Liberty University honors founder Dr. Jerry Falwell at library groundbreaking. The Liberty University Web site. Accessed August 11, 2018, from http://www.liberty.edu/news/index.cfm?PID=18495&MID=49773

Chapter 12: Leadership Post-Disaster

1. Ersing, R., & Kost, K. (2011). *Surviving Disaster: The Role of Social Networks*. Oxford, England: Oxford University Press. p. 22.

2. Psychologists for Social Responsibility. Groupthink. The PSYR Web site. Accessed August 11, 2018, from http://www.psysr.org/about/pubs_resources/groupthink%20overview.htm

3. Landesman, L. & Weisfuse, I. (2014). *Case Studies in Public Health Preparedness and Response to Disasters*. Burlington, MA: Jones and Bartlett Learning. p. 220.

4. Baker, L. & Cormier, L. (2015). *Disasters and Vulnerable Populations: Evidence-Based Practice for the Helping Professions*. Danvers, MA: Springer Publishing Company. p. 100.

Chapter 13: Dealing with the Stress

1. The Mayo Clinic. Job burnout: How to spot it and take action. The Mayo Clinic Web site. Accessed August 11, 2018, from https://www.mayoclinic.org/healthy-lifestyle/adult-health/in-depth/burnout/art-20046642

2. Pierson, A. (2017). *George Muller of Bristol*. CreateSpace Independent Publishing Platform.

3. Priscilla, D. (2009). *Crisis and Disaster Counseling*. Washington, DC: SAGE Publishing. p. 36.

4. Farrar, S. (2004). *Overcoming Overload: Seven Ways to Find Rest in Your Chaotic World*. Colorado Springs, CO: Multnomah.

Chapter 14: Keeping Spirits High

1. Harrison, K. (2008). *Just in Case: How to be Self-Sufficient When the Unexpected Happens.* North Adams, MA: Storey Publishing. p. 61.

Chapter 15: When Bad Stuff Happens

1. Quote attributed to Jerry Falwell, Sr. written on a plaque by his grave.

Chapter 16: Fear

1. Latimer, S. (2016, April 10). Remember Who You Should Fear – Part 1. Survivalblog. Accessed August 11, 2018, from https://survivalblog.com/remember-who-you-should-fear-part-1-by-sarah-latimer/

2. Novick, L., Morrow, C., & Mays, G. (2008). *Public Health Administration: Principles for Population-Based Management.* Sudbury, MA: Jones and Bartlett Publishers. p. 704.

3. Addley, E. (2009, July 17). 'We always said a pandemic was not a matter of if, but when'. The Guardian. Accessed August 11, 2018, from https://www.theguardian.com/world/2009/jul/17/london-tower-hamlets-swine-flu

4. Berger, H. (2011, November 11). Next pandemic is 'not a matter of if'. The National Web site. Accessed August 11, 2018, from https://www.thenational.ae/uae/science/next-pandemic-is-not-a-matter-of-if-1.430997

5. *The Hot Zone* by Richard Preston, *Spillover* by David Quammen, and *Flu* by Gina Kolata are all excellent books that further touch on this subject. I highly recommend each of them if you are interested in pandemics, infectious diseases, or medical history.

6. Deuteronomy 31:6; Joshua 1:9; Isaiah 41:10/43:1; Matthew 8:26; Mark 4:39-40; John 14:27 just to name a few.

7. Matthew 7:7-11 – "Ask, and it will be given to you; seek, and you will find; knock, and it will be opened to you. For everyone who asks receives, and he who seeks finds, and to him who knocks it will be opened. Or what man is there among you who, if his son asks for bread, will give him a stone? Or if he asks for a fish, will he give him a serpent? If you then, being evil, know how to give good gifts to your children, how much more will your Father who is in heaven give good things to those who ask Him!...";

Luke 11:5-13 – And He said to them, "Which of you shall have a friend, and go to him at midnight and say to him, 'Friend, lend me three loaves; for a friend of mine has come to me on his journey, and I have nothing to set before him'; and he will answer from within and say, 'Do not trouble me; the door is now shut, and my children are with me in bed; I cannot rise and give to you'? I say to you, though he will not rise and give to him because he is his friend, yet because of his persistence he will rise and give him as many as he needs. So I say to you, ask, and it will be given to you; seek, and you will find; knock, and it will be opened to you. For everyone who asks receives, and he who seeks finds, and to him who knocks it will be opened. If a son asks for bread from any father among you, will he give him a stone? Or if he asks for a fish, will he give him a serpent instead of a fish? Or if he asks for an egg, will he offer him a scorpion? If you then, being evil, know how to give good gifts to your children, how much more will your heavenly Father give the Holy Spirit to those who ask Him!"

8. Matthew 22:36-40; Mark 12:28-33; Luke 10:25-28

9. Ackerman, C. (2018, May 1). Self-Fulfilling Prophecy in Psychology: 10 Examples and Definition. The Positive Psychology Program Website. Accessed August 11, 2018, from https://positivepsychologyprogram.com/self-fulfilling-prophecy/

10. There's actually some debate as to whether or not this quote belongs to Twain. For more info on the subject, check out the Freakonomics website at http://freakonomics.com/2011/04/25/quotes-uncovered-twain-or-not-twain/

11. Quote on a plaque at Jerry Falwell, Sr.'s grave.

Chapter 17: What is the Role of the Church Post-Disaster?

1. Pierson, A. (2017). *George Muller of Bristol.* CreateSpace Independent Publishing Platform.

2. This particular quote by Joel Salatin can be found in a number of his books, but for the sake of ease you can also find it here at https://modernfarmer.com/2015/10/farming-advice-joel-salatin/ . He's a very interesting guy. I highly recommend checking out his writings and interviews.

3. Diep, F. (2017, November 6). Church shootings are becoming much more common. The Pacific Standard. Accessed August 12, 2018, from https://psmag.com/news/church-shootings-are-becoming-much-more-common

4. Carter, J. (2017, November 6). How Common are Church Shootings? The Gospel Coalition website. Accessed August 12, 2018, from https://www.thegospelcoalition.org/article/common-church-shootings/

5. The Associated Press. (2017, November 6). A list of some U.S. house of worship shootings since 2012. The Salt Lake Tribune. Accessed

August 12, 2018, from https://www.sltrib.com/news/ nation-world/2017/11/06/a-list-of-some-us-house-of-worship-shootings-since-2012/

Chapter 18: Disaster Denial
1. Luther, D. (2018, February 8). The Brutal Truth About Violence When The SHTF. The Organic Prepper website. Accessed August 12, 2018, from https://www.theorganicprepper.com/selco-truth-violence-shtf/
2. Nelson, J. (2013, March 14). Why You're in Denial About Disasters. Fox Business website. Accessed August 12, 2018, from https://www.foxbusiness.com/features/why-youre-in-denial-about-disasters
3. Bliss, L. (2015, July 21). Why You Don't Really Care About the Next 'Big One'. CityLab website. Accessed August 12, 2018, from https://www.citylab.com/environment/2015/07/why-you-dont-really-care-about-the-next-big-one/398969/
4. Baker, L. & Cormier, L. (2015). *Disasters and Vulnerable Populations: Evidence-Based Practice for the Helping Professions*. Danvers, MA: Springer Publishing Company. p. 99.
5. Kapucu, N., & Ozerdem A. (2011). *Managing Emergencies and Crises*. Burlington, MA: Jones and Bartlett Learning. p. 63.
6. Priscilla, D. (2009). *Crisis and Disaster Counseling*. Washington, DC: SAGE Publishing. p. 13.
7. Morris, C. (2018, April 18). 42% of Americans Have Less Than $10,000 Saved for Retirement. The Fortune Website. Accessed August 12, 2018, from http://fortune.com/2018/04/18/americans-save-less-than-10000-for-retirement/
8. ThePatriotNurse. (2016, September 1). CHEAP Dollar Tree Medical Supplies – Prepping Low on Cash. YouTube. Accessed August 12, 2018, from https://www.youtube.com/watch?v=CBcb8RcEmUg

Chapter 20: Beginning to Prepare
1. The 9/11 Commission Report. Accessed August 12, 2018, from https://www.9-11commission.gov/report/911Report.pdf
2. Stein, M. (2008). *When Technology Fails*. White River Junction, VT: Chelsea Green Publishing. p. 96.
3. Ibid., p. 97.
4. Parrett, C. (2011, January 1). LDS Preparedness Manual. The Survival Mom website. Accessed August 12, 2018, from https://thesurvivalmom.com/wp-content/uploads/2010/08/LDS-Preparedness-Manual.pdf

5. LaPierre, W. (2010). *Safe: How to Protect Yourself, Your Family, and Your Home.* WND Books. p. 16.

6. Landesman, L. (2011). *Public Health Management of Disasters: The Practice Guide.* Washington DC: American Public Health Association. p. 189.

7. Logue, V., & Logue, F. (2004). *The Appalachian Trail Hiker.* Birmingham, AL: Menasha Ridge Press. p. 42.

8. Cobb, J. (2014). *Prepper's Long-Term Survival Guide: Food, Shelter, Security, Off-the-Grid Power and More Life-Saving Strategies for Self-Sufficient Living.* Berkeley, CA: Ulysses Press. p. 22.

9. Lennquist, S. (2012). *Medical Response to Major Incidents and Disasters: A Practical Guide for All Medical Staff.* NYC, NY: Springer Publishing. p. 59.

10. Rawles, J. (2009). *How to Survive the End of the World as We Know It.* Westminster, MD: Plume. p. 35.

11. KB6NU's No Nonsense Technician Class License Study Guide can be found at https://www.kb6nu.com/wp-content/uploads/2015/03/2014-no-nonsense-tech-study-guide-v20.pdf

12. Lennquist, S. (2012). *Medical Response to Major Incidents and Disasters: A Practical Guide for All Medical Staff.* NYC, NY: Springer Publishing. p. 60.

13. Baker, L. & Cormier, L. (2015). *Disasters and Vulnerable Populations: Evidence-Based Practice for the Helping Professions.* Danvers, MA: Springer Publishing Company. p. 26.

14. Kapucu, N., & Ozerdem A. (2011). *Managing Emergencies and Crises.* Burlington, MA: Jones and Bartlett Learning. p. 87.

15. Rawles, J. (2009). *How to Survive the End of the World as We Know It.* Westminster, MD: Plume. p. 80.

16. Pearson, C. (2004). *NOLS: Cookery. (5th edition).* Mechanicsburg, PA: Stackpole Books. p. 5-6.

If you enjoy backpacking, or have any intention of ever bugging out, you need to not only read this book, but practice what is within the pages. The NOLS is king when it comes to preparing for surviving outdoors, and this book is a wealth of information on a subject that may not be as exciting as tactical training, but that will make your life infinitely more enjoyable at least 3x/day.

17. Ibid., p. 7.

18. Ibid., p. 8.

19. Parrett, C. (2011, January 1). LDS Preparedness Manual. p. 23. The Survival Mom website. Accessed August 12, 2018, from https://thesurvivalmom.com/wp-content/uploads/2010/08/LDS-

Preparedness-Manual.pdf

20. I believe this study is groundbreaking. Infertility seems to be on the rise, and I believe that this may be one of the culprits. This study is the reason that ibuprofen is no longer used within my house. Tylenol and aspirin are what we use for aches and pains. Ibuprofen is no longer welcome.

Kristensen, D., Lethimonier, C., Mackey, A., Dalgaard, M., Masi, F., Munkbol, C., et al. (2018, January 8). Ibuprofen alters human testicular physiology to produce a state of compensated hypogonadism. Proceedings of the National Academy of Sciences of the United States of America. Accessed August 12, 2018, from http://www.pnas.org/content/early/2018/01/03/1715035115.full

21. *KNACK First Aid* by Buck Tilton, Emergency War Surgery from PrepperPress, *NOLS Wilderness Medicine* by Tod Schimelpfenig, *Where There is No Doctor* by Jane Maxwell21

22. Lewis, P. (2017, April 1). Medical Preparedness. The Rural Revolution Blog. Accessed August 12, 2018, from http://www.rural-revolution.com/2017/04/medical-preparedness.html

23. The entire series of the excellent *Survival Guns* books can be found at PrepperPress.com. I have been around guns my entire life, but was surprised to find out just how much I didn't know. These books serve as an excellent reference, and I highly recommend them.

24. Rawles, J. (2009). *How to Survive the End of the World as We Know It*. Westminster, MD: Plume. p. 55.

25. Lewis, P. (2015, June 2). Review: the Seven Core Areas of Preparedness. The Rural Revolution blog. Accessed August 11, 2018, from http://www.rural-revolution.com/2015/06/review-seven-core-areas-of-preparedness.html

Chapter 21: Using Technology to Help Prepare

1. Landesman, L. (2011). *Public Health Management of Disasters: The Practice Guide. Washington* DC: American Public Health Association.

Unfortunately, I have lost the page number for this one.

2. Delaware County A.R.E.S. Amateur Radio Emergency Service. Accessed August 12, 2018, from http://www.k8es.org/ares/html/what_is_ares.html

Chapter 22: Increasing Your Resilience

1. Falk, B. (2013). *The Resilient Farm and Homestead*. White River Junction, VT: Chelsea Green Publishing. p. 32.

2. Cobb, J. (2014). *Prepper's Long-Term Survival Guide: Food, Shelter,*

Security, Off-the-Grid Power and More Life-Saving Strategies for Self-Sufficient Living. Berkeley, CA: Ulysses Press. p. 10.

3. Christopher, J. (2016). *The Death of Grass*. The STYLE Press.

A great post-apocalyptic novel that will have you frustrated with the stupidity of the main characters. No one really seems to give a crap until things are too late. I suppose one could draw a parallel between this book and the stupid behaviors that will be displayed by those who didn't prepare before a disaster.

4. Fisher, L. (2011). *Crashes, Crises, and Calamities: How We Can Use Science to Read the Early-Warning Signs*. NYC: Basic Books. p. 156.

I tend to like Len Fisher's books, and this one was interesting, but the title was slightly misleading. I didn't really feel like crashes, crises, and calamities were truly discussed until the last few chapters of the book. The beginning seemed to be filler science to me.

5. Ibid., p. 157-168.

6. Gillespie, D. & Danso K. (2010). *Disaster Concepts and Issues*. Alexandria, VA: Council on Social Work Education. pg. 74.

7. Fisher, L. (2011). *Crashes, Crises, and Calamities: How We Can Use Science to Read the Early-Warning Signs*. NYC: Basic Books. p. 153.

8. Ibid., p. 169.

9. Kloos, B., Hill, J., Thomas, E., Wandersman, A., Dalton, J. (2011). *Community Psychology: Linking Individuals and Communities*. Belmont, CA: Wadsworth Publishing. p. 258.

10. Fisher, L. (2011). *Crashes, Crises, and Calamities: How We Can Use Science to Read the Early-Warning Signs*. NYC: Basic Books. p. 152.

Chapter 23: Financial Preparation

1. Kapucu, N., & Ozerdem A. (2011). *Managing Emergencies and Crises*. Burlington, MA: Jones and Bartlett Learning. p. 40.

2. I think this is possibly one of the coolest examples of prepping the news has ever seen. Check out the pictures of this in action sometime. It's absolutely fascinating.

Skaggs, H. (2016, June 12). Texas Man Uses Massive Inflatable Dam to Save House. The Wide Open Country website. Accessed August 12, 2018, from http://www.wideopencountry.com/houston-man-uses-massive-inflatable-dam-save-house/

3. Ramsey, D. (2009). *The Total Money Makeover*. Nashville, TN: Thomas Nelson. p. 144.

All of Dave Ramsey's books are excellent, but this is probably my favorite. If given the chance, I highly recommend attending one of his *Financial Peace University* courses. The information that you'll learn within (either the course or the book) will help you to be a better budgeter.

4. Just like his books, Ramsey's website is packed with top-quality information that you need to know if you want to make wise money decisions. I would keep tabs on this if I were you.

Cruze, R. (2018, February 7). *Money Ruining Marriages in America: A Ramsey Solutions Study.* The Dave Ramsey website. Accessed August 12, 2018, from https://www.daveramsey.com/ pr/money-ruining-marriages-in-america

5. Rawles, J. (2009). *How to Survive the End of the World as We Know It.* Westminster, MD: Plume. p. 262.

6. Quite possibly one of the most fascinating pieces that Lewis has ever written (and her entire blog is great). This is the protective buffering action of homesteading/prepping in action. Where the rubber meets the road.

Lewis, P. (2015, July 4). Cash under the mattress or chickens in the yard? The Rural Revolution blog. Accessed August 12, 2018, from http://www.rural-revolution.com/2015/07/cash-under-mattress-or-chickens-in-yard.html

7. Bartholomew, M. (1981). *Square Foot Gardening.* Emmaus, PA: Rodale Press.

One of the best gardening books ever written. I created eight of these beds shortly after reading this book, and quickly paid for them with the crops that were produced from each. They made a significant dent in my grocery bill for the price of a small amount of labor.

8. Falk, B. (2013). *The Resilient Farm and Homestead.* White River Junction, VT: Chelsea Green Publishing. p. 162.

The best permaculture book ever written. If you are a homesteader, you need to read this book. For those not familiar with the term, permaculture is the act of making a homestead self-sufficient, efficient, and sustainable. This book will help you to better understand the *science* behind how your homestead works from a productivity standpoint.

9. Colossians 3:2 – Set your mind on things above, not on things on the earth.

Luke 16:13 – "No servant can serve two masters; for either he will hate the one and love the other, or else he will be loyal to the one and despise the other. You cannot serve God and mammon."

10. Now this is *spooky*. One of the reasons that proper OPSEC is a must.

Mariotti, S. (2017, December 6). When Owning Gold Was Illegal in America: And Why It Could Be Again. The Huffington Post. Accessed August 12, 2018, from https://www.huffingtonpost.com/ steve-mariotti/when-owning-gold-was-ille_b_10708196.html

11. Rawles, J. The Precepts of Rawlesian Survivalist Philosophy. Survivalblog. Accessed August 14, 2018, from https://survivalblog.com/precepts/

12. Ramsey, D. (2009). *The Total Money Makeover*. Nashville, TN: Thomas Nelson. p. 55.

13. This is actually just one potential source of where the term "shot glass" came from. Nobody's really positive.

14. Zerpa, F. (2018, May 4). In Venezuela, a Haircut Costs 5 Bananas and 2 Eggs. Bloomberg website. Accessed August 12, 2018, from https://www.bloomberg.com/news/articles/2018-05-04/in-caracus-venezuela-a-haircut-costs-five-bananas-and-two-eggs

15. Rawles, J. (2009). *Patriots: A Novel of Survival in the Coming Collapse*. Berkeley, CA: Ulysses Press.

16. Rawles, J. (2009). *How to Survive the End of the World as We Know It*. Westminster, MD: Plume. p. 269.

Chapter 24: Safety

1. Lennquist, S. (2012). *Medical Response to Major Incidents and Disasters: A Practical Guide for All Medical Staff*. NYC, NY: Springer Publishing. p. 322.

2. Baker, L. & Cormier, L. (2015). *Disasters and Vulnerable Populations: Evidence-Based Practice for the Helping Professions*. Danvers, MA: Springer Publishing Company. p. 162.

3. Luther, D. (2018, February 8). The Brutal Truth About Violence When The SHTF. The Organic Prepper website. Accessed August 12, 2018, from https://www.theorganicprepper.com/selco-truth-violence-shtf/

4. Baker, L. & Cormier, L. (2015). *Disasters and Vulnerable Populations: Evidence-Based Practice for the Helping Professions*. Danvers, MA: Springer Publishing Company. p. 158-159.

5. Actually, that number's around 17% or so. Miller, S. (2016, December 13). 1 in 6 Americans Takes a Psychiatric Drug. Scientific American website. Accessed August 12, 2018, from https://www.scientificamerican.com/article/1-in-6-americans-takes-a-psychiatric-drug/

6. LaPierre, W. (2010). *Safe: How to Protect Yourself, Your Family, and Your Home*. WND Books. p. 270-271.

7. This is Gibb's Rule #11, to be specific. Hoffman, K. (2017, July 26). 36 Rules of Life from 'NCIS's' Leroy Jethro Gibbs. The Odyssey website. Accessed August 12, 2018, from https://www.theodysseyonline.com/life-rules-nciss-leroy-jethro-gibbs

8. Rawles, J. (2009). *How to Survive the End of the World as We Know It*. Westminster, MD: Plume. p. 51.

9. Byerly, C. (2010). The U.S. Military and the Influenza Pandemic of 1918 – 1919. *Public Health Reports*, 125(Suppl 3), 82-91. Accessed August 12, 2018, from https://www.ncbi.nlm.nih.gov/ pmc/articles/ PMC2862337/

10. Landesman, L. (2011). *Public Health Management of Disasters: The Practice Guide*. Washington DC: American Public Health Association. p. App. K.

11. Welcome to the South.

The Associated Press. (2018, June 17). US woman fights off rabid bobcat, strangling it with bare hands. The Guardian website. Accessed August 12, 2018, from https://www.theguardian.com/us-news/2018/ jun/17/georgia-woman-strangles-rabid-bobcat-self-defense

12. Coyne, C. (2013). *Doing Bad by Doing Good*. Stanford, CA: Stanford Economics and Finance. p. 158.

13. McKay, K., & McKay, B. (2010, December 9). A Deadly Ritual: 5 Men Who Died from Shaving. The Art of Manliness website. Accessed August 12, 2018, from https://www.artofmanliness.com/ articles/a-deadly-ritual-5-men-who-died-from-shaving/

14. Luther, D. (2018, February 8). The Brutal Truth About Violence When The SHTF. The Organic Prepper website. Accessed August 12, 2018, from https://www.theorganicprepper.com/selco-truth-violence-shtf/

15. Quote from Dennis Wholey, author and TV host. Accessed August 14, 2018, from https://quotefancy.com/quote/758711/Dennis-Wholey-Expecting-the-world-to-treat-you-fairly-because-you-are-a-good-person-is-a

16. Luther, D. (2018, February 8). Selco: The Brutal Truth About Violence When the SHTF. The Organic Prepper website. Accessed August 14, 2018, from https://www.theorganicprepper.com/selco-truth-violence-shtf/

17. Game theory is a statistics and probability approach to making decisions. It helps us to make the best decision possible. It's fascinating to study at first, but quickly grows stale. Every book discusses the same problems and concepts. For a good primer, read Presh Talwalkar's *The Joy of Game Theory*.

18. Quote by Doug Patton: conservative writer. http:// www.oregonrepublicanparty.org/quotes/author/Doug%20Patton

19. I recall reading this from Ayn Rand's *Capitalism: The Unknown Ideal*, I believe.

Rand, A. (1966). *Capitalism: The Unknown Ideal*. NYC: Signet Books.

20. Terry, P. (2011, September 25). Beans, Bullets, Band-Aids, and Bibles: Faith When the World Falls Apart. Survivalblog. Accessed August 12, 2018, from https://survivalblog.com/beans-bullets-band-aids-and-bi-1/

Chapter 25: OPSEC

1. I've seen a lot of people analyze the laws here and proclaim that the government doesn't actually have the capability to do this. I claim that as pure garbage. History pretty much proves that government does what it wants.

Jorgustin, K. (2016, March 8). Anti-Hoarding Laws Will Enable GOV to Take Your Food Storage. Modern Survival Blog website. Accessed August 12, 2018, from https://modernsurvivalblog.com/ preps/anti-hoarding-laws-will-enable-gov-to-take-your-food-storage/

2. Usafeaturesmedia. (2016, March 9). Government will use anti-hoarding laws to take your food, water, and supplies. BugOut News website. Accessed August 14, 2018, from http://www.bugout.news/2016-03-09-government-will-use-anti-hoarding-laws-to-take-your-food-water-and-supplies.html

3. Rawles, J. (2009). *How to Survive the End of the World as We Know It*. Westminster, MD: Plume. p. 221.

4. Mitnick, K. (2017). *The Art of Invisibility*. NYC: Little, Brown, and Company.

I highly recommend that every prepper with a computer read this book. It is *the best* book on cybersecurity that I have ever read.

5. Emerging Technology from the arXiv. (2015, July 31). How Far Can the Human Eye See a Candle Flame? Technology Review website. Accessed August 12, 2018, from https://www.technologyreview.com/s/539826/how-far-can-the-human-eye-see-a-candle-flame/

6. Lodge, S. (1997). Type of People Who Settled Here. Shelby County History website. Accessed August 12, 2018, from https://www.shelbycountyhistory.org/schs/pioneers/typepeoplelived.htm

7. Basaraba, S. (2018, June 11). A Guide to Longevity Throughout History, From the Prehistoric Onward. Very Well Health website. Accessed August 12, 2018, from https://www.verywellhealth.com/longevity-throughout-history-2224054

8. Fleming, T. (2011). What America was Really Like in 1776. Brumbaugh Wise website. Accessed August 12, 2018, from http://www.brumbaughwise.com/history-1/america-1776

9. Ken, H. (2011, August 4). The "Average Life Expectancy" Myth.

Passion for the Past Blog. Accessed August 12, 2018, from https://passionforthepast.blogspot.com/2011/08/average-life-expectancy-myth.html

10. Howard, C., & Holcombe, A. (2010). Unexpected changes in direction of motion attract attention. *Attention, Perception, and Psychophysics.* *72*(8), 2087-2095. Accessed August 12, 2018, from http://www.psych.usyd.edu.au/staff/alexh/research/papers/Howard Holcombe_APP_2010.pdf

11. Kellene. (2011, February 28). Ten Principles of Preparedness: #1 Spiritual. The Preparedness Pro website. Accessed August 12, 2018, from http://www.preparednesspro.com/ten-principles-preparedness-1-spiritual

Chapter 26: The Ethics of Forced Quarantine

1. Upshur, R. (2003). The ethics of quarantine. *Virtual Mentor, 5*(11), 393-395. Accessed August 12, 2018, from https://journalofethics.ama-assn.org/article/ethics-quarantine/2003-11

2. Reed, M. (2015, May 6). Quarantine: Ethical Considerations for Public Health Officials. Penn State Public Health Preparedness website. Accessed August 12, 2018, from https://sites.psu.edu/workworthdoing/2015/05/06/quarantine-ethical-considerations-for-public-health-officials/

3. Lieberman, R. (Producer), & Torme, T. (Writer). (1993). *Fire in the Sky.*

I've not actually seen this movie, but I do know what it is about. I like to watch clips of famous monster movies and read plot synopses to stoke the fires of story writing. So if this movie is filled with profanity, sexual content, and inappropriateness, you'll have to forgive my ignorance.

4. Pope, S., Sherry, N., & Webster, E. (2011). Protecting Civil Liberties During Quarantine and Isolation in Public Health Emergencies. Law Practice Today website. Accessed August 12, 2018, from https://www.americanbar.org/publications/law_practice_today home/law_practice_today_archive/april11/protecting_civil_liberties_d uring_quarantine_and_isolation_in_public_health_emergencies.html

5. Rand, A. (1966). *Capitalism: The Unknown Ideal.* NYC: Signet Books. p. 328.

6. Pickover, C. (2012). *The Medical Book: 250 Milestones in the History of Medicine.* NYC: Barnes and Noble. p. 298.

Fascinating book on medical history that you can get from Barnes and Noble.

7. Arkell, E. (2014, December 25). What the City of New York Did to "Typhoid Mary" Was Pretty Horrific. The io9 website. Accessed August 12, 2018, from https://io9.gizmodo.com/what-the-city-of-new-york-did-to-typhoid-mary-was-pre-1674812001

8. Eswaran, V. (2014, October 31). Quarantine: Ethical and Legal Battle for Human Rights during Public Health Emergencies. Emergency Public Health website. Accessed August 12, 2018, from https://emergencypublichealth.net/2014/10/31/quarantine/

9. I really enjoy Answers in Genesis' work. For self-study regarding apologetics, evolution, and the like, I strongly recommend their website.

Gillen, A. (2007, June 10). Biblical Leprosy: Shedding Light on the Disease that Shuns. Answers in Genesis website. Accessed August 12, 2018, from https://answersingenesis.org/biology/disease/biblical-leprosy-shedding-light-on-the-disease-that-shuns/

Made in United States
Orlando, FL
22 October 2023

38114025R00138